# PARADOXES OF PROTEST

*Black Student Activism in a White University*

# Paradoxes of

# PROTEST
*Black Student Activism in a White University*

WILLIAM H. EXUM

TEMPLE UNIVERSITY PRESS
Philadelphia

TEMPLE UNIVERSITY PRESS, PHILADELPHIA 19122

© 1985 by Temple University. All rights reserved

Published 1985

Printed in the United States of America

Library of Congress Cataloging in Publication Data

Exum, William H., 1942–
Paradoxes of protest.

Bibliography: p. 241
Includes index.
1. Afro-American student movements.   2. Afro-American
college students—Political activity—History—20th
century.   3. New York University—Students—Case studies.
4. Afro-American student movements—New York (N.Y.)—Case
studies.   5. College integration—New York (N.Y.)—Case
studies.   I. Title.
LC2781.7.E95   1985      378'.1981      85-2680
ISBN 0-87722-377-7

# Acknowledgments

I would like to thank publicly a number of those who have, in various ways, provided much appreciated help for this study. First, I am grateful to the Ford Foundation, whose assistance gave me the time and financial support to carry out some of the original research on which this study is based. Without such support it would have been significantly more difficult to accomplish.

Second, I would like to thank the many persons in University College—administrators, faculty members, and particularly black students—who provided critical information and let me impose on their time and patience.

Third, a number of persons have read and commented on various drafts and versions of this work. I am especially grateful to Edward W. Lehman, Caroline H. Persell, Richard Sennett, Robert W. Friedrichs, and Raymond Hall. My work has benefited materially from their always constructive criticism and perceptive suggestions. Special gratitude is due Arlene Kaplan Daniels, whose tireless encouragement and constant support in this project and many others has meant so much.

# Contents

# Preface

The years following 1960 were among the most tumultuous in recent American history. Groups long excluded from participation in society and its institutions demanded greater access. Groups already enjoying the benefits of such participation sought increasingly to redefine, if not restructure, the way the system operates or their own place in it. Some rejected the system altogether. In one way or another, each questioned or protested against things as they are and suggested or demanded changes in both social structure and social process. Women, opponents of American involvement in Indo-China, minority groups, young people—all expressed dissatisfaction with American society and its institutions as they experienced them. College students and blacks occupied a central place in the period's discontents and produced some of its most memorable images: the sit-ins and Freedom Rides in the South; the March on Selma and the various marches on Washington; the Columbia Bust and the emergence of armed black students from a Cornell University building.

In these pages we look at one important segment of these recent protest phenomena—the black student movement in the predominantly white university. Four college generations have now graduated since black student activism emerged on white campuses. This seems an appropriate time for an examination of the movement and its origins, development, and consequences with the advantages that retrospective analysis can provide, particularly since issues of racial equity and the democratization of higher education remain unsolved and past gains appear to be eroding (note, for example, the apparent decline in black student enrollments since 1976; see American Sociological Association, 1982; Fiske, 1981; National Advisory Committee on Black Higher Education, 1981).

As an illustrative example of the black student movement and its accomplishments, I examine the movement in University College, an undergraduate liberal arts division of New York University, one of the largest private universities in the nation. The discussion principally covers the period of greatest student unrest (1966–1972), as well as some continuing issues.

I look at University College for several reasons. First, during the period examined I was a black graduate student at NYU and then an instructor in University College. Thus, I had a chance to observe events in the University and College intimately and occupied roles that gave me access to many of the participants in these events. Second, although media attention to black student protest tended to focus on nationally prominent institutions (e.g., Harvard, Columbia, Cornell, and Northwestern), or institutions where black unrest was especially intense and prolonged (e.g., San Francisco State), these institutions are not necessarily representative, nor are the experiences and protests of black students at them indicative of the full range of experiences in all institutions. An examination of events in an institution that received little national media coverage and no scholarly attention can give us a clearer view of this range. Third, NYU is one of the largest universities in the country and is located in the largest metropolitan area, which has a very large black population. Thus, the role of the institutional bureaucracy and the impact of events in the black community off campus should be easier to discern than in schools located in an area with a smaller black population. Fourth, the University's stated goal of being a "school of opportunity" would, on the surface, seem to suggest that it would be receptive to black students. However, University College's aspirations to be an elite institution and its history of hostility to new, "alien" students are equally critical. The unique qualities of the University and the College, as well as their similarities to other institutions, make an investigation of unrest there instructive for understanding the larger phenomenon of black student activism.

Essentially this is a case study of the on-campus black student movement and an analysis of its impact and the reasons for its successes and failures. It presents a historical reconstruction and sociological interpretation of the movement's origins and development. The primary emphasis is on institutional structure, institutionalized values, collective experience and action, and change through time. Methods used in collecting data for this study are discussed in Appendix C.

In general terms, my principal concern is with those factors: (1) producing black student discontent in the white university and leading to the emergence of the movement; (2) determining the movement's character and ultimate fate; (3) stemming from the role of the university or college as the organizational setting for the movement; and (4) having a role in limiting the kinds of change achieved.

There are several reasons why such an examination is important. First, understanding the past—what happened, and how, with what consequences—helps us understand more effectively the present situation of black students in white institutions as well as continuing problems of racial interaction and equity on campus. Such understanding makes clear that neither the conditions that produced protest, nor protest itself, have entirely disappeared from white institutions.

Second, there is a need for systematic information about black student unrest in white colleges and universities. Some detailed accounts appear in the literature about student discontent (e.g., Anthony, 1971; Edwards, 1970, 1971; Napper, 1973; Willie and McCord, 1972), but most have been impressionistic, even when informative and valuable.[1]

Third, there is a continuing need to understand that the problems of black students in these institutions originate in important respects in the institutions themselves. This study reminds us that the black student movement develops in great measure out of students' *on-campus* experiences, experiences that include discrimination and alienation. Neither discontent nor the movement is simply imported to campus, nor is unrest the work of outside agitators or a handful of disgruntled misfits. The students' discontent suggests some of the more significant, if less visible, consequences of the limited desegregation of higher education so far achieved.

Fourth, for both observers and those attempting change, this examination demonstrates that ideology and rhetoric are no substitute for clear strategy, effective organization, and concrete programs, and that unity is not easily achieved. It illustrates the importance of the organizational character of the college or university as the setting for reform efforts. And it shows the weight of individual black students' values and aspirations in determining their on-campus actions.

Fifth, it is important to understand not only black students' desire for recognition of their capacity to run their own affairs, but also the kind of place they have tried to make for themselves (and for blacks to follow) in the white institution. They have attempted to create a place that is physically and psychically secure, socially and politically strong, educationally beneficial, and personally fulfilling. They have attempted to make the university responsive to their needs, more representative of the larger society in the diversity of its members, and more sensitive to its moral and social obligations in the services it provides. In a larger sense, they have attempted to have the black experience and black cultural values legitimated and incorporated into national culture through the university's gate-keeping functions in the preservation and production of knowledge.

In these attempts there have been both important successes and failures. This fact raises broader questions. How well has higher education served black Americans in recent years? What impact has the black student movement had on black students and on white colleges? Why has there been apparent lessening since 1971 of on-campus political activism by black students, and how real is this apparent decline?

This study is also about the nature of the university, particularly as it has been experienced by black students. It is concerned with social change, particularly the possibility and difficulty of achieving—and maintaining—change in the university. Thus, we are ultimately concerned not just with the activities of black students in a given university, but with assessing the causes and effects of efforts to reduce racial inequality in a key sector of American life. To quote a recent observer: "We hear voices all around us saying that the sixties failed. Nonsense; the score is only now being settled" (Kaplan, 1976:31). This book is part of the effort to assess that score.

# PARADOXES OF PROTEST

*Black Student Activism in a White University*

# Introduction

The beginning of widespread campus unrest is commonly dated from events at the University of California, Berkeley, in 1964. On-campus activism by black students in white colleges and universities is sometimes, though not altogether accurately, dated from 4 April 1968, the date of the assassination of Martin Luther King, Jr. Black activism in white colleges was especially widespread in the closing years of the 1960s. For example, the American Council on Education (Bayer and Astin, 1971) found that in 1968–69, 57 percent of all campus protests involved black students. A study conducted by the Urban Research Corporation (1970) found that in the first half of 1969 alone, black students, who then were less than 6 percent of the total college population, were involved in 51 percent of all protest incidents, though in 1970–71 their involvement had declined to 36 percent of all incidents.[1] Further, significant black student unrest continued after 1970–71, though on a reduced scale and with less publicity, occurring, for example, at Harvard, Columbia, and SUNY-Cobleskill in 1971–72; at Rutgers, Brandeis, and Antioch in 1973; at Brown, Michigan, and Boston College in 1974–75; at Princeton and Stanford in 1977–78; and at Purdue and Northwestern in 1980–81. In short, the black student movement in white colleges and universities is not dead even now.

Black student efforts at social change predate both Martin Luther King's assassination and the Free Speech Movement at Berkeley, a prime example being the civil rights activities of black students in the South, which began in 1960. These early protests differed in significant ways from contemporary black campus unrest. To understand either, a brief discussion of important events prior to 1968 is necessary.

Before 1960 black students appeared to many to be among the most nonpolitical and least protest-prone groups in American colleges. In the words of one observer, they were "individualistic, assimilationist, and

3

politically indifferent" (Skolnick, 1969:xxii). This historical absence of activism was partly due to the lack of higher educational opportunities for all but a small number of blacks. One consequence was a heightening of the social, as well as economic, value of college attendance and graduation. College attendance received a kind of internal and external validation likely to predispose black students against action that would jeopardize their standing as students and thus endanger their future standing as members of the black middle and upper classes.

The absence of activism also reflects the authoritarianism of college administrations in those days, particularly those in black colleges, which then enrolled the overwhelming majority of black students. In these schools there has always been a greater acceptance of the principle of *in loco parentis* by administrators, faculty, and, to a lesser degree, students.[2] Full implementation of this principle seems to have been expected by many parents and by the larger society. In such circumstances administrations did not hesitate to use academic sanctions, notably suspension and expulsion, to suppress student discontent.

This tendency was reinforced by the fact that most of the black colleges located in the South were dependent upon the good will of the surrounding white community for racial peace, and not infrequently for financial support as well (see Thompson, 1973, for a discussion of this historical condition). Student protest, by rocking the larger boat of southern society and the southern way of life, could seriously jeopardize the college's position. This gave administrators and faculty an additional incentive to suppress student activism, as can be seen in their negative reactions to the first sit-ins of the early 1960s (see Lomax, 1963; Miles, 1971).

Student unwillingness to take the chances of activism was reinforced by the hostility of the surrounding society to blacks in general. Black students in particular could easily be perceived by many southern whites as examples of "uppityness" and as sources of contamination. Thus, activist students faced not only academic sanctions but other potential dangers as well, especially if their protest was aimed at off-campus conditions (Wolters, 1975).

Despite all these obstacles, the level of protest at black colleges should not be underestimated. Black student protests (involving student strikes, picket lines, mass expulsions, police intervention, and presidential resignations) occurred during the 1920s at several black colleges, including Knoxville College, Fisk, Florida A&M, Howard, Lincoln (Pa.), and Shaw universities (Altbach, 1974; Bowes, 1964; Graham, 1969; Lipset and Raab, 1970; Miles, 1971; Rosenthal, 1975).

Protest before World War II was aimed primarily at reforming and restructuring black higher education; postwar protest included civil rights demands along with campus reform goals.

The 1920s saw a number of important events: the Harlem Renaissance and Marcus Garvey's black nationalist activities reached their peak; the National Association for the Advancement of Colored People (NAACP), the Urban League, and the black press were growing, as were black businesses and other institutions. In addition, there was the impact of W. E. B. Du Bois, symbol and leader of the "New Negro" movement (see Wolters, 1975). As Miles (1971:193) has noted, "The principles of this movement—political assertion and a celebration of negritude—naturally had special influence among students and intellectuals. Its currents provided the political impetus and the educational content for the demands of student rebels at such colleges as Howard, Fisk and Hampton." Similarly, the late 1940s and the 1950s were a period of intensified and expanded civil rights activity in the larger society by such groups as the Congress of Racial Equality (CORE) and the NAACP.

Protests by CORE and the NAACP, significant in themselves, provide support for the basic assumptions of this study. One is that black student activism is influenced by, and occurs within the context of, off-campus developments in the larger black community. A second assumption is that there is a continuity between earlier black student protest and that of more recent years: that "the programs of race radicals of the 1920s and 1930s are among the gut issues of the contemporary black student movement" (Miles, 1971:196).[3] Between the demands of the 1920s and those of the 1960s, "the connecting link is the belief that the peculiar circumstances of the Afro-American's sojourn in this country mandate a special approach to the education of black youth" (Ballard, 1973:3). However, while the content of demands has remained similar, the focus in contemporary black student protest has shifted to the white college and university.

Historically, black students attending white colleges faced on-campus discrimination, segregation, and exclusion to the point that they were "denied practically every right except that of attending classes" (Wolters, 1975:316). Because they were so few on any one campus, problems of adjustment, mobility aspirations, the push to assimilate, and the necessity of handling discrimination more or less alone left little energy for activism (cf. Naughton, 1972). As Ballard (1973) and others have indicated, the psychological pressures on early black students in these schools were intense.

Nevertheless, many black students, individually and in groups, protested against the discrimination and exclusion they experienced in those white colleges that would admit them, particularly during the 1920s. In this case, "the 'integrated' black students . . . , like their brothers and sisters on the predominantly black campuses, were not docile accommodationists"; they "consistently fought against racial discrimination on their campuses" (Wolters, 1975:314–15).

Furthermore, these black students took pride in their survival in the white institution. Many achieved superior academic records. Nor were they "whitewashed" in the process (see Aptheker, 1969; Ballard, 1973; Wade, 1976; Wolters, 1975). After all, these were the college generations that produced such men as Allison Davis, Sterling Brown, Mercer Cook, Robert Weaver, Montague Cobb, Rayford Logan, Paul Robeson, Ralph Bunche, and William Hastie.

During the first half of the century the absence from the larger society of a political, change-oriented ideology that legitimized protest, and particularly the absence of a climate of opinion receptive to collective black protest, created a situation inimical to black student activism, despite widespread dissatisfaction among blacks with American society and its institutions. Yet activism and protest by black students expanded dramatically in 1960 with the beginning of sit-ins, wade-ins, pray-ins, Freedom Rides, and other efforts. Black students in black colleges were in the forefront of these initial efforts. In part, this seemingly sudden appearance of black student activism, focusing on discrimination in the South, was a continuation of discontent and protest already experienced, but rarely publicized, in a number of black (and white) colleges. The sit-in in Greensboro by four black North Carolina A&T students in February 1960 was "the spark that would ignite the smoldering discontent" (Rosenthal, 1975:119) already present among black collegians.

Their discontent was also part of the new social and emotional climate among blacks that had been building at least since the Supreme Court's 1954 school decision. In the years following *Brown* v. *Board of Education*, blacks increasingly saw the status quo as unacceptable and change as possible and necessary. This new climate lessened fears, particularly among southern blacks, of the consequences of activism and enjoined struggle by emphasizing its necessity and benefits. The successful Montgomery bus boycott of 1955–56 reinforced these views by showing what could be accomplished by direct action. At the same time, these developments, by raising expectations and lowering fears, may well have produced higher levels of frustration and active discontent—especially among the young—with the still-slow pace of racial change in society.

One result of these and related developments was that during the late 1950s a new generation came of age who had had rather different socializing or politicizing experiences than their parents (e.g., the impact of the Montgomery bus boycott and the confrontations at Little Rock and elsewhere, the actual experience of some desegregation in public schools) and faced a changed or changing social reality. In this same period college and societal control over young people was, for a variety of reasons, beginning to lessen or become more problematic (see Flacks, 1971*b*).

In short, a number of events and developments, on and off campus, combined to produce the emergence in 1960 of an unprecedented level of black student activism that was to last through 1964 and 1965. The passage of civil rights legislation in those years was the culmination of a phase of political effort by blacks, including students.

The contemporary phase of black student activism began between 1966 and 1967. The catalyst in this new development seems to have been twofold. The urban rebellions that peaked in the summers of 1964–67, and the frustrations they symbolized, were one factor. The disappointments and loss of momentum of civil rights activities were a second. During this time blacks came increasingly to realize that previous efforts had failed to alter in a fundamental sense the lives of the majority of blacks in white America. The tense, "hot" summers of these years helped promote awareness of the intractability of discrimination and the institutional basis of racism and "the discovery that anger can produce more action than suffering and pleading" (Long, 1970*a*:462). These lessons were first demonstrated by blacks in the ghetto and made acceptable, even attractive, to black students through their explorations of the concepts of institutional racism and Black Power. Their experiences on the white campus often reinforced them.

As a result, the black student movement after 1965 differs from that of just a few years earlier (see Orum, 1972*b*, for an alternative discussion of this difference). First, the target was different. In the early 1960s protest was aimed at society in general, especially southern society, not the white university. Part of the reason for this shift may lie in the increasing number of black college students in white institutions. As late as 1964 blacks were fewer than 3 percent of all college students and were heavily concentrated in the black colleges and universities. However, black college enrollment doubled between 1964 and 1970 (Henderson and Henderson, 1974; Janssen, 1972), with the greatest portion of this increase occurring in white colleges and universities. By 1968, 64 percent, and by 1972, 75 percent, of all black college students were enrolled in white colleges, with blacks accounting for 8.7 percent of all college enrollments (American Council on Education, 1973; Blackwell, 1982; Hechinger, 1980). Seventy percent or more of all black students continue to be enrolled in predominantly white institutions (Astin, 1982; Astin and Cross, 1981).

Second, the shift in target also meant a change in goals and objectives. The objective was no longer change in laws or in southern customs and traditions. The contemporary black student movement envisaged change in one of society's most central institutions, the university.

Third, in large measure the participants were different. During the protests of the early 1960s, black students often worked closely with whites, students and non-students, to achieve common objectives. This kind of interracial cooperation was more often the exception than the rule in recent actions—with important implications for the black student movement.

Fourth, the style of protest and activism was different. Earlier protest was explicitly non-violent. This stance has not always been taken in contemporary black (or white) student activism (see Bisconti, 1970). Black students have not always hesitated to employ the threat of defensive violence (as seen, for example, in events at Cornell in 1969), or to use methods of direct confrontation when all other means of achieving goals seemed ineffective.

Fifth, the organization of the movement and of protest was different. Earlier activities were conducted through nationally (even if loosely) affiliated and coordinated structures such as CORE or the Student Nonviolent Coordinating Committee (SNCC). In the contemporary black student movement, national coordination and affiliation is absent. However much they may know of events in other schools, each group of black students in each college has been, and remains, essentially independent.

In sum, since the mid-1960s black student protestors have emerged in a new place, the white campus, and in new guises and roles—as members of black student unions, concerned about on-campus as well as societal issues, directly confronting the university and often acting as spokesmen for the large black community as well as for themselves.[4]

This study looks especially closely at the black student movement in one white university in order to increase our understanding of the movement in many colleges and universities. I give particular attention to the development of the movement in New York University's University College. As a large, urban university, NYU is particularly appropriate for an examination of recent activism on university campuses. Because its history and character proved to be relevant to the career of the black student movement there, a brief discussion of the institutional setting of the movement is helpful.

NYU was chartered in 1831 and opened in 1932 at Washington Square in Manhattan with University College as its first, and for some years only, unit. Unlike many private colleges and universities, NYU was founded explicitly to serve the general population of New York City—the "laboring classes" and the "mechanics" in the words of Albert Gallatin, one of its founders—by providing a "useful and practical education" instead of the classical curriculum oriented toward Greek, Latin, and philosophy (T. F. Jones, 1933). In practice, however, University College, in both curriculum and student body, deviated rather markedly from its founding philosophy. It adhered firmly to the concept of a liberal arts education traditionally conceived. Both socially and academically, University College was throughout its history considered the most elite of all the University's undergraduate divisions (e.g., a males-only admissions policy was in force until 1959).

In 1894 University College moved to University Heights in the Bronx. This move was viewed by the University as a way to enhance the College's competitive position vis-à-vis the elite colleges with which it identified and competed by creating a more bucolic and tranquil campus than was possible in the bustle of Manhattan. It remained there until 1973, when it moved back to Washington Square and merged with the University's other undergraduate liberal arts college.

That early move to the Heights had two consequences relevant to the career of the black student movement. First, it began NYU's development as a multicampus university whose central administration, with the final power in settling internal disputes, remained in Washington Square. Second, the move to the Heights intensified the question of the role of University College—whether the school was to be an elite oasis of calm and splendid isolation from the city, or whether it was to serve the city and its diverse people. The struggle between involvement and detachment continued as the city grew past the Heights, and as the surrounding neighborhoods slowly changed from predominantly white to predominantly black and Puerto Rican. When black students became active on campus in the late 1960s, the ethnic and racial character of these neighborhoods brought to the fore once again the issue of institutional involvement in the larger community.

Several decades earlier the University's commitment to its founding philosophy had been tested by the great waves of immigration that lasted from the end of the Civil War until 1924, when severely restrictive immigration legislation took effect. The response of University College demonstrated that many in the institution opposed any attempt to make it in fact a school of opportunity. Given its location in New York City, the major port of entry for immigrants, it was only a matter of time before NYU and University College had to face the consequences of immigration. The fact that the University was not tuition-free delayed but did not prevent its confrontation with the new population of the city.

It came in 1913 when the College introduced a medical preparatory course designed to prepare students for entry into NYU Medical College. Requiring only fifteen credits from city-approved high schools, entrance to the medical course was significantly easier than entrance to the College's bachelor's degree program. The result was that College enrollment tripled between 1912 and 1916 (T. F. Jones, 1933). The great majority of the new students were either immigrants or the children of immigrants, a fact that caused great consternation on campus:

> Now, however, with the arrival of the pre-medical students, came a sudden and overwhelming influx of young men who seemed, rightly or wrongly, to the students of older American stock, to be distinctly alien to their own manners and habits of thought. The social conflict that ensued may easily be exaggerated; but the University College of 1917 was a very different place from that of 1913. (T. F. Jones, 1933:255)

While members of most ethnic groups then in New York City were represented among these "alien" young men, the majority were apparently Jewish. The "old Americans," those whom we would today call WASP, were primarily of British or northern European Protestant background.

By 1917 intergroup prejudice, social dissension, and conflict on campus had reached serious proportions, fueled by a concern with preserving "Americanism" and "American values" in the College. In addition, many faculty members and students of older stock felt that academic standards were being lowered by the influx of new students; severe congestion in classrooms and laboratories added to social tensions.

Faced with this situation, the faculty became convinced of the need for some means of more closely restricting entry into the College "in order that men obviously unadapted to college work may be sifted out"

(T. F. Jones, 1933:231). In 1919 the College introduced rigorous entrance examinations, only partly academic in content and intent. Writing in 1933, Jones notes that University College had "the merit or demerit, as only the future may decide, of being among the first of American colleges to provide personal and psychological examinations for entrance" (T. F. Jones, 1933:235).

From the point of view of the College, these examinations had several desirable results. They drastically curtailed, even if they did not eliminate, the entrance of "alien" and "unworthy" students. They enhanced the socially elite status and aspirations of the College. And they improved the "quality," academic and otherwise, of the student body.

The College's response to the changing ethnic composition of New York City, as reflected in its student body, was in line with much of the thinking of the period. A number of "old Americans" held extremely ethnocentric, indeed racist, views, and many societal institutions, including those of higher education, were marked by a variety of discriminatory policies and practices, directed against both white ethnic students and the relatively few black students then present. University College was not atypical (see Steinberg, 1971, 1973). Nonetheless, its response was a systematic and deliberate compromise of the purpose for which the University was founded.

Through the 1930s and into the 1940s, University College remained predominantly Anglo-Saxon in composition. By the late 1940s and into the 1950s, the faculty and administration were still significantly WASP, but the student body had a much larger "alien" (predominantly Jewish) population. Before the Second World War the prevailing attitude was that such students were not really wanted and would not be encouraged. In later years with increasing demands from various groups for admission to colleges across the country, this attitude changed. The necessity of accepting Jews began to be viewed with composure, if not always pleasure. More important, the task of "Americanizing" these students became a dominant goal among many members of the faculty and administration. Such a view was not unknown in earlier years, as Jones (1933) implies, but it was never as fully accepted as in the postwar years.

From 1919 through the 1940s, the more blatant kinds of social discrimination and prejudice gradually declined, but did not entirely disappear. A student in University College in 1947 describes the atmosphere: "The University College of Arts and Pure Science offered compulsory ROTC, clasp-hands-on-desk discipline, an ancient faculty, a persistent strain of anti-Semitism and a kind of justifiable paranoia among cadres of young Jews" (Kahn, 1971:61). During the 1950s and into the 1960s the progressive "de-WASP-ing" continued. By 1970 the college's student body was generally believed, by students and outsiders alike, to be predominantly Jewish.

In the years before 1966, when University College had only fractional black representation in its student body, black students were welcomed no more readily than other "alien" students. Particularly during the first decades of this century, the rising tide of racism and ethnic and color prejudice confronted black students at NYU with discrimination in almost every aspect of their college experience. Indeed, the situation was so bad that during the 1920s black students there approached the NAACP for legal aid. The most publicized instance of discrimination occurred in 1927 when a black football player was benched in order not to offend an opposing team from the University of Georgia, an act that led columnist Heywood Broun to characterize the football coach as "the gutless coach of a gutless college" (Wolters, 1975:317). "The NAACP publicized the situation, threatened legal action," and after protracted negotiations, "got the university to promise to mend its ways. Yet discrimination persisted; the only change was in the official rhetoric" (Wolters, 1975:320).

Black students in NYU, like those in other white colleges of the period, were not all inclined to submit silently to discrimination. Explaining the decision to call in the NAACP, Thomas W. Young, a black freshman, used language with a remarkably contemporary ring when he stressed that it was

> essential . . . to keep striking back at every injustice and mis-
> treatment. . . . If New York University knows that for every offence there
> is a strong organization ready to "strike back" she will not be so incon-
> siderate in her actions. She is fully capable of paying the price each time, it
> is true, but she will not be willing to pay if she knows that it will be
> exacted every time. (Wolters, 1975:315)

The development of restrictive examinations and procedures in University College was an early indication of the still current tendency in much of academia to control the size and composition of the student body through admission systems based on "objectively determined merit." Many have seriously questioned the basic assumptions behind this tendency as well as the tests supported by it (see, e.g., Astin, 1982; Ballard, 1973). The contemporary concern often expressed, in University College and elsewhere, about the maintenance of "standards" following the admission of "different" students from "disadvantaged" backgrounds reflects the same kind of status fears and prejudices as in the earlier era (see, e.g., Lavin, Alba, and Silberstein, 1981). When black students arrived in University College in large numbers during the late sixties, many already in the College responded with the same feelings and attitudes, if not policies, as in the earlier period. And black students in turn responded with protest and activism, providing evidence of continuity with earlier black responses to discrimination.

There is a significant irony here. Jews, earlier the target of much opposition and discrimination, by the late 1960s were perhaps the largest ethnic group in the college. Despite the College's history of anti-Semitism and the tradition of Jewish liberalism and involvement in black civil rights efforts, Jews were among the major opponents of black student efforts—if only because they had become part of the "establishment" of the College. This response had important implications for black-Jewish relations on campus and the career of the black student movement.

Finally, between 1956 and 1966 NYU undertook a major shift in educational philosophy and policies aimed at making it a university of the first rank. Implementation of these goals began in 1963 and, despite some subsequent modifications and delays, continues. In the process, the University's character, structure, and image were transformed. Every unit of the University was affected, including University College.

Whether they approved of the changes or resisted them, people at all levels in the University were well aware that changes were occurring. During the sixties and into the following decade, an atmosphere of change was prevalent. Change seemed both possible and necessary. In such a climate, students (or others) can come to feel that certain features of the status quo need not endure, and that it is both possible and desirable for the changes they support to be implemented. Put simply, this atmosphere can produce both conflict and the desire for other and further changes. As I shall argue, this was apparently the case in University College.

In sum, the character of University College, molded by its history, is relevant to the development of black student activism there. Although some features of University College are unique, restrictive access and on-campus discrimination have been widespread in American higher education (see, e.g., Meier and Rudwick, 1973; Steinberg, 1971, 1973; Synnott, 1979; and Weinberg, 1977). In University College, as in other schools, they helped to shape black students' experience on campus.

## CHAPTER I

# To Change a World: Activism and Movement

*P*ower *concedes nothing without a
demand; it never has and it never will.*——Frederick Douglass

Social protest and social movements are collective activities aimed at producing measurable alteration in some aspect of the world deemed unsatisfactory or unacceptable by those seeking change. Indeed, the terms are often used interchangeably to describe these efforts. However, social protest and social movements are not identical. On the one hand, they are intimately related, since the former is often the tangible, visible expression of the latter; on the other, protest may also be an ill-coordinated, spontaneous, one-time event. Black student activism and protest—lasting over several years, occurring in colleges and universities across the country, and often reflecting a high degree of organization and coordination on a given campus—has been very much a part of a coherent social movement.[1] Student beliefs, values, and experiences have provided both the basis and the justification for these collective actions. They are a critical element in the development of the black student movement.

Similarly, activism must be understood separately from ideology, however closely they may be connected in practice. Ideological beliefs are a necessary basis for action, but holding beliefs critical of the status quo does not necessarily produce activism. We must also distinguish between ideological discontent and ideological anger. It is ideological anger, expressed through organization and collective action, rather than discontent per se, that tends to produce active protest. In all these things, the black student movement, like student movements in general, shares characteristics common to all social movements. In this chapter we look briefly at conceptions of social movements and their applica-

tion to the black student movement. I introduce the three primary
theoretical perspectives that will be used to analyze the movement in
University College and suggest a kind of development model of the
movement.

## SOCIAL MOVEMENTS AND THE BLACK STUDENT MOVEMENT

Social movements belong to that category of phenomena sociologists
commonly term "collective behavior," a broad category that includes
crowd behavior, the actions of violent mobs, and spontaneous upris-
ings or revolts. Although such behavior may occur in the course of
social movements (cf. Evans, 1973), social movements differ from other
forms of collective behavior. They are more highly organized, and they
tend to have a coherent ideology and system of beliefs and to select
targets, goals, and tactics much more deliberately (though there may be
a great deal of emotion involved). Movements generally develop traditions and have more stability and continuity through time than spontaneous outbursts or other forms of collective behavior.

In defining social movements, their traits, and their characteristic
development, we are faced with almost an embarrassment of riches.
There is a long tradition of sociological investigation and interest in all
forms of collective behavior. One consequence is a voluminous (though
not always consistent or integrated) literature, both theoretical and
empirical, on social movements.[2]

The general view is that social movements arise because people who
are in some way dissatisfied with their life situations or the world
around them "mobilize to reconstitute the social order" (Smelser,
1963:315) by seeking to implement some set of beliefs, norms, or
values. Movements can grow out of shared feelings and experiences of
"cramp" or a subjective sense of "repression," or both (Killian, 1964).
A social movement, then, is the expression of "socially shared activities
and beliefs directed toward the demand for change in some aspect of the
social order" that involves "more or less explicit rejection of dominant
practices or beliefs, and attempts to bring about change against the
resistance of prevalent belief and authority" (Gusfield, 1970:218). It is
a collective effort to solve a common problem. In effect, a social
movement is "a group venture extending beyond a local community or
single event and involving a systematic effort to inaugurate changes in
thought, behavior, and social relationships" (King, 1961:27).

Generally speaking, social movements follow a similar pattern of development. They have a beginning, or emergent, phase; an organizational phase; an active phase; and a phase in which institutionalization and routinization occur.[3] All social movements eventually change in structure, membership, and/or goals; not infrequently, they disintegrate or disappear.

All social movements possess an ideology or generalized beliefs that provide a rationale for their existence. All possess an organized structure in some form and degree. At the center of this structure are one or more organizations that determine much of the movement's activity and influence its development. All movements possess rules or expectations (even if loose and flexible) for membership and member behavior, as well as goals to be achieved or implemented. Organization, internal expectations, and external goals all tend to reflect the movement's ideology (see, e.g., Lipsky, 1968; Turner, 1970).

Further, all movements at some point in their history are likely to face the same general problems: (1) overcoming resistance and efforts at control by opponents; (2) recruiting members; (3) maintaining commitment, morale, and group cohesion over time; (4) resolving the question of leadership effectiveness and continuity; (5) achieving success and coping with failure; and (6) maintaining effectiveness and continuity.[4] However, movements are not all the same. They tend to vary in terms of internal structure and organization, membership, orientation to the world, activities, goals, social impact, and other dimensions. Such empirical differences have led observers of social movements to develop a variety of typologies as a means of distinguishing between kinds of movements and accounting for these differences.[5]

One of the most useful typologies is that of Neil Smelser (1963), who distinguishes between norm-oriented and value-oriented movements. In Smelser's view, a norm-oriented movement envisions reconstituting the normative order: changing particular rules or norms. Value-oriented movements foresee a reconstitution not only of norms but of fundamental values as well. In these movements the entire value system is questioned. Norm-oriented movements are essentially reformist, not revolutionary. Changes in institutions, social policies, or practices may be sought by both types of movements as part of the effort to change norms or values.

Smelser's distinction provides a useful framework for analysis of black student values, beliefs, and experiences because it stresses actor orientations and goals, a crucial perspective in understanding the sociological character of black students' efforts. It is also helpful because it suggests that the two kinds of movements will develop different approaches, strategies, tactics, and goals. Moreover, if we view the distinction as part of a continuum rather than a dichotomy (a view implied in Smelser's usage), it helps us illuminate the different stages and variable character of the black student movement over several years. Black students were not always entirely clear or consistent on what they were doing or why. For example, black students have sought reconstitution of important parts of the white university's normative order, as well as the policies and practices that reflect that order. As in other normative movements, this effort has been carried out by a clublike organization that acts as an organized interest group—in this case, black student unions. And, as in the other norm-oriented movements, black student unions have become pressure groups in the face of perceived university unresponsiveness to black student concerns pursued through regular channels. Finally, black students' efforts to change admission procedures so that more minority students would be admitted, or to change curricula through the development of black studies programs, reflect the norm-oriented side of the movement (Corson, 1970; Grier and Cobbs, 1968; Krueger and Silvert, 1975; Ladner, 1967). Their activism in the university also represents an attempt to reconstitute their immediate world and through it the larger society. Certainly many of their ideological beliefs were premised on the assumption of the evil, pervasiveness, and intractability of white racism and the need to fight it vigorously. Their actions on a wide variety of grievances were justified on these grounds and, during the period of most intense protest, often escalated to include more severe measures when other avenues of seeking change were perceived as inadequate or unavailable.

It is this seemingly contradictory character that led some observers to see black student activism as norm-oriented (e.g., Horowitz and Friedland, 1970; Lipset, 1971) and others to see it as strongly value-oriented (e.g., Cass, 1969). Viewing Smelser's orientations as representing two poles of a continuum allows us to resolve this apparent inconsistency and to see the movement as more norm-oriented at some stages and more value-oriented at others. This typological distinction thus allows us to appreciate some of the nuances of the movement's transformation through time and the vicissitudes of fortune.

A second theoretical key is provided by what has come to be called the resource mobilization perspective. Unlike Smelser's approach, whose stress on values, beliefs, and orientations leads to a focus on grievances and motivations, resource mobilization theory emphasizes the kind and variety of resources available to a movement, the effective-

ness of the means used to mobilize resources, the supports and constraints the movement faces, its linkages with other groups, and the
social control efforts exercised against it by authorities and opponents.
This perspective is particularly interested in the strategic and tactical
dilemmas faced by movements, in the relative costs to members of
participation, and in the effects on mobilization, participation, and
success of the pre-existing social relations of members and sympathizers. More generally, it is concerned with the dynamics of movement
development and change through time and with the influence of setting
on mobilization efforts and the movement's career. (For good discussions and applications of the resource mobilization perspective, see
Oberschall, 1973; Tilly, 1978; and Zald and McCarthy, 1979.)

Black students, as members of a historically subordinated minority
and as students, faced critical problems of resource acquisition, mobilization, and management. These problems, as much as the beliefs and
grievances that impelled them to collective action, played a critical role
in the history of their movement. As we shall see, the history of the
movement in University College demonstrates that having a "right-
eous" cause and widely shared grievances is not sufficient to achieve
lasting success if problems of resource mobilization are not effectively
resolved. The resource mobilization perspective will help us illuminate
this aspect of the movement's career.

Further, through its emphasis on the setting in which a movement
occurs, resource mobilization theory leads us directly to the third
theoretical key in this analysis of black student activism: the fact that it
occurs and is contained within a large-scale bureaucratic organization,
the university. Several observers (e.g., Etzioni, 1964) have stressed the
differences between complex organizations and societies, and the great
bulk of the work on social movements has looked at movements
occurring in society, not within an organization. However, I believe
Zald and Berger (1978) are right in arguing that social movements may
also occur within organizations; that social movement theory is applicable to organizational as well as to societal settings; that resource
mobilization theory is particularly useful in this case because the organizational setting has built into it significant problems of resource
mobilization for movement members; and that we should never underestimate the role of internal social movements as a source of organizational change.

When we look at universities and see more black and other minority
faces among the students and faculty than in the years before black
campus activism; when we consider the curricular changes that have

occurred in many institutions; when we see administrative offices concerned with minority or community affairs—when, in effect, we examine the variety of organizational changes that occurred in American higher education during the 1960s and 1970s, it is clear that black students were important agents of such changes. However, it is equally clear, as this study will demonstrate, that the fate of the movement was shaped by the university's character as a bureaucratic organization and by the mobilization constraints inherent in the status of student.

The relevant organizational qualities of the university include the following: a hierarchy that centers power and authority in the hands of chief administrative officers; a division of authority between administrators (who control the purse strings, have the power to hire and fire, and get the final say in a wide range of policy matters) and faculty (who claim pre-eminence in matters of curriculum and educational policy); an emphasis on rational discourse and maintaining a normative consensus based on collegiality and compliance with organizational rules and traditions because of a belief in their legitimacy; limited coercive power on the part of authorities; the relative powerlessness of students (who are both clients and low-status members of the organization); and traditional policies (e.g., an undergraduate curriculum designed to be completed in four years) that produce constant turnover in the student population, thereby creating serious problems of continuity for any student movement. Lack of continuity between student generations makes the cost of mobilizing resources for this kind of mass movement particularly high.

All of these features, in varying degree, are shared by University College and NYU with other universities. One of the unusual features of NYU was its division into separate campuses, with the Heights campus enjoying only a limited degree of autonomy. Real power to resolve many of the issues raised by black student protest rested with the central administration at Washington Square. Further, the division made it difficult for black students on the two campuses to coordinate their activist efforts, with important consequences for the movement in University College.

Finally, it is important to stress the influence of organizational setting for the black student movement because the movement highlights a subtle but significant paradox that results from the university's organizational character. On the one hand, the university tends to emphasize community and collegiality, caring and responsiveness, as well as commitment to common values, among its members. On the other hand, these emphases engender in students expectations of responsiveness and concern that are bound to be unmet in some degree and that can form the basis for organized protest. Students are not the only constituency of the university. Equally, although stressing collegiality and community helps maintain normative consensus, it also obscures the hierarchy and the asymmetrical distribution of power in the university. Students may discover that they have no real power in determining many of the policies which directly affect their lives on campus. One result may be student discontent. As I shall argue, this was certainly the case in the black student movement.

## THE BLACK STUDENT MOVEMENT
### A DEVELOPMENTAL MODEL

Social movements do not appear full-blown in a society or an organization. Rather, they develop over a period of time, though the emergence of a movement may appear sudden. The black student movement is no exception.

The emergence and development of the black student movement was significantly influenced by a number of factors both internal and external: (1) off-campus events and on-campus conditions, the movement's context and environment; (2) the traits of black students themselves; (3) their shared experiences and reactions; (4) the formation and character of the black student union, its mobilization, and its goals; and (5) the actions of college authorities. Its development can be analyzed as the result of a developmental sequence of the kind discussed in more general and theoretical terms by Jessor (1968), Seeman (1971), and Stinchcombe (1964). The factors noted above are interrelated elements and components of this sequence. The sequential model argues that off-campus events (including those in which students may have directly taken part) and the experiences of black students on campus, which are determined in large part by the organizational character of the institution, combine to produce a sense of disjuncture, alienation, and inauthenticity in many. In the impelling and legitimizing context of ideological beliefs derived from external sources and from shared collective experience on campus, it leads to the organization of black students—specifically, the formation of the black student union.

Once formed, the union becomes the mechanism for expressing dissatisfaction with a still-alienating environment, arguing the need for change, and mobilizing resources to produce that change. Thus, organization facilitates collective action and behavior that, given an appropriate precipitating event, can become open and large-scale protest. Activism by black students and the black student union produces responses and control efforts by university authorities. These efforts by both the union and the authorities, as well as movement success or failure, influence the experiences and further actions of black students in a kind of continuing feedback loop.

Over time, diverse outcomes of this developmental history are possible, ranging from total success, full achievement and institutionalization of all goals with substantial rewards for members, to total failure, the collapse of the movement, and the disintegration and disappearance of both the movement and its organization(s) with virtually no rewards for members. In the chapters that follow we shall see how this developmental sequence worked out in University College as black students there attempted to change their world.

## CHAPTER II

# A Summoning Historical Time

*M**any reasons indeed have caused
Negroes, . . . to join the several protest movements. They may generally be
stated as combinations of private experiences or emotions engaging with
public events in the context of a summoning historical time.*——Robert
Coles (1964:307)

## THE MOVEMENT'S CONTEXT: OFF-CAMPUS EVENTS

The campus is the immediate social and physical environment for
students, the place where most of their energies and efforts are centered
for the period of their college years. For black students, however, the
frame of reference often includes the larger off-campus black community. Off-campus events were an influential part of the context of the
development of the black student movement, not least for their role in
the political socialization of black students both before and after they
arrived on campus.

Most important were events that heralded significant developments
in social and political beliefs among blacks, whether in their evaluation
of problems faced or in proposed solutions or both. Especially crucial
was a growing acceptance among blacks of the necessity of black unity,
self-help, collective effort, and active protest, including that targeting
basic institutions in the society. In essence, these events signaled the
development of a militant kind of collective race consciousness.[1] In this
regard, black students have been both followers and in the forefront of
the larger civil rights movement (Krueger and Silvert, 1975; Miles,
1971; Perkins and Higginson, 1971).

There were several such developments during the 1960s.[2] Events
occurring between 1964 and mid-1968 nationally and in New York

City were of particular importance for the emergence of the black student movement in University College. First, 1964 through 1968 were pivotal years for the black community and the larger civil rights movement. Numerous black communities across the nation were in flames, their residents filled with anger, rebellion, frustration, and despair. This discontent reflected the failure of the civil rights movement to achieve fundamental change in the structure of American society or in the life of the average urban black, highlighted the apparent intransigence of white-dominated society, and suggested to many the need for new approaches and redoubled efforts to achieve black liberation.

Many of those interviewed for this study (who were either in high school or just beginning their college careers at the time) remembered being very much impressed by these urban disturbances. For some, the urban riots were their first sign of the great distance still to go in achieving real change and the depth of anger and despair among many blacks—a first awareness, in effect, of how deeply wrong things were for blacks. In some students from more "advantaged" backgrounds, this awareness produced discomfort. As one student put it:

> When the riots first started in Harlem and Watts, in 1965 I think, I remember being really surprised and a little scared. I didn't really understand what they were all about. As they went on summer after summer I remember each year being less surprised and more angry. I was mad at blacks for burning their own homes, I was mad at whites for causing the whole thing because they were so racist. And I guess I was mad at myself for not having known about what was really happening. (Student Interview no. 4)

Or, as another student described his reaction to the riots: "They blew my mind and opened my head to what was really going down" (Student Interview no. 2).

Second, during 1966 and 1967, many of the political goals of the civil rights movement to that point appeared to have been largely won, while the philosophy and tactics that had dominated its efforts came under serious questioning. These were years of consolidation of previous achievements, critical examination of the movement's direction, and fragmentation over goals and tactics.

Black leaders were forced to recognize the extent of the still-unfilled aspirations and needs of the black masses. There was growing awareness that the real problems were not discriminatory laws alone, but also black self-hatred, uncritical acceptance of white standards, economic inequity, powerlessness, and institutional racism and its consequences. This was a time, in effect, when new directions and emphases came to the fore in response to the recognition of both changed and unchangizg conditions.

In 1966 Stokeley Carmichael became chairman of SNCC. In that same year, when James Meredith's march through Mississippi ended with Meredith's being shot, Carmichael voiced the call for Black Power. Thus, in the Mississippi delta the ideology of Black Power received its first explicit enunciation.[3] It rapidly became a matter of national concern: whites were apprehensive and rejected it; blacks variously endorsed, rejected, or redefined it. Carmichael in the next few years appeared all over the country at colleges and universities and in black communities "urging black people to unify and, by collective effort, seize power" (Anthony, 1971:9).[4]

Eventually, many black leaders of all degrees of militance came to embrace the concept in some form, though the definitions tended to vary widely from Roy Wilkins to H. Rap Brown. Despite such variations, the idea received widespread discussion and increasing acceptance within black communities and leadership groups. Included in such discussions were the views of Malcolm X and the Black Muslims, who explicitly rejected integration with whites and called for separate black development. The Black Panthers contributed black nationalist ideas to the broadening stream of power-oriented ideological programs.

The Black Panther Party had been founded in November 1966 by a group of students (including Huey Newton and Bobby Seale) who were members of the Afro-American Student Union at Merritt Junior College in Oakland, California (Anthony, 1971). This is an early indication of the importance of the black student union. Further, with the exception of Malcolm X, the leaders in the growth of the new ideologies were almost all black students: Stokeley Carmichael, H. Rap Brown, and the leaders of SNCC generally; Bobby Seale, Huey Newton, and many others.

Although such developments were picked up and elaborated by other groups, black students were in the vanguard on and off campus. Although it was the masses of blacks who were in rebellion in urban centers across the country, it was often black students who formulated or articulated the grievances of their brothers and sisters in the ghetto (see Anthony, 1971; Edwards, 1970).

The ideological developments of this period, though not always explicitly anti-white, did not generally encourage white participation in the black struggle, except possibly as loose allies working in their own communities. This emphasis on collective effort and black control over black liberation was carried over into the developing protest by black students in white colleges, where it often appeared to lead to strong separatist tendencies.

Third, during this period of ghetto unrest and ideological shifts, works of tremendous influence were published and contributed to these developments. The year 1967 saw the publication of *Black Power* by Stokeley Carmichael and Charles Hamilton. *Black Rage* by William H. Grier and Price Cobbs, Eldridge Cleaver's *Soul on Ice*, and the *Report of the National Advisory Commission on Civil Disorders* (generally known as the Kerner Commission Report) were all published in 1968.

These works explain the origin and character of black anger and legitimize its use in the black struggle. The Kerner Report, for all its flaws, was the first official recognition by an establishment body of the reality of white racism, not only in individuals but in American society and its institutions. The validity of the concept of racism in analyzing and fighting racial problems was firmly established for blacks, who all along had been aware of the reality behind the term. In the process, the report's indictment of whites and white society as the source of black oppression gave strong support to the idea that blacks must find ways to racial change through their own efforts.[5]

Fourth, events in other colleges between 1966 and 1968 were also an important part of the context for the black student movement in University College. By the fall of 1966, colleges and universities had already begun to experience some student protest, primarily over Vietnam and related issues, but also to some extent over campus conditions (see Peterson, 1968a and 1970). In the majority of these instances the protesters were white, and their protest escalated after 1966.

As late as 1966 black student protest was either absent or insignificant in most white colleges (though not in black ones; see, e.g., Rosenthal, 1975). Through the fall of the 1966, black students in white schools were not, in general, visibly active on campus, though things were beginning to heat up at some colleges, one prime example being San Francisco State.[6] By the end of 1967, however, black student activism had begun to reach large proportions; 1968 witnessed an even higher incidence of black protest in white colleges; and 1969 brought perhaps the peak of black student activity (Astin and Bayer, 1971; Bayer and Astin, 1969; Lemberg Center, 1968–69; Urban Research Corporation, 1970).

In addition, protest activities by black high school students began appearing by the end of 1967 and were widespread by the spring of

1968 (Lemberg Center, 1968–69). Thus, in the following years some black students would arrive on campus already possessing a "raised consciousness"—in effect, socialized for on-campus political activism.[7]

The growing black (and white) student activism in white colleges and universities and in junior and senior high schools across the country provided an example and symbol for black students in schools that had not yet experienced black protest. Finally, the assassination of Martin Luther King, Jr., symbolized for many blacks the frustration of the civil rights movement, the limited effectiveness of non-violent approaches, and the endurance of hate in American race relations.

In New York City the 1967–68 school year saw several local developments that were critical for black/white relations in the city generally and were an important part of the context of the movement in University College. One was the continuing series of controversies concerning Intermediate School 201, a public school in Harlem. These centered on several issues, among them the character of the school and its staff; its educational philosophy and program; its role in the community; and parents' role in the school. The local Harlem community, the central Board of Education, the local board of education, and the United Federation of Teachers (UFT) were all involved.

A second development was the controversy over decentralization and community control of the public schools in the Ocean Hill–Brownsville school district in Brooklyn, which began in September 1967. In May 1968 the UFT called a strike of teachers against the local Ocean Hill–Brownsville school board. By September 1968 the teachers' strike had become citywide. The local community in Ocean Hill–Brownsville was actively involved, as were the city's black and Jewish populations (the local community and local school board were predominantly black; the UFT, in the community's view, predominantly Jewish). Protest spread in city high schools, triggered in many cases by the Ocean Hill–Brownsville controversy and largely involving black and Puerto Rican students. The teacher strike continued for weeks as tensions between the black and Jewish communities in the city rose. These tensions remained high for months.

As Ritterband (1974) points out, the school controversies were basically a struggle between ethnic communities, rather than labor-management disputes. Ethnic power concerns rapidly replaced educational ones. One consequence was a permanent strain within the old liberal Jewish-black coalition in New York and a polarization of the black and Jewish communities.[8] As we shall see, these developments

were an important element in the history of the black student movement in University College.

A third crucial development during this year was growing student
unrest and discontent at colleges and universities in New York City
itself, and especially at Columbia University. The unrest at Columbia
culminated in the spring of 1968 in an escalating series of building
occupations and other actions, leading to what has come to be known
as the Columbia Bust (see Cox et al., 1968). In these efforts black
students' concerns and actions played a crucial, perhaps catalytic, role.

In short, in the years leading up to the emergence of the movement in
University College, a number of off-campus events, national and local,
produced the climate for black student protest there. However, these
events were only part of the context. On-campus conditions and black
students' own characters and experiences were also crucially important.


## THE MOVEMENT'S CONTEXT: CONDITIONS ON CAMPUS

The immediate social context for the development of black student
movements is the campus itself. Conditions in the college or university,
with off-campus events, provide both the context and the climate for
activism. Some of these conditions are shared by all colleges to some
degree. Others are determined by factors peculiar to each college.
On-campus conditions are important in two senses. First, some of them
can produce strain and discontent in black students. Second, by providing a precedent, an example of action, or a source of discontent, or even
by raising student expectations, they often serve to legitimize black
student actions to redress perceived inequalities.

Conditions common to most American colleges and universities stem
from the organizational character of academic institutions, their collective developmental history, or their role in society. Colleges have, for
example, historically been responsive and innovative, though often
only following internal or external pressures for change, especially
from students (see, e.g., Otten, 1970; Rudolph, 1965, 1966). Thus,
students in the past two decades could look at the history of higher
education and ask, if change has happened in the past, why not now?

Second, the history of most academic institutions is one of increasing
tolerance, even on sectarian campuses, of a variety of viewpoints and
organized student groups. Thus, current generations of students can

find ample precedent for organizing and expressing their views and interests. Third, by the time blacks began to arrive in larger numbers on white campuses in the 1960s, other minority students had already developed organizations for essentially "self-serving" purposes, whether religious or ethnic or some combination. These organizations—of Jewish students, Catholic students, Chinese students, or other groups—were already accepted as legitimate on campus. Thus, there was ample precedent for the emergence of black student unions, even though their own actions and the liberal, integrationist ideology dominant on many campuses made them appear separatist to many whites.

Fourth, although it is certainly true that black student unions were, and are, often much more explicitly concerned with sociopolitical issues than many white student groups, nonetheless white students on many campuses exhibited concern with sociopolitical issues before and after black students arrived. Whether this involved participation in civil rights efforts, tutoring disadvantaged children, or some other programs, black students could find in such activity both precedent and legitimation for their own orientations. (Eichel et al., 1970, and Otten, 1970, discuss some of these issues in reference to specific campuses.)

Fifth, faculty and administrators often applauded and encouraged the social activity of white students. Indeed, they themselves often took actions indicative of a social conscience: helping fund student efforts, taking part as individuals in civil rights efforts, or, in a number of instances, voluntarily taking steps to increase the numbers of minority students *before* there was great pressure from activists to do so (see, for example, Peterson et al., 1978).

Thus, black students found both legitimation and precedent for their own organizations and activities, whatever their differences from those of other students. Yet because of ideological beliefs in white intransigence, the puzzlement, confusion, or hostility of whites on campus in response to black student organization and activity was perceived by black students as racism and deliberate hostility to blacks in general. (This is only one of the many ways in which black students and white students experience the white college differently.)

Sixth, such problems of differing perceptions occur in a context where the power relationship between authorities and all students is strongly asymmetrical, despite the stress on community. All students experience relative powerlessness, and authorities have tended to resist student demands for what they perceive as truly fundamental or radical change. Moreover, students are only one of several constituencies that look to the college to meet their interests and needs. Academic institutions are gate-keepers to status, hold the key to upward mobility, and play a central role in the labor market. As a result, competition, even conflict, between interest groups is endemic and must be attended to by institutional authorities. Thus, although academic history and tradition provide some precedent and legitimation for black students' expectations of responsiveness, the structural and political character of the white university create barriers. Frustration and discontent have often resulted.

In University College most of these conditions were already in existence when black students arrived in 1966 and 1967. Several specific conditions are especially worth noting: endemic conflict with and isolation from Washington Square, the administrative center and the largest campus of NYU; prior organization by students of other racial or ethnic minorities; on-going student activity expressing social concern and political consciousness; previous College responses or voluntary actions symbolizing such concern and consciousness; on-going educational and structural innovation in the College, indicating that it was a place open to new ideas and policies; and evidence of the College's acceptance of some degree of responsibility to the neighborhoods surrounding it.

I have already noted the programs aimed at enhancing NYU's academic stature that began in 1963. By 1966–67 such changes were well under way in all units of the University, including University College, often producing conflict, resistance, or unhappiness (Baldridge, 1971). Discontent itself, in such an atmosphere, acquired a certain legitimacy.

In University College, conflict between the college and the central administration centered on: (1) whether to continue graduate programs at the Heights (Dean's Report, 1967–68); (2) the desire of the college's faculty and administration to modify substantially the all-University department system (Baldridge, 1971); and (3) the acceleration of the centralization of authority in the offices of the president and chancellor, with corresponding decreases in the individual autonomy of the University's campuses and divisions. The last trend was especially resented in the College because it served to heighten its already strong sense of being a stepchild or second-class citizen within the University. Many felt that the College already had too little autonomy (see Baldridge, 1971, for detailed discussion of this point).

Though not a party to these conflicts, the black student movement could not escape some of their consequences. For one thing, the continuing drive for centralization meant that there were few major issues that College authorities could manage without reference to the central administration. As a consequence, many problems raised by student activism, black or white, could not be resolved by College authorities alone.

As noted above, by 1966 and 1967 student organizations of a basically ethnic character were already well-established. Hence, the formation of a black students' union did not involve a drastic departure from existing tradition, although they are frequently explicitly political and activist in their aims and actions, while the more traditional groups often are not. Similarly, we should distinguish between traditional collegiate activities and political activities. Political activity on campus contributes to a climate conducive to the development of the black student movement. Such activity—like the prior existence of ethnic student organizations—legitimates student political concern and action (particularly where these have administrative approval or faculty support), and provides an example from which black students may learn or profit; and moreover, it indicates tolerance of certain kinds of student beliefs, concerns, and activities.

From September 1966 through March 1968, there was a great deal of political activity in University College. Many—faculty members and administrators as well as students—saw such activity as good and right. The 1966–67 school year opened with an editorial in the student newspaper, the *Heights Daily News* (HDN), praising the changing times and student participation in poverty and racial equality programs on "progressive" campuses, including University College. In the fall of 1966, several such projects were under way.[9] Though not funded by either the college or the university, they had the sanction and official recognition of the college. Most were run and staffed by college students. In many instances, the driving forces behind these programs were black students.

These and other student projects led the director of student affairs to note publicly the decline of student apathy and the increase in student activity of all kinds at the Heights. It was, in his opinion, a "wonderful" development; the students were the "most interesting and exciting group of students" he had worked with (HDN, 4 Oct. 1966).[10]

The dean of the College was moved to report approvingly at the end of the school year that "student life as distinct from academic life was thriving. Of all the on-going student associations, only those with religious affiliations gave the Director of Student Affairs and his staff much concern" because of declining activity and membership (Dean's Report, 1966–67).

These activities did not lead to protests and took place off campus. Incidents of on-campus student protest in the College involved white students almost exclusively. Throughout 1966–67 there were protests over library reforms and cafeteria services. In December 1966 one of the largest protests occurred in opposition to proposed tuition rises (Baldridge, 1971; HDN, 7 Dec. 1966). At least a thousand students demonstrated at Washington Square, and a smaller number at the Heights. Agitation over the library and cafeteria service continued during the fall of 1967. Additional protests over on-campus recruiting by the Dow Chemical Company and the retention of ROTC on campus during this fall semester were part of student opposition to the Vietnam War.

Not only students of liberal or radical left political persuasion were active during this period. Both the Heights Conservative Club and the Young Americans for Freedom (YAF) were quite active during 1966–68. Indeed, in February 1968 YAF staged a demonstration against recruitment on campus by IBM. Arthur Watson, chairman of IBM, was burned in effigy in protest against IBM's sale of computers to Eastern European nations (HDN, 12 Feb. 1968).

Indeed, so much student activity seemed to be occurring in the University that the chancellor felt it necessary to clarify the institution's stand on student demonstrations. His clarification was carried in all the student newspapers, appearing in HDN on 5 December 1966. The chancellor emphasized that the University would "do everything possible" to avoid calling in the police and instead would concentrate on the use of disciplinary actions to prevent or control disruptive or violent demonstrations.

The editorial stance of HDN was indicative of the climate of opinion in the College during this time. In its editorials and to some extent in the features chosen, HDN provided strong, continuous support for activities expressing sociopolitical concerns. For example:

> Now that the South Bronx Project is undertaking an ambitious plan of community action to improve education in a ghetto, it deserves even more enthusiastic support than it received the past year. Originating in an endeavor to bring tutoring to the disadvantaged youngsters of the South Bronx, it has now expanded to the role of an organized pressure group. . . . The augmented ambitiousness of the Project appears to be accompanied by increased maturity and dedication on the part of the

Heights organizers. . . . The University has given its sanction to the South Bronx Project, a most desirable affiliation in view of its motto, "a great university is a great city." In doing so, it chooses a good means of proving that it does not consider its passive presence as sufficient contribution to New York. (*HDN*, 27 Oct. 1966)

The paper applauded the University and College when they supported such activities and roundly condemned them when they did not.

Two years ago in our April Fool edition we presented a story about the Heights receiving an award from the white citizen's council for maintaining the best color scheme on campus. We believe that this jest is not very far from the truth. In reality, our campus, a major constituent of the world, a university which prides itself on attacking the social problems of our city, has an infinitesimally small number of Negroes. . . . Surely among the more than 1,100,000 Negroes in New York City, there are a substantial number of students qualified to enter NYU who are economically unable to attend. We believe the University should give preferential treatment to qualified Negro applicants and grant not one or two, but dozens of scholarships. . . . It is the responsibility of a "responsible urban University" to help in every way to alleviate the vicious cycle of prejudice and poverty. (*HDN*, 14 Oct. 1966)[11]

*HDN* also consistently supported the aims, if not always the tactics, of student protests and demonstrations. In commenting on the formation of the Commission on Student Participation by the University Senate following the tuition protests, *HDN* editorialized:

The University Senate's action seems to be a direct outgrowth of last December's protest over the tuition increase. In a way, it is unfortunate that positive action can not be taken without so much preliminary screaming and yelling. Nonetheless, the Senate's action is concrete evidence that student protests are heard. A student group which, in the future, suspends its protest activities because "it won't do any good" should take the present lesson to heart. (*HDN*, 8 Feb. 1967)

In addition, *HDN* provided a forum for the expression of opinion by its readers, faculty members and administrators as well as students. Throughout 1966–67 both the "Campus Mail" (the letters to the editor) and a special column written by students carried an extended, often heated, dialogue between students of various political persuasions about such issues as Black Power, integration, civil rights, and poverty. Before the formation of the black student association, virtually all of the participants were white. As discussion turned more and more to the black student association itself, black students began joining in, although the debate remained largely a debate among whites.

College officials also showed social concern. During 1966–67, for example, the College made some tentative moves toward remedying a situation that, though not specifically focused on black students, could not fail to affect them—namely, the inadequacy of scholarship and financial aid funds. The dean of University College in his 1966–67 Report lists this issue as one of the top priorities for College action: "Of applying freshmen for Sept. 1967, 633 asked aid; of these 533 qualified; we could make offers to only 169. In total we aided only 12.5% of our students in 1966–67, a figure not to be broadcast among colleges comparable to ours."

In his report the following year, the dean indicated that by the time the 1967–68 academic year was well under way, the College had already begun taking steps to bring in more black students. This was partly on the College's own initiative, but it was also due to prodding by black students, as well as of events off campus.

> Before the Martin Luther King, Jr., assassination, University College was already in high gear in attempting to recruit Negro and other disadvantaged students and even in working out educational support programs to sustain the effort. University College is pleased to report that prior to the King assassination, it was actively engaged in recruitment with the help of the now defunct ACCESS and of Mr. [Bill Moore], a 1968 graduate. Prior to this tragedy, thirty-two black students had already been accepted. (Dean's Report, 1967–68)[12]

The Dean found it worthwhile to add a further explanation of admissions practices, possibly in response to questions raised in the College about the maintenance of "standards" (a not uncommon reaction to increased minority admissions).[13]

> Another area in which University College has been forehanded in its admissions policies is in its flexibility with respect to SAT scores. A few minority group students have lower scores than usual but not necessarily defective backgrounds or defective capacity. Most of those admitted could come in under any standard. Those needing help or hand-tailored programs will get them. University College had been working out an educational support program before this term was applied to it. . . . We have every confidence that we can identify students who may benefit from the University College experience and that we can take care of them after they have come to our campus. (Dean's Report, 1967–68)

Despite these assurances, as we shall see, some members of the faculty and administration appear to have felt that incoming minority and black students were not fully qualified academically. This attitude toward black students' capacities and backgrounds continued after 1967–68.

In other efforts to meet the social concerns of students and faculty members, the College, along with other units of the University, joined the College Bound Program, run by the New York City Board of Education and aimed at getting promising graduates of the city's high schools, especially minority students, into colleges and universities in the city. The fall of 1967 also saw the first offering of courses related to black studies. The impetus seems to have come from a few faculty members and individual students, both white and black. The courses, primarily in African history and civilization, together formed the nucleus of an African Studies minor.

During 1966–67 University College generally showed itself willing to make changes in response to faculty and administration efforts and student concerns. Changes were implemented in these years in the areas of curricular expansion and enrichment; academic programs, majors, and minors; evaluations of student academic progress and work; student participation; and administrative expansion. (For a more detailed presentation of these various innovations, see Appendix A.)

University College, while traditionalist in some respects, was by no means rigid or unchanging. Nor was it completely unaware of the community around it and its possible role in that community.

> Less obviously pressing in the local administration sense is the high desirability for the College to play a large role in the affairs of its immediate locality. You [President Hester] have already announced your intention to organize and head a group of University people to study the situation and the needs of the Bronx, especially the West Bronx. A study having been made, implementation of its recommendations must become a first priority for the College administration. (Dean's Report, 1966–67)

In short, the climate of University College between 1966 and 1968 did little to hinder and much to encourage the growth of the black student movement. Conflict was endemic within the College and University. Several ethnic groups had already organized. Political activity was under way, frequently with direct or indirect College support. Student protests on a number of issues had already begun. The College had been highly responsive to internal pressure for innovation, though some changes within the larger University were resisted as inimical to its interests. There was evidence of some acknowledgment by the College of its public responsibility, and some College-initiated actions could be seen as expressive of social concern.

Finally, in some respects University College was more like an autonomous small college than an integral part of a university: for example, its relatively small student body; its low student-faculty ratio and the resulting close interaction between students and faculty; the relative accessibility of administrators to students. Certainly this was the image that was constantly emphasized. It depended in large part on the belief that this was an institution where student-faculty-administration relations had always been close and good, communications excellent, and student views promptly taken into consideration. The image seems to have been strong in the late sixties (see Dean's Reports, 1966–67 and 1967–68). However, it was held more by faculty members and administrators than students and did not accurately reflect student experiences. During this period students were not members of any official College committee and did not participate in decisions other than those specifically related to student affairs—discipline, extra-curricular activities, and so on. Even here, student participation was largely observational and advisory.

This was the university context for the development of the black student movement. As we shall see in the following chapter, black students' characteristics, which tended to be different from those of white students, produced in this setting an experience of disjuncture, alienation, and inauthenticity. Belief in the necessity of unity and collective action in these circumstances made organization—in this case the formation of the black student union—virtually inevitable. Once formed, the organization provided the mechanism for the full emergence of the movement.

# CHAPTER III

# "Being Black Was Hard Work"

*P*olitical stability and instability are, *ultimately, dependent on a state of mind, a mood, in society. . . . It is the dissatisfied state of mind rather than the tangible provision of "adequate" or "inadequate" supplies of food, equality, or liberty which produces the revolution.*——James C. Davies (1971:136)

## BLACK STUDENTS: CHARACTERISTICS AND BELIEFS

Their own characteristics and beliefs help to shape the campus experiences of black students and their evaluations of these experiences and of the white college generally.[1] They are, in addition, a principal element in the articulation of the individual with the group, and of both individual and group with the social structure of the college. Hence, they have been significant in the development of the black student on white campuses.

The rather large literature on black students in white colleges and universities suggests that, for the period we examine, black students, compared with whites, are older at entry; more urban and less suburban; from lower socioeconomic backgrounds; more likely to be public school graduates and to be less well prepared academically (though, perhaps paradoxically, they have higher educational and mobility aspirations); and somewhat *less* likely to drop out because of academic failure. They also tend to be more instrumental and vocation- and career-oriented.[2]

Black students are more aware of and sensitive to social and political issues, as well more politically cynical and sophisticated—in the strategic and tactical, if not philosophical, sense—than are white students. They are further to the left, more militant, have lower needs for social approval (at least from non-blacks), and less need to conform to white, middle-class standards.[3]

Perhaps most significant are the findings pertaining to their expectations of the white college. In spite of ideologies critical of white institutions, black students, before enrolling, are more likely than white students to expect the college to be practical in its orientation (in the sense of providing them with job-related skills) and more sensitive and responsive to social issues and to them than other societal institutions (see, for example, Proctor, 1970; Simon, 1969; and Willie, 1981). This is not to say that these students have an especially positive view of the white college, but only that they tend to view it more favorably than they do other societal institutions.

As a result, many black students come to school with some initial trust in the white college, a trust perhaps heightened by the provision of financial aid and support services. However, their experience in many white colleges—frequently one of hostility, mistrust, isolation, frustration, and superficial relationships with other students and with teachers and administrators—usually fails to fulfill these expectations (see Willie, 1981). Once enrolled, black students tend to be measurably less satisfied than white students with the help given them by the college (Centra, 1970a; Simon, 1969; Walters, 1974). This situation, which creates strain and discontent, is a major source of criticism of the college and a central element in the development of activism, particularly where the institution has by its own actions helped raise expectations and then not met them. In short, black students' backgrounds and expectations are likely to make them aware of and sensitive to injustice, frustrated by the white university's unresponsiveness, and willing to act on such feelings to produce change.

What about the black students who were enrolled in University College in 1966–68? What were they like, and what were their experiences and activities in the College?[4]

There were relatively few black students in University College before September 1968. Out of an entering freshman class of 459 in September 1966, fewer than one percent were black. This ratio seems to have been fairly typical for the school. The total number of blacks in the freshman class entering in 1967 increased to 13 out of 563 (Dean's Report, 1967–68), largely because of increased recruiting efforts. Even counting transfer students, there were still only a small number of black students on campus between 1966 and 1968, perhaps 25 at most, and the majority were new, either freshmen or transfers.

On the basis of available evidence, before September 1967 they were, with the large exception of race, rather like other students. That is, they came from middle-class families, with fathers and/or mothers in professional, managerial, or technical occupations. In terms of academic preparation, these were students who would have been admitted to this college, and many others, under any circumstances. College attendance was as natural for them as for their white counterparts. Their secondary school preparation was good, and their SAT scores were like those of whites. Most paid their own way, though some were on full or partial scholarship.

They tended to be more urban than white students, though they were more suburban than black students entering after September 1968. That is, they were drawn from a slightly larger geographic area than subsequent black students, most of whom seem to have come from New York City or the greater metropolitan area.

These students appear to have had few major problems of adjustment to the campus; few reported overt racial hostility. (Administrators interviewed likewise report very few explicit racial incidents.) They seem to have been fairly well integrated into the life of the College, many taking full part in campus organizations and activities. Some became dorm presidents, athletic captains, and members of student government. In general, black students before 1967 were more or less like earlier generations of black students in white universities: unorganized, few in number, taking as full a part in campus activities as allowed, or as individual initiative provided, and essentially apolitical in any active sense, particularly in terms of on-campus conditions. As one former student put it: "We were dance teachers. Most of us dug it pretty much." Significantly, he went on to add after a moment's reflection:

> Of course, for a lot of whites, that's *all* we were, dance teachers. I never felt they ever really knew me, let alone understood or cared. You know, I learned some important stuff when I was in school. For one thing, I never really knew what it was to be black, to *feel* black, until I was in college. Most of all, I found out that being black was hard work! (Student Interview no. 7)

For this student and others, being black in the College meant dealing with an alienating setting every day they were on campus.

## DISJUNCTURE, ALIENATION, AND INAUTHENTICITY

For many black students, the white college represents a new setting and experience for which little in their background has prepared them.[5]

Their attributes and expectations make them, as a group, different from their white fellow students, a difference others on campus respond to in negative or patronizing fashion.

> When the blacks arrived on the campuses in larger numbers in 1966, 1967 and 1968 they found several assumptions operative. One assumption was that they should be grateful for this big break; two, they should be ready to prove their capacity and should, if need be, sacrifice to compete successfully; three, they should emulate "white" standards of social decorum; four, their success would pave the way for others and for enlargement of programs for the "disadvantaged"; five, the best thing for blacks to do is to learn to maneuver the "system," get the skills, join the five-figure suburbanites, and become a role model for young blacks in the ghetto. These assumptions were radiated to blacks, not in a manual, but in the unspoken words that one read in smiles, handshakes, announcements, committee appointments and all the rest. They got the message. (Proctor, 1970:48)

The message black students received was one of patronization and denial: of their identity as blacks, of their past and present, and of their aspirations. Their on-campus experiences, as well as off-campus influences, led them to see the white university as, like the larger society, "racist, corrupt, morally bankrupt, and unresponsive to the oppressed" (Kauroma, 1971:66).

As a result, black students were likely to experience discontinuity and stress on the white campus (cf. Boyd, 1974b; Willie and McCord, 1972; Willie, 1981). A crucial consequence was alienation. Wegner (1975) suggests that alienation is a likely result of disjuncture and incompatibility between the personal characteristics of individuals on the one hand and social settings and situations on the other. As a number of observers have noted, alienation from the white college has been high and widespread among black students.[6]

Alienation of individuals and groups from social institutions, organizations, and systems of belief is often of central importance for collective protest in general (Gurr, 1970; Gusfield, 1970; Hajda, 1961; Paige, 1971; Smelser, 1963), and has been an important determinant of student protest in particular (Miles, 1974). It is equally important in the emergence of the black student movement. In this regard, black student activism can be understood as stemming from collective attempts to cope with students' problems in the white setting—"relevance, estrangement, and identity" (Bunzel, 1969). The white college becomes the target of such collective efforts because black students tend to blame the institution for feelings of alienation, feelings that may not have existed or been manifest before matriculation (Burbach and Thompson, 1971).

Alienation is not easy to define. As a concept it embraces a rather wide range of phenomena.[7] Following Etzioni (1968a) and Gould (1969), I view alienation here from the perspective of the actor, rather than in terms of a societal norm or some hypothesized ideal condition or as a global concept referring to a state widespread in the larger society. By alienation I mean "the degree to which a man feels powerless to achieve the role he has determined to be rightly his in specific situations" (J. P. Clark, 1959:849); it is a "syndrome consisting of feelings of pessimism, cynicism, distrust, apathy and emotional distance" (Gould, 1969:40). Hence, the alienated person is "one who has been estranged, made unfriendly toward, his society and the culture it carries" (Nettler, 1957:671).

Alienation here refers: (1) to black students' feelings of isolation in and estrangement from the college; (2) to their feelings of estrangement from work in the sense of curricular and learning experiences in traditional form (cf. Clignet, 1974); (3) to their feelings of betrayed trust; and (4) to feelings of meaninglessness and the sense that campus experiences have little relevance to the larger society, past experiences, or future aspirations.

There is a distinction between active and passive alienation (Etzioni, 1968a). Those who are passively alienated tend to be apathetic, acquiescing to and often not fully aware of those forces creating their alienation. The actively alienated, on the other hand, are generally conscious of their condition and actively "strive to transform it" (Etzioni, 1968a:619). Ideological beliefs are central in creating such an awareness and in legitimating subsequent action. This was, and is, especially true for black students (see Gurin and Epps, 1975).

The existence of such active alienation suggests that one commonly recognized dimension of alienation—powerlessness—may *not*, contrary to what many have suggested (e.g., Crawford and Naditch, 1979; Seeman, 1971; Silvern and Nakamura, 1971), necessarily lead either to apathy or to purely expressive action. Rather, the alienated may feel a sense of efficacy, personal or collective, that leads them to take sustained rational and instrumental action, especially in the context of supportive ideological beliefs. This has been true of blacks in general and black students in particular (Caplan, 1971; Forward and Williams, 1971; Gurin and Epps, 1975; D. I. Warren, 1975).

Both active and passive alienation are created by social conditions and structures. These may be not only alienating, but also inauthentic. Etzioni (1968a:619–620, 635) states the problem clearly.[8]

A relationship, institution, or society is *inauthentic* if it provides the appearance of responsiveness while the underlying condition is alienating. Objectively, both alienating and inauthentic conditions are excluding, but inauthentic structures devote a higher ratio of their efforts than alienating ones to concealing their contours. . . .

Inauthentic institutions seem to have (a) a comparatively high investment in manipulative activities . . . [and] (b) interrank (or status) strains resulting from the split between the appearance of community and the underlying bureaucratic reality (*above and beyond* the strains resulting from alienation itself). (Emphasis in original)

The person who is alienated feels estranged and powerless and sees no meaning in what he does; the person who is "involved inauthentically" feels "cheated and manipulated" and "that he has been made . . . to bless his captors if not his tormentors" (Etzioni, 1968a:633). The contemporary college or university, in which an emphasis on community hides the reality of hierarchy and inequality, is experienced by some students as an inauthentic institution. This is even more true in the case of black students in white colleges and universities.

Hence, many black students in white institutions are likely to be actively alienated in settings that for them are inauthentic. Their movement represents the attempt to reduce such conditions in what they have perceived to be a racist and alienating institution. To quote Allen Ballard (1973:72):

The storms that ensued across the country, then, were of multiple genesis, but their essence was the same: "If you're going to admit us to the university," Black students were saying, "and are unable to provide the environment in which we Black people can feel human, then we ask the right to create those structures within the university that will enable us to do so."

In University College in the years immediately preceding 1968, it appears that the principal source of disjuncture was the fact that black students were racially different from the majority of the students. This difference should not be minimized. The fact that most of these students came from backgrounds that harmonized with those of other students in the College may have mitigated the sense of disjuncture for them, compared with black students in later years. Or this sense may simply have been more repressed, as it often was by black students on white campuses (see Wade, 1976; Wolters, 1975).

It is difficult to determine precisely the degree of alienation experienced by black students in University College. Their apparently high degree of participation in campus activities would seem to indicate that for participating students, at least, alienation either was not extreme or was more or less effectively handled. We might recall here the student who felt that he was appreciated primarily as a dance teacher. However, another former student, who was in the College during 1966 and 1967, suggests that much discontinuity and alienation was repressed and not openly admitted:

> Looking back, I realize that all of us, each in our own separate ways, was doing a lot of repressing and denying of the little things that made us feel uncomfortable and strange on the campus. Some things were not so little. That's why we had to get together to try to change things. (Student Interview no. 9)

At that point alienation may have seemed unavoidable and inherent in the College experience—something to be endured. The view that it was *not* to be endured became increasingly prominent as a result of changes in attitude in the wider black community.

Between the fall of 1966 and the assassination of Martin Luther King in April 1968, black students' actions and beliefs in University College underwent a profound change. This shift, as I have suggested, took place in the context of important off-campus developments. It both preceded and followed the growth, in 1967 and early 1968, of black student organization on campus, a development that was critical in the emergence of the black student movement in University College.


## THE ORGANIZATION AND EMERGENCE OF THE MOVEMENT

The disjuncture and alienation experienced by black students on white campuses have been a critical factor in their organization.[9] This collective response was encouraged by their acceptance of ideologies stressing solidarity, unity, and collective struggle against racism. The result was the formation of black student unions, the general term for organizations with a variety of formal names: Black Student Union, Association of Afro American Students, Allied Black Students. All these organizations share certain traits: they are exclusively black in membership, monolithic in appearance, highly self-conscious, and motivated by sociopolitical concerns.

The term "black student union," then, refers specifically to those organizations formed in the mid- and late sixties explicitly to foster solidarity and unity, black culture, and significant change in the university or college. Among the first such organizations were the black student unions at Columbia and Harvard, formed in 1963; that at Cornell, formed in 1965; and that at San Francisco State, formed in 1966 out of a previously existing group, the Negro Students Association (Barlow and Shapiro, 1971; Pinkney, 1975; Strout and Grossvogel, 1971). Specifically excluded from this discussion are student groups of the more traditional sort—fraternities, sororities, student government, general service organizations, and political groups like the Young Democrats.

Black student unions have been crucial for black student activism in white colleges for several reasons: their function in meeting various student needs; their concentration on cultural, psychological, or collective social identity; their role in the growth of student values and ideological beliefs; their development of a sense of collective competence; and their use as a mechanism for expressing collective purposes and discontents.

The union can serve to mitigate the strain of being in the white university and to meet needs (met for other students by fraternities, service organizations, or other traditional groups). It provides a setting that is not white and in which, therefore, relaxation, security, and escape from the pressures of the university are ostensibly possible. The organization may help in individuals' personal adjustment to the university, not least by functioning as a supportive peer group (see, e.g., Willie and McCord, 1972). Relatedly, it can provide a group in which friends can be made somewhat more easily and with less anxiety over rejection or self-compromise than in white-dominated groups (assuming, of course, that the organization is not itself torn by internal factionalism or a subject of controversy among black students). Several of the former students I interviewed who were involved in the early years of the black student organization in University College felt very strongly about its supportive role. As one put it, "I finally felt that I was with people like me, who knew what I felt because they felt the same way" (Student Interview no. 3).

In addition, the union often provides social, cultural, and recreational events and alternative educational experiences, both within the union and in the programs and events it sponsors. It also provides a forum for collective discussion and sponsors speakers, panels, and other activities with a political focus. In this regard, the black student organization has had an important role in the growth of social and political views among students, especially views critical of white society in general and the white college in particular. It frequently provides a kind of collective reinforcement and legitimation for beliefs (see, e.g.,

Harding, 1969), [10] especially where it serves as the basic source of social life and recreational activities for black students. In this regard it has been as much a political organization as a social one. As we shall see, this was very much the case with the black student organization in University College.

In addition, the organization has played a highly significant role in black students' sense of collective competence. [11] By its very existence it has given a tangible, concrete form to ideological beliefs about black unity and solidarity. It provides a continuing sense of corporateness, of we-ness, that is important in maintaining a sense of efficacy in confronting and managing the social world of the university; in this sense, member commitment and cohesion are crucial. Finally, once formed, the organization has generally been the unit with which the college deals when questions or issues relevant to black students arise. This negotiating role is important in maintaining a sense of collective competence and efficacy.

This sense of collective competence has, in turn, been a central factor in the development of the movement. It has had the most powerful effect when combined with the disappointment of high expectations and consequent lowered trust in the institution. Where black students' sense of collective competence has remained high, their critical view of the white college has been maintained, and their expectation of college responsiveness has been dashed, the circumstances are ripe for black student protest and the active expression of discontent. This is shown clearly in the history of the black student movement in University College. As Gamson (1968:48) notes, "a combination of a high sense of political efficacy and low political trust is the optimum combination for mobilization." [12]

It is under these circumstances that the black student union has achieved its most visible significance. It was, and remains, the vehicle through which collective discontent is expressed and efforts at producing change in the college or university are generally channeled. The organization is, in short, the heart of the black student movement. We can see this in the development of the black student union in University College.

On 14 December 1966 ACCESS (Afro-American Cultural and Educational Student Society) held its first meeting, and the first black student organization in University College came into existence. Four principal aims of ACCESS were enunciated at this meeting: (1) recruiting more black students into the College; (2) creating special programs at NYU (i.e., University College) to aid the poor and the disadvantaged; (3)

giving black students a sense of unity; and (4) in the words of Bill Moore, first president of the organization, "finding and expanding ways of making white middle-class NYU more meaningful to the black student" (HDN, 15 Dec. 1966). The appearance of ACCESS was the first overt indication of the impact of off-campus developments and on-campus experiences on black students in the College and a sign of a major shift in their views and objectives. ACCESS and its activities became a source of much discussion and debate during the spring term of 1967, especially in HDN.

At least some of the initial aims of ACCESS—for example, increasing the number of black students and creating special programs—had been promoted earlier in editorials in HDN. Thus, some sentiment in favor of such changes may be presumed to have existed on campus already. However, it had not produced extensive action by the College, perhaps because there was no organized, coherent pressure behind it. If this was the case, the existence of ACCESS meant a real change in the situation. Indeed, to bring such pressure was one of the reasons for its formation.

At its 15 February 1967 meeting (as reported in HDN), the activities and plans of the new organization were outlined further. The emphasis on recruitment continued, and some students began initial steps toward this end. Coordination was planned, and in a few instances begun, with similar organizations at other colleges in the New York area. An "Upward Bound"–type program was planned for later in the spring, both to benefit high school students and to recruit black students to NYU. An important goal was to obtain official support and sponsorship for such a program. "The university's interest in our program is the critical factor," Bill Moore noted in an article in HDN on 15 February. All this is significant: the relatively modest, reformist, norm-oriented nature of the students' goals; the absence of any fundamental challenge to the College; the acknowledgment of the necessity for official support and sponsorship of a student-initiated program; and the use of persuasion and conventional means to achieve the organization's goals. Official sponsorship, of course, would represent a concrete, tangible commitment from the administration, which would improve the chance of achieving those goals. Although the formation of the organization, its formulation of a program, and the beginning of efforts to implement it can be seen as indicating the emergence of the black student movement, the goals and tactics of ACCESS at this point reflected moderate political beliefs and educational goals as well as the basic legitimacy of the institution among a majority of black students.

On 7 April three committees of ACCESS announced their plans in

*HDN*.[13] The Social Committee revealed plans to hold a party and to invite black students from all colleges in New York City. The Education Committee disclosed its plans to join the newly formed Intercollegiate Education Committee (comprising the education committees of all black student organizations in colleges and universities in New York City), and announced a College Day and open house to be held for black and Puerto Rican high school students. The Cultural Committee announced that it was in the midst of compiling a list of publications pertinent to black students, separate from and independent of the College library. In addition, under the aegis of the committee, an Afro-American History Club was in the planning stages.

These announcements are worthy of note for several reasons. First, they show the degree of organization already existing by this time. Second, they illustrate the essentially cultural and educational, as opposed to political, aims of the black students then in University College. Third, they provide some indication of their perception of their own needs and interests. Finally, and perhaps most important, they demonstrate that black students at this time were not actively challenging the prevailing structure of power and authority within the College. In short, they provide further evidence of the reformist, norm-oriented character of the movement at this early stage of its career.

During this time, the central aim of ACCESS, recruitment of more black students, was not forgotten. Many of its members, particularly Bill Moore, were actively engaged in recruitment efforts. Indeed, the admissions office, announcing in May that incoming freshmen were "the strongest class we have ever had" (*HDN*, 11 May), was moved to note the close cooperation of ACCESS. Furthermore, an administrator in the College reported, "ACCESS was tremendously helpful in recruiting black students. I just wish they had continued to be the leadership group we dealt with in later years. They always struck me as a level-headed group" (Administrative/Faculty Interview no. 4). Given that only thirteen black students actually entered with this class, however, their efforts, for whatever reason, do not seem to have achieved the success that many students desired.

As the school year of 1966–67 closed, ACCESS was faced with internal dissension and division. The split seems to have been based on political differences between a more moderate group, apparently led by senior Bill Moore, and a more militant one, apparently led by sophomore Edson Lawrence. This development was the first case of internal dissension within the black student movement at University College. At the time I interviewed those students who were in ACCESS, they described a period of intense discussion and no little hostility among factions in the organization. The moderate students seem to have felt that more could be gained by working through channels, while others argued that working in the traditional way would only produce co-option. As one student put it, "Those of us who wanted to work with the University were always arguing with those who felt that would be giving up the game" (Student Interview no. 1). The immediate consequence was a change in organization the following year.

Black students engaged in no activity during the summer. The school year of 1967–68 opened quietly, with little indication of the activities, or even the existence, of ACCESS. The first concrete evidence of a shift in black student views came in a column in the 9 October 1967 edition of HDN written by a black student, Thomas Sutcliffe. In this article, entitled "Violence Is American," Sutcliffe asked, "Why are white Americans so horrified at the violent reaction of the black man and the prospect of black revolution?" Violence, he argued, has accompanied every radical and important change in America and been subsequently rationalized and justified because of the benefits of such changes. Negotiation, attempts at legal redress through the courts, nonviolent protest, appeals to whites, "were to no avail." Hence, "if nonviolence doesn't work, what is there left for blacks to do? There are two choices: to give up the struggle for equality, or to pursue it more belligerently. The status quo is unacceptable." Sutcliffe concluded by noting that the failure of nonviolence is

> conclusive proof that white America will never respond to nonviolence and is in reality asking for violence. The riots are the first step toward fulfillment of this request. . . . It is up to white people to solve this problem. They caused it, they prolonged it, and they, too, must end it. It is not a question of Afro-Americans being ready; the question is are whites ready? Time is running short. A revolution may be closer than you think. Black people will come to violence only with sincere racist help. Think about it, white people!

Though debate over political issues continued in HDN, there was no published reaction to Sutcliffe's column. In the previous year, when extensive discussion of civil rights issues appeared in the paper, a column like this would likely have provoked a great deal of response. This lack of published response by whites to the statements or actions of black students was a common pattern during 1967–68.

On 13 November a column appeared in HDN entitled "Uncle Tom's Myth: Whitewash," written by Edson Lawrence, "president of *Katara,* the Afro-American organization of NYU" (that is, of University College; it was common practice for members of the College to refer to it as the University). This was the first indication that ACCESS no longer existed and that henceforth the black student organization was to be known as Katara, a Swahili word connoting power and liberation.[14] Katara, a very different organization, was the result of the split that had developed in ACCESS the previous spring. It was a much more overtly political organization than ACCESS, and its leaders appear to have been more militant. A student who strongly agreed with the change in operations described Lawrence and the other new leaders as "tough, right-on guys who knew what they were doing, and knew we had to fight the University for whatever we were going to get" (Student Interview no. 3).

In the column Lawrence announced a change in self-image and a changed perspective on the world among black students. Essentially, the article was a celebration of the death of Uncle Tom and of the Negro. "They say you should speak only good of the dead. Uncle Tom is dead. Good! The black man who has replaced him has re-defined the black man's role in America's white society." The white-determined and imposed term "Negro" was categorically rejected, as were behaviors or persons who conformed to either the meanings or the implications of the term.

> The black man who has replaced Tom is not one of these "responsible" Negroes. He rejects "whitenization." . . . He rejects the lie that all goodness and beauty is white. . . . He no longer thinks purely in terms of his own physical comfort. More and more he organizes with his black brothers, silently building black power to use the economic and political potential of black people for the benefit of black people. Instead of begging for tasteless crumbs at the white man's table, he'd rather bargain from a position of unified strength—man to man. He's not necessarily anti-white, but he is pro-black.

Lawrence stressed that "black," formerly a term of derision and denigration, henceforth would be the only acceptable term by which to refer to Afro-Americans. These changes in attitude and action by blacks were things white America and its institutions, and some Negroes, were going to have to get used to and accept.

> Can you dig it, white America? Then get yourself together! 'Cause my brothers and I, this new breed, no longer ask for your goodwill to take another hundred years to give us equality. We already know we're equal and we're demanding our share as equals. We don't need you as our

leaders. We already have our own. We'll make our own mistakes and claim our own victories. As for those few sons of Uncle Tom who are still around, don't think we don't see you sneaking kneels in the white man's temples, slobbering over his discarded trash (sacrificial pigs). We don't hate you. Far be it from us to make you look foolish to hate yourself. You're already doing that yourself.

Sutcliffe's and Lawrence's columns gave notice not just that a new kind of black student group had appeared on campus, but that former conceptions and modes of interaction between blacks and whites were no longer to be considered automatically good and valid. Both warned whites, in effect, to change their ways of seeing and dealing with blacks or face serious efforts by blacks to change their situation.

The first semester ended and the second began with no further public action or pronouncement of any kind by Katara. Early in the second semester, Katara released an official statement (published in the 8 Feb. 1968 HDN) in which many of the ideas articulated by Sutcliffe and Lawrence were elaborated and presented as group policy. The statement berated whites for past injustices and took them to task for present racism in all forms. Participation by whites in the black struggle—especially "white liberals" and whites who assumed leadership roles—was emphatically rejected. So were white views of what should be done to accomplish racial change, especially when they implied any kind of white-controlled timetable for achieving goals; gradualism and "go slow" approaches were no longer acceptable.

As in the earlier statement, "Tomming" as an appropriate mode of behavior for blacks was rejected, along with the name and implications of "Negro." Further, black students proclaimed their refusal to be bought off, co-opted, fragmented, or split up by authorities of any kind. they would remain unified to the end. Finally:

> As black students we pledge to use our talents in black communities for the benefit of the black man. We will teach ourselves and our children the true heritage and pride of the black man. We will unite and develop the economic and political potential of our people. Black unity is black power. With power, the black man will end the racist exploitation of black people. Toward this end we stand united!

With this statement the campus was once more put on notice that this was indeed a different group of black students from those who had attended the College in previous years. In many respects it was a Declaration of Independence and a Declaration of Principles in one and served the same sort of public notification and belief-enhancing function for its members. The statement can be seen as a kind of oath or pledge of allegiance by black students, to each other and to the black communities across society. Most important, it (along with the special columns in HDN in the fall) indicates that despite the absence of public visibility and overt action, significant developments had occurred among black students. The disappearance of ACCESS (largely due to a kind of coup d'état by younger students and the impending graduation of seniors like Moore) and the appearance of Katara were an important outward sign.

In retrospect, the period from late spring 1967 to spring 1968 seems to have been one of strategic withdrawal, a loin-girding time. During these months of public silence, important developments in generalized beliefs and shifts in leadership occurred.[15] As one student put it: "We spent a lot of time getting ourselves together—talking, arguing, holding meetings, etc. Always realizing more and more just what shit whites— yeah, even the University—had been handing us" (Student Interview no. 6). Almost every meeting of Katara in these days was a kind of consciousness-raising session in which black history and thought were presented, various sociopolitical ideas and positions critically examined, and the beauty of blackness and the power of unity consistently stressed. The individual and collective self-worth of black people and the necessity of collective action were a constant theme.

The 8 February statement in some ways signaled the end of the period of strategic withdrawal. It was followed in a few days by a column in the 12 February HDN (whether it was deliberately scheduled for appearance on Lincoln's birthday is unknown) written by Katara leader Todd Little and following along the same lines as the earlier statements. In it he asserted that white racism was responsible for "planting and cultivating the seeds of revolution in the black community." Liberalism was only a façade for racism. Moreover, he argued, too often and in too many places, blacks have been exploited by other minorities further up the "success or status ladder." It was time for blacks to stop begging; they had a right to demand, and to use violence if necessary: "Whether white Americans are able or unable to see the signs, the hour of decision is rapidly approaching, and you as the oppressor will greatly influence what decisions we, as the revolting people, will make."

Little's column was one more indication of the on-going process of consciousness-raising, self-definition, and analysis that marked this period. It provided further rationale for separation from whites in the liberation struggle and for collective effort and black self-reliance "in our quest for dignity, unity and power." Moreover, it gave further evidence of an acceptance, at least in rhetoric, of non-traditional tactics of struggle. Taken together, this column and previous statements signaled Katara's readiness for public activity.

Neither this statement nor the earlier ones provoked any recorded reaction in the College, although public campus commentary of some kind would have been likely the previous year. This silence, whatever its causes, represents a breakdown in interracial communication and seems to have affirmed for black students both the correctness of their analysis and a sense of collective competence, particularly since the silence of whites was accompanied by continued efforts on the part of the College to increase its recruitment of black students.

The period from December 1966 through March 1968 was a critical one for the development of the black student movement in University College. Prior to 1966 black students seem to have accepted the legitimacy of the University without open question, showing a certain basic trust in it and a sense of confidence in themselves as *individuals*. In their backgrounds, aspirations, and on-campus activities, they do not appear to have been markedly different from their white contemporaries, or from the relatively few black students who attended white colleges and universities at that time.

December 1966 to March 1968, however, saw significant changes. During these months students began to organize and crucial shifts in black students' attitudes toward themselves and toward whites took place. These shifts led to changed views of the white university. A decline in trust and in belief in its legitimacy characterized these changing views. A sense of collective competence seems to have grown apace, encouraged indirectly by off-campus events, more directly by College actions, and deliberately by Katara. These developments were accompanied by what were apparently increasing difficulties in interracial communication on campus and by pressures on black students to join the organization and give its goals precedence.

Up to this point Katara's publicly articulated views were different from ACCESS's and more directly challenging to the status quo. At the same time, they were not nearly as specific as those of ACCESS and focused more on general societal issues than on College ones. Yet, while the movement's rhetoric at this point was of the value-oriented type, its actions were not. Indeed, as we have seen, there was very little public action of any kind between September 1967 and March 1968. The movement was norm-oriented in conduct at least.

However, with the development of organization and the articulation of changed beliefs, an increasing sense of competence, and decreasing trust in the College, all the preconditions for the active expression of black student discontent were met. Thus, what was said of black students at other colleges was true of black students in University College by the beginning of April 1968: "The black student activists in '68 closed ranks among themselves in order to become more clearly defined and have the advantage of collective effort" (Anthony, 1971:12). It remained only for some precipitating factor to set off active protest. Ideological mobilization had begun, and an organizational infrastructure was already in place. The first phase of black student activism was finished.

## CHAPTER IV

# "This Place Has Gotta Change"

*A*n *apparent paradox . . . tends to develop in the dynamics of education systems. Modern systems of education, on the one hand, draw men into the orbit of the societal center and generate intensified participatory activity; on the other hand, they engender a tendency to a more fully articulated protest and dissent.*——S. N. Eisenstadt (1972:17)

By the spring of 1968, the movement in University College was fully developed, an organization was in place, and initial activism had produced some limited success in increasing the admission of black students. The most active efforts, including large-scale protest, were still to come. In all of these efforts, we can see the varying roles of off-campus events, black students' on-campus experiences, and their interactions with others in the College in influencing the direction and focus of the movement. There were essentially six phases of black student activism in University College. In the preceding chapter I discussed the first phase, which involved the development of ACCESS/Katara and the organization's initial activities and successes.

The second phase of activism was precipitated by the assassination of Martin Luther King, Jr., and involved much more intense activity. It was marked by extensive mobilization by the movement of its resources and efforts and the presentation of its first full demands for change. In this phase the movement was programmatic, primarily concerned with change in the College, and, in several senses, successful. The third phase of activism, which occurred the following fall, was the most intense in the movement's history, involving building occupations, the calling out of New York City police by the college provost, student strikes, and weeks of student agitation in what came to be known as the Stone affair. The focus during this phase was centered more on persons than programs; it involved extensive mobilization of the membership but ultimately produced two major crises for the movement and failed to achieve its main goal. In this chapter we will examine these two phases of activism in some detail. In the following chapter I will discuss phases four through six of the movement and its ultimate disintegration.

## PHASE 2: APRIL TO SEPTEMBER 1968

The murder of Martin Luther King on 4 April had a profound effect on blacks around the country. Some of the most serious urban disturbances in American history took place in black ghettos following his death. Black students, especially those on white campuses, were equally affected. Like black students around the nation, those in University College reacted with shock, grief, and anger. The King assassination symbolized the intransigence and totality of white racism. It called into question the continued viability of the approach King embodied and, for many, pointed up the need for different strategies and tactics, as well as new targets. After the assassination many vowed to let the world know that things had to be—were *going* to be—different. For black students in the College, the assassination represented the final impetus to a trend that had been developing all year.

After the initial shock and disbelief, white students, faculty members, and administrators at NYU began asking themselves how and why such a thing had happened. What could the University, as a place of humanity, reason, and good will, do to help remedy the ills suffered by black Americans? What could it do to implement the ideals King worked so hard to foster? The University authorities closed the school, canceled classes, and held memorial services in all the various divisions, including University College. At the College the administration scheduled an all-campus symposium for 10 April—after school reopened—the topic of which was to be "The Negro and the University."

Throughout the week from 4 to 10 April Katara held a series of meetings, trying to decide how to react as a group, both to the death and to the College's actions. As might be expected, there was a great deal of anger and hostility toward whites. Some felt that they should strike or otherwise refuse to participate in College routines. When the plans to hold the symposium were announced, there was widespread sentiment against attending—the meeting was viewed as a waste of time.

At this point the faculty advisor to Katara played a decisive role.

Professor Catherine Curtis of the anthropology department, though white, had been chosen by Katara as sponsor because, in her words, "they knew I was sympathetic and knew I would leave them alone." In a meeting with Katara during this week, she finally persuaded the members that they should attend the proposed symposium at least "long enough to make a dramatic exit." Accepting this advice, they spent the time remaining before the symposium determining how to make their attendance productive for future change. The participation of as many black students as possible was solicited, with the result that the overwhelming majority of black students in the College attended these sessions. Out of these deliberations came agreement on a list of demands for the College authorities.

The symposium, held as scheduled on 10 April in Gould Memorial Theater, was well attended by students, faculty members, and administrators. College administrators, after paying homage to King, described efforts to admit more black students and their successes to that point: at least thirty-two black students had been accepted for the fall semester of 1968 before the assassination. Other administrators described the tutorial and counseling programs in the ghettos of New York City in which students and the University were involved. White students and faculty members then expressed their opinions about the meaning of Dr. King's life and death, the needs of blacks and other minorities in a white society, and the goals and responsibilities of the University in relation to these needs.

Black students were silent through most of these discussions. At this point Edson Lawrence, president of Katara, gained the floor and, after some remarks about King and the meaning of his death in relation to the white university, presented Katara's list of six demands for immediate acceptance and implementation: (1) hiring of more black faculty members and administrators, persons who would be knowledgeable about the concerns and problems of black people; (2) expansion of the curriculum to include the study of Africans and their descendants throughout the world, particularly in the United States; (3) induction of Martin Luther King and Malcolm X into the Hall of Fame;[1] (4) establishment of a University-financed community center in the College's immediate neighborhood, to be run by the community to serve its own purposes; (5) abolition of white fraternities that discriminated against blacks;[2] and (6) the inclusion of African history among the courses required for freshmen and sophomores to meet the general education and distribution requirements for the B.A. degree. Unlike black student unions at other schools, Katara made no demands for more black students, an indication of its recognition that the College had already begun to take steps in that direction.

Lawrence concluded by saying that the symposium was a white idea and reflected a white problem; black people would take care of their own. Whereupon, before there could be any response, black students rose as a body and left the meeting. This was a deliberate move, planned for maximum impact and intended to convey the importance of their demands, the seriousness with which black students viewed the issues, and their opposition to compromise. (The walk-out was, of course, a common tactic during the 1960s.)

This episode marks the beginning of Katara's public activism—the first public presentation of *demands* focusing on the institution. Moreover, it was the first walk-out by black students from any meeting, public or private, with others in the College community. Needless to say, it created some consternation and not a little shock among whites at the meeting. Some were offended that black students left without waiting for a reply. Others felt that the demands were extreme and did not deserve serious discussion. Still others took them seriously, felt they had merit, and insisted that steps to implement them begin forthwith.

Whatever further actions may have been planned by Katara are not known, though there had been vague talk among some students of a class boycott or a sit-in. What might have happened in the absence of official response is a subject for speculation; however, immediate action by the central University administration effectively forestalled more serious steps on the part of black students.

The following day, 11 April, the University Senate approved a five-point plan aimed specifically at combatting racism in NYU. First, there would be an immediate increase in the recruiting of minority students, particularly blacks and Puerto Ricans.[3] Second, a Martin Luther King Scholarship Grant Program would be established to ensure aid for any minority student who needed financial asistance, but "who could not qualify for normal scholarship assistance because of inadequate secondary school records" (New York University, 1971). Since regular scholarship funds had already been awarded by this time, the University undertook a $1 million fund drive to finance the program, and the admissions office was directed to find suitable candidates for admission that September despite the late date. An educational support effort was established as part of this program. Third, existing undergraduate educational support and remedial programs would be strengthened.[4] Fourth, the University Senate endorsed the introduction of new courses and announced plans to establish the Martin Luther King Institute for

Afro-American Affairs as a primary means of increasing the University's research and instruction in areas dealing with blacks. And, fifth, the University would engage in intensive recruitment and appointment of black faculty members and administrators for all its divisions (there were virtually none at the time).

The University's response to Dr. King's death was swift, positive, and concrete. Many of the goals and demands of black students, at the Heights and at the Square, were ostensibly accepted. Whether or not it was aware of developments in University College the preceding day, the senate's action in effect nipped in the bud the possibility of serious black student protest in the College. Nor were College authorities unresponsive.

On 17 April HDN announced the organization of six joint student-faculty-administration committees in the College to attack racial problems and deal with the specific demands of black students. Each committee was to concentrate on one of the following issues: (1) curriculum changes; (2) the establishment of a community center; (3) the problem of discrimination in fraternities; (4) summer programs to benefit neighborhood children and youth, principally tutorials and recreation programs; (5) the MLK Institute for Afro-American Affairs and the question of its relation to University College; and (6) a Harlem Independent Board of Education.[5] (Neither summer programs, the MLK Institute, nor a Harlem Board of Education were among the initial Katara demands.) The school year ended with all six committees meeting and with expectations of appreciable results soon.

When one looks back, it is clear that Martin Luther King's assassination led to the first serious, large-scale, public black activism in the College. It could have impelled the movement toward more radical action, perhaps violence, as certainly happened on other campuses and in numerous urban communities.[6] It did *not* have this effect, because of swift, concrete responses by both the University and the College, which pre-empted black students' issues and concerns and removed any immediate justification for further, more extreme activion or protest.

The response of the authorities could, from their perspective, be seen as both morally right and politically effective. The "testing" could also be seen as successful from the student viewpoint. Not only did the institution seem to be taking positive action, but its reaction to student concerns and demands reinforced the sense of collective competence of black students as a group.

By showing itself responsive, however, the University created the expectation that such responsiveness would continue. In effect, it not only confirmed the efficacy of black students as a group, but also raised their expectations for continued progress and responsiveness. Equally important, such responsiveness may have engendered a certain amount of trust in the institution. Given the militant and highly politicized orientation that developed, as we have seen, before King's assassination, this likely was a rather tenuous trust. Nonetheless, by the summer of 1968, many black students in the College had reason to believe that their hopes had some justification.

During the summer the first of the summer programs proposed in April got under way. Geared primarily for neighborhood children, it was officially sponsored by the College, used College facilities, and was staffed by student volunteers (predominantly black). The programs appear to have been a success from the beginning. The intensive recruitment of black students begun by the College in the aftermath of King's death continued through the summer, with many black students participating in these recruiting efforts. University College also expanded its earlier educational support efforts during the summer. As the dean put it,

> This summer [we are] counselling many incoming students. Those who have need of it have been enrolled in a special reading course offered by our American language institute. Some of these and others have been enrolled in a special course in English Composition. We have every confidence that we can identify students who may benefit from the University College experience and that we can take care of them after they have come to our campus. (Dean's Report, 1967–68)

Black students were also engaged in their own activities. As black freshmen were accepted for admission, members of Katara immediately contacted them to encourage and ensure their acceptance of admission. Between June and September Katara members held meetings with groups of incoming freshmen to acquaint them with each other, with the College, with black students already enrolled, and with Katara and its activities. In the process, these new students were exposed, before actual entry into the College, to the views and attitudes of Katara members, and the growth of shared beliefs and viewpoints was fostered.[7] Such consciousness-raising, whether it was intended to or not, accomplished a basic, initial mobilization of students.

Other members were planning a series of orientation activities for black freshmen in September. (It seems that Katara had at least the tacit permission of the College administration to take over major responsibility for the orientation of new black students.) In the words of a student involved in these activities, "We knew what we wanted to do with these students—what they should know, how we could help them. We knew we could do a better job than white counselors" (Student Interview no. 5).

Obscured for the moment in all this activity was the fact that the College had not yet implemented all the demands from the previous spring. Further, many in the college held covert negative images of black students, especially of the new students entering in September, and often assumed that they had marginal academic preparation, backgrounds of hard-core poverty, and families with severe social as well as economic difficulties. Many (if not all) were stereotyped as unlikely to make it without special and extensive help from the College to overcome their various deprivations and inadequacies. Even with special assistance, few expected them to exhibit marked academic achievement in any great numbers.

In the words of one College faculty member, who seemed to express the opinion of many, "NYU gets the marginal black; good blacks go elsewhere. I have often argued that given our black students, unless NYU provides intensive special programs for them, they would suffer such adjustment problems, academic and personal, it might be better to have no black students at all" (Administrative/Faculty Interview no. 4). Such views may reflect sincere concern, but they assume, almost a priori, the inferiority of black students in the College. Black students entered the College perceived by some as a threat—to academic standards and related values, if in no other way. These views, which echo sentiments expressed in the College several decades earlier, indicate that some faculty members had low expectations of students' abilities, with consequent possibilities for self-fulfilling prophecies in student performance. Such attitudes may have reduced black students' willingness to accept the status quo in the College. Certainly they were important in determining the quality of their experience and the character of their grievances.

Thus, when school opened in September 1968, potentially troublesome conditions were present. On the one hand, black students' expectations of College responsiveness and continued progress in their own endeavors were high and rising. Concurrently, their sense of their own collective competence had been bolstered, while many continued to hold views of whites and white institutions that called for constant struggle against them. On the other hand, the College had been responsive to black students, without acceding to all their demands, while there were decidedly mixed feelings on campus about black students in general. In retrospect it is clear that conditions on campus were such that if there was a threat to or reversal of continued progress by black students, or if there was major College resistance to change or a cessation of perceived responsiveness, black student protest would erupt.[8] Though it was not apparent at the time, events in the weeks following the opening of school provided just such a threat of reversal.

Much more visible at the start of the 1968–69 academic year was the fact that the entering freshman class—626 students—was the largest in the College's history. More dramatically, it contained approximately 70 black students, the largest number ever. This enrollment represents better than a fivefold increase in black admissions since September 1967, when 13 black students entered in the freshman class.

With the return of approximately 25 upperclassmen, there were about 95 black students on campus, 4 percent of the total student body of 2,261. Almost three-quarters were incoming freshmen. This seems to have been one reason for Katara's eagerness to meet with or at least contact incoming students over the summer and for its virtual take-over of orientation activities for new black students. A large group of new students represented a real challenge to the consensus and cohesive relations among black students that Katara had been striving to achieve.

Of the 70 new black students, 59 were MLK scholarship recipients. This represents a real achievement for a program that came into existence only four months before the start of the new school year. These numbers were, however, hardly likely to quiet fears that the campus was being flooded with inferior students.[9] The academic preparation of many (though not all) of the new black students was somewhat less complete than that of incoming white students, but there was a wide variation. All the black freshmen admitted, MLK and non-MLK, appear to have met the basic standards of the College without too much difficulty, and at least in the official view of the administration, their admission did not represent any serious lowering of standards (see Dean's Report, 1967–68).

They were greeted by the full array of orientation activities that Katara had been planning all summer, including a series of forums at which invited speakers presented a spectrum of conservative, moderate, and radical political views on black issues. Discussions were held about majors and career possibilities; campus life and experiences; past Katara activities; and plans for Katara, including discussions of needed changes in the College and its relationship to the surrounding black and

Puerto Rican neighborhoods. In addition, films of the Howard University demonstrations of the previous year were shown and analyzed.

There were also a full range of entertainment activities, including concerts, barbecues, and parties. As a Katara officer explained, the purpose of this orientation was to

> let the freshmen know that they're not alone on this campus, that NYU is not an impossible school and that they are not being left to sink or swim. Our main job will be to keep them here for four years, have them graduate and go back into the black Community and help build it up.[10]
> (Todd Little, quoted in HDN, 18 Sept. 1968)

At the same time, these orientation activities can be seen as a means of strengthening the political position and power of Katara as a campus organization.

The first indication that Katara did not intend to waste time beginning its activities for the year came in its budget request and announcement of its plans for the coming months.[11] An article in the 19 September HDN revealed that Katara had requested $1,400 for 1968–69 from the Student Governing Board (SGB), the student agency responsible for distributing operating funds to recognized student organizations. Of this amount, $500 was earmarked for communications, $600 for educational purposes, and $300 for traveling expenses incurred in visiting other colleges and attending conferences and meetings.

Katara's request precipitated a minor crisis within SGB, and an impasse quickly developed between the board and Katara. The request for $1,400 was a very large one, inasmuch as SGB reportedly only had $11,000 for *all* clubs. Moreover, it had already granted Katara $950; hence, the request raised Katara's total proposed funding to $2,350. The administrative staff in the student affairs office and most of the students on SGB viewed the request as excessive, unfair, and not serious. On the other hand, some administrators were inclined to grant Katara the money, arguing in part that black students were new on campus and needed to build up the facilities and resources to carry out an on-going program as other student organizations had in the past.[12]

Cognizant of its audacity in the face of SGB's budgetary constraints but convinced of the justice of its request, facing resistance from SGB but enjoying some administrative support, Katara from the first took the position that its request was completely justifiable given the needs of black students and its planned program of activities. The request was not open to discussion as far as black students were concerned. For over two weeks Katara failed to send representatives to either regular or specially scheduled meetings of SGB to discuss it.

During this impasse the director of student affairs, who was also the SGB advisor, announced that SGB was trying to get more money for Katara from the newly opened MLK Afro-American Student Center downtown and that plans for a similar center at the Heights had been temporarily suspended pending a meeting of SGB with the newly appointed director of the center, James Stone.[13]

The confrontation between SGB and Katara was finally resolved on 7 October with the announcement that Katara would get $250 instead of the requested $1,400. Added to the $950 already granted, this came to a total of $1,200, more than 10 percent of SGB's total budget. Though it was short of the original request, getting any money at all in the face of strong opposition was a kind of victory for Katara. This peaceful and relatively successful outcome helped to maintain the high level of expectations held by black students toward the College. It further confirmed their sense of collective competence, while the opposition to the request strengthened their belief in the virtue of maintaining a somewhat wary stance toward the white College.

Their wariness was reinforced by the controversy surrounding the appointment of James Stone as director of the MLK Afro-American Student Center downtown, which was then reaching a climactic stage and making the University a very tense place.

## PHASE 3: SEPTEMBER TO NOVEMBER 1968

Following the assassination of Martin Luther King, black students at the downtown campus had proposed that the University establish a student social and cultural center—the Martin Luther King Afro-American Student Center—where black students could meet and hold activities. It was to be a place where they could "be themselves," foster solidarity, and promote black culture. The director of the center would be black, hold official administrative status within the University, and have as his basic responsibility service to black students and to the center.[14]

The University accepted this proposal, in principle, in April 1968. Formal approval was given at the beginning of the summer, and plans were begun to open the center in the coming fall at Washington Square. The search for a director began immediately and continued throughout the summer. Black students from both campuses took a lively interest and were given a major role in the search. By August it had become clear that the leading candidate was James Stone, a public school teacher and community leader in Harlem who had been intimately involved in controversies over the public schools there the previous school year. Almost from the time his name first arose, his candidacy was strongly and consistently supported by the black students involved in the search for a director, not least because of his consistently pro-black and militant stances in the Harlem school disputes.[15] By the end of summer, however, as his candidacy looked more and more likely to be successful, voices began to be raised questioning his fitness for the job. Opposition came from alumni, students, faculty members, the press, people in and out of academia—all white, many Jewish. It centered on charges that in his activities and statements during the Harlem school disputes Stone had shown himself to be anti-Semitic.

In the summer of 1968 tensions between the black and Jewish communities in New York City were reaching new peaks over conflict between community school boards and the United Federation of Teachers in Harlem and Brooklyn. These controversies, and the charges of racism and anti-Semitism that they engendered, had received intensive media coverage for months. As a result, sensitivities were acute. University College, with its many students and teachers of Jewish background from the New York City area, could not remain unaffected by these off-campus developments. The black-Jewish confrontation that developed in the University over Stone must be seen in the context of these larger confrontations. It illustrates, in fact, how interethnic community power conflicts can be transferred to and acted out in the urban university, whether private or public. Urban universities that have a significant enrollment from the local area are not immune to conflicts in their host cities. For them there is no such thing as an ivory tower.

Though Stone and black students denied the charges of anti-Semitism, these reached such a level that the University's president, James Hester, felt compelled to launch an official blue-ribbon, "bipartisan" investigation. Former Supreme Court Justice Arthur Goldberg (Jewish) and Federal Judge Constance Baker Motley (black) were appointed to search for any substance in the charges. After interviews with Stone himself and a careful review of his statements and actions, Goldberg and Motley concluded that he was not anti-Semitic. As a result, his appointment as director of the Martin Luther King Afro-American Student Center was officially announced on 19 September by President Hester, who thus responded to the urging of black student leaders, the NYU Student Presidents Conference,[16] and others within the University that Stone be appointed. Failure to hire him in the face of black students' intense desire for his appointment would, they felt, create black resentment toward the University, as well as further heightening tensions between black and Jewish students.

Appointing Stone met black students' wishes but did not mitigate the discontent of his critics, both in the University and outside. Opposition ran so high that on 30 September 40 white students walked out of a meeting they had requested with President Hester at the Heights to protest against the appointment. Their walk-out came after they received no indication that the appointment would be rescinded; it was a protest against Stone's alleged racism and anti-Semitism, as well as an expression of anger toward the president.

In HDN the following day, Hester justified Stone's appointment and attempted to calm the situation by arguing that the Afro-American Student Center grew out of black students' requests following King's death and the choice of Stone out of their requests for a director who would act as their advisor and be sensitive to their needs and interests. The University was bound to honor their requests. In the final analysis, the president concluded, it came down to a personal decision on his part as to whether Stone was anti-Semitic. And though Stone had made statements that were open to more than one interpretation, Hester did not believe him to be anti-Semitic. Therefore, he stood by the appointment and hoped that the University could get on with its more important business.

Hester's effort, however, did not calm the furor. Discontent continued unabated in many quarters. Alumni contributions to the University as well as the private funding of the MLK scholarship program, dried up (Administrative/Faculty Interviews nos. 2 and 5). As attacks on Stone grew, so did the determination of black students, both in University College and at Washington Square, to keep him. While recognizing that his retention would be controversial, most seem to have felt that they, the University, and Stone himself could weather the storm. The constant reaffirmation of the appointment by President Hester led many to believe that the administration would not give in to pressure. As a kind of counterpressure, however, they continually let it be known through rallies that they were behind Stone and wanted him to remain as director of the center.

Yet the furor over Stone created disillusionment among black students at both campuses, increasing their distrust of the University and of whites in it. They began to worry that their expectations, as well as gains already won, were being threatened. Their hostility and resentment toward whites correspondingly increased, as did on-campus interracial tensions. As one black student then in the College observed: "These whites were finally showing their true colors. They were just as racist as we suspected they were" (Student Interview no. 9).

In the midst of this conflict, Stone was attempting to get operations under way at the student center and to get to know and be known by as many black students as he could. His actions at this point convinced black students that his identification was with the students first and the University second. In this he very much fulfilled their expectations of the kind of director they wanted. As part of this effort to introduce himself to black students, and perhaps also to calm the furor over his appointment, Stone accepted an invitation to speak at an open meeting in Gould Memorial Chapel at the Heights. The meeting was held on Tuesday, 8 October.

That evening the chapel was filled to its limits. Virtually every black student at the Heights attended, as did a large proportion of the College faculty, administrators, and white students. With the full attention of all present, Stone proceeded to give a forceful speech. In it he advocated two standards: one for whites (largely the one dominant in society), and one for blacks that would allow them to do things forbidden to whites in order to achieve freedom and liberation. In the course of his speech describing and analyzing American society, Stone lumped together presidential candidates Richard Nixon and Hubert Humphrey and Albert Shanker, the president of the teachers' union, as "racist bastards." Though black students present cheered throughout, this speech caused consternation among Stone's white supporters and those heretofore willing at least to accept him, and it deeply offended many others. A number of whites in the audience walked out at various points in his presentation.

As might be expected, rather than calming opposition, this speech created even more controversy and proved to be the last straw for the administration. The following morning, 9 October, the *New York Times* published an editorial calling Stone an anti-Semite and urging that his connection with the University be ended. The University administration found itself with progressively fewer options, especially as Stone refused to retract any of his statements. Pressure for his dismissal mounted all day. For example, though it was not widely known at the time, individual faculty members in University College on the night of 8 October and throughout the following day advised the dean of the College that they intended to move either for Stone's official censure or "for removing our own black students from Mr. [Stone's] jurisdiction" (Dean's Report, 1968–69).

By the morning of Thursday, 10 October, the decision to relieve Stone of his duties had been made.[17] The assistant chancellor for student affairs met with Stone to inform him of the decision. The chancellor of the University concurred in the recommendation, and it was presented to President Hester. By late that morning word of Stone's dismissal had already circulated among students at Washington Square. During the day black and white radical student groups there met in closed session to decide on steps to take. Participating in the meeting were the Black Allied Student Association (BASA), the Peace and Freedom Party, the Young Socialists League, Students for a Democratic Society (SDS), and other groups and individuals, all of which, except BASA, were white.

Just before their closed meeting, black and white student groups published two sets of demands. Black students demanded that "[Stone] be taken care of," since his reinstatement seemed impossible; that they be allowed to pick his replacement; and that his replacement be given a contract that could not be terminated at the University's discretion (New York University, n.d.a, student broadside, 10 Oct. 1968). The white students' presentation rejected the University's right to fire Stone—"if the Black community hired him, the Black community should be the ones to fire him"—and they vowed to support black students in their actions (New York University, n.d.a, student broadside, 10 Oct. 1968).

During the meeting agreement was reached to call for a student strike starting the following day and to form picket lines at all entrances to classroom and other University buildings at the Square. The strike was to extend at least through the following Monday and was to end only with the full reinstatement of Stone as director of the student center. Black students, who had seemed to accept the dismissal as a *fait accompli,* during the course of the meeting apparently moved closer to the more militant position of the white students who rejected the firing.

It was in this context that Stone, with the permission of the University Senate, appeared at its regularly scheduled meeting at 2:00 P.M. that same afternoon, accompanied by his lawyer and three black student leaders from Washington Square; all but the lawyer made statements. Following these presentations President Hester indicated that he was going to accept the recommendation for dismissal. After extended debate, the senate voted overwhelmingly (43 to 2, with 3 abstentions) to support the president's decision.

In an article in *HDN* the following day (11 October), President Hester gave the official reason for Stone's removal, stressing that he was removed because of "the incompatibility of many of his actions and public statements with the requirements of his position at the University," and because of his resulting inability to meet the objective of the center—"to work toward improving relations among all religious and ethnic groups."[18]

Surprisingly, neither the president nor the senate seems to have anticipated the reaction of black students, despite their intense support for Stone and the call for a student strike that had already been issued. Neither the president nor other members of the central administration ever officially notified the College of Stone's dismissal. The College's students, faculty, and administrators received word late in the afternoon and evening of 10 October, largely through word of mouth, telephone, or news broadcasts. Though many white students and faculty members welcomed the dismissal, there was some opposition at the Heights from white students. For example, an editorial in the 11 October HDN (which went to press late on the night of 10 October), vigorously condemned the firing.[19] Once more black students found support for their position among their white peers.

At its regular 5:00 P.M. meeting that Thursday, 10 October, Katara was informed by members returning from downtown that Stone had been fired. Shortly thereafter the dismissal was verified on radio news reports. Black students in University College began preparing for protest action. First, they decided to adjourn the meeting until 9:00 P.M. so that Katara could communicate with black students at Washington Square, after which they would meet again to decide on steps to take in concert with black students downtown. (This attempt to communicate with black students downtown was followed by many others in the days ahead.) In their initial contact with the Square, Katara was told that BASA had already occupied a building; only the next day would members find that this had not been true.

The regularly scheduled meeting of SDS began at 6:30 P.M. that evening and was promptly informed, first by Katara and then by radio and other sources, that Stone had been fired. SDS immediately decided to adjourn until 10:00 P.M. and in the interim to find out what Katara planned to do. In the confusion of activity and rumor on campus, the impression was somehow conveyed that this was to be an open, general meeting. As a result, the SDS meeting was swamped with an overflow crowd of white students of various views. During a heated and intense discussion of Stone and his dismissal, SDS proposed a mass hunger strike, a blockade of the College faculty meeting scheduled for the next

day, and a take-over of Philosophy Hall, which housed many administrative offices, all to continue until Stone was reinstated.

At this point the College provost, J. Grant Neal, responding to a call
from the dean, Wright George, entered the meeting and offered,
although he fully supported the decision on Stone, to try to get representatives of SDS and Katara into the upcoming faculty meeting. Neal's
appearance and statement began a shouting match between himself,
SDS, and others. Seeing that the meeting was out of control, SDS
members left to hold their meeting in more private circumstances. With
them went other white students who sympathized with their position.

Meanwhile, the postponed meeting of Katara had reconvened, and it
was decided that black students would occupy Gould Student Center.
While some Katara members worked on plans and began preparations
for the occupation, Todd Little and a few others went to Philosophy
Hall, where the mass meeting was still in progress.

Expecting to meet with SDS, they found Provost Neal and many other
students instead. Gaining the floor, Little spoke to several points. He
noted that Stone was one of the first people chosen by black students, as
well as one of the first administrators chosen by students of any sort. He
accused the administration of lying: they had promised not to pressure
Stone or censor his public statements and to support his efforts as a
University administrator. His dismissal proved that the administration
could not be trusted. Furthermore, Stone, contrary to what Hester
asserted, was at NYU specifically for black students, not to form bridge
between black and white. Little then called both Hester and Neal senile
as well as untrustworthy. He accused the Heights administration, as
personified by Provost Neal, of not having "done a damn thing for the
black student," of being paternalistic and racist, while Stone was "for
us 100 percent." Little welcomed white support for black students'
opposition to the dismissal and announced that there would be a
protest by black students at 10:30 the next morning on the Mall. He did
not reveal that Katara had already decided on a rather different form of
protest.

After some further unproductive exchanges between Little, the provost, and others, the black students left to meet with SDS. In this
meeting, SDS members informed Katara that they would do whatever
black students wanted, at which point they were told of Katara's plans
to occupy the Student Center. Little and other black students told the
white students that they welcomed white support; SDS could do whatever it felt was best, including occupying a building if it chose—that

would be graphic and important support—but the decision was theirs. Black students would take responsibility only for their own actions. Actions would be coordinated, but the two groups would not occupy the same building: each should preserve its freedom and independence of action.

After SDS decided to occupy Gould Memorial Library, Little and the other black students left the meeting. Both groups agreed that they were acting in support of Katara's demand that Stone be reinstated and given a hearing before a group in which black students were represented, and that the charges against him should be clearly spelled out.[20] Both SDS and Katara then proceeded to make plans for their separate occupations. Thus, by 3:00 A.M. on Friday, 11 October, plans were well under way for the most dramatic episode of protest in the College's history.

Just how SDS mobilized its members and supporters is not clear. Katara, however, had been preparing for some form of action from the time it received word of Stone's dismissal. After the decision to occupy the Student Center was made, members immediately set about preparing for the occupation.[21] While some collected items like blankets and food, others visited the dorm rooms of black students living on campus to make sure they knew what was happening and to encourage each of them to participate in the occupation. Intense pressures, both social and moral—what some students felt were arm-twisting tactics—were applied to achieve the fullest participation from black students. From all indications physical threats were not employed, but other pressures were intense. Where possible, those who lived off campus were reached and urged to return to the campus to participate.

Gould Student Center closed at 11:00 P.M. as usual that Thursday evening, though the staffs of the radio station and HDN remained in their offices by permission of the administration. They would remain, locked into their offices, throughout the occupation of the building, providing continuous if limited coverage of events inside.

> At some time after midnight two black students were admitted to the building by a member of the WNYU staff in response to their request to submit a statement to the news media, and these two students never left. Between 4:30 and 6:00 they let in other black students in small groups until there were perhaps 50 such students in the building. (Haines Commission Report, 1968:3)

Thus, rather more than half the black student population of the College participated in the occupation.[22] Both students in the building and administrative observers report that the majority of the participants inside were freshmen; this is not surprising, since the great majority of black students in the College were freshmen.[23]

White protestors began their occupation of the library at about 5:00 A.M., gaining entry through an unlocked rear window. Approximately sixty students then held the building. More than ninety would finally occupy it before the occupation was ended.

By 6:00 A.M. on Friday, both Gould Student Center and Gould Memorial Library were firmly in the hands of student protesters. By this time Provost Neal, Director of the Student Center Kurt Mann, Assistant Provost Arnold Hirsch, and Professor Jon Lewis, the College ombudsman, had all been informed that the buildings were occupied. Lewis and Hirsch had already reached the campus. Both tried to reach Todd Little inside the Student Center by phoning WNYU but were unsuccessful. Students in the radio and HDN offices had been locked in and had no way to inform members of Katara of the efforts to reach them.

By 6:30 A.M. Neal announced that he would use "any means necessary" to eject students from the Student Center and the library. To quote from his statement to the Haines Commission:

> At 7:30 I concluded that the students could not be removed without the help of more force than I had available on campus. At this point there were only a handful of people on campus outside the buildings and I hoped that if we could take action quickly, it would be possible to complete the job before any substantial number of students had appeared on campus who might find it attractive to take sides in the matter. (Haines Commission Report, 1968:4)

Without consulting his assistant, the dean, or any other faculty members or administrators on campus, the provost decided to call in the police to remove students from the buildings.

> Prior to calling the police, the Provost called President Hester to inform him of the situation and of his decision to summon police aid. He did not ask for the President's approval of this action, being perfectly willing to take full responsibility for it, but he did give the President the opportunity to object, which the President did not do. President Hester has told the commission that he considers this to have been the proper and correct procedure under the circumstances. (Haines Commission Report, 1968:5)

At 7:20 A.M. the provost phoned the 56th Police Precinct:

> My attempt to enlist the help of the police was not fruitful for quite a while. The police change shifts at 7:30 and it was not until nearly 8

o'clock that men began to appear on campus who had the authority to summon any substantial number of men. They told me immediately that it would take them more than an hour to bring in the number of men they considered necessary to carry out a job of this kind without risk of losing control.[24] I protested that the students almost certainly would be well behaved and would probably vacate the building under the influence of a small number of police, but I was dealing with men whom I did not know well and they were not willing to take a chance. (Quoted in Haines Commission Report, 1968:4–5)

It was apparent that the police did not want a repetition of the events at Columbia University the previous spring. Not until 10:00 A.M. or later could a sufficient number of police be assembled, and 10:30 was set as the time to remove the students. Following Provost Neal's call, the police immediately prepared for action. Both faculty members and students report seeing plainclothesmen and undercover agents on campus before ten, some in "student-style" civilian clothes and others with police riot helmets and gear visible in the back of their cars.

As the provost and the police made arrangements to remove the students, the situation was rapidly changing in both buildings and outside on the campus.

At about 7:00 Sgt. [James] of the campus security force followed two students in through the window, was able to break through the barricaded chapel door and confronted the students on the library stairs. He asked them to leave, and they asked him to leave, but no threats were made on either side. He then removed the barricades from the front door without resistance from the students and opened the door. (Haines Commission Report, 1968:5)

Professor Rob Nicholas was already at the library door when the campus guard emerged, and without objection from the students he stayed to help keep the door open and to act as an intermediary between SDS and those outside the library. (No faculty member appeared at this point to perform these functions for black students.) Nicholas, attempting to maintain dialogue and communications with the students (though acting essentially on his own authority), agreed to communicate their demands to the administration and accepted their condition that no one would enter the building without their consent. Their demands boiled down to a pledge to support whatever Katara wanted: "We will act only according to Katara's explicit instructions" (quoted in HDN, 14 Oct.). SDS followed this line throughout the Stone crisis.

In the Student Center, meanwhile, Katara had changed its deployment within the building in response to the increased anxiety and uncertainty, especially among the women and freshmen occupiers, occasioned by the mustering of the police. The students believed (as do many blacks) that in any confrontation police deal more brutally with blacks than whites. These fears were intensified by a report (later proved false) that the police whom the students could see assembling from the windows in the Student Center were part of the Tactical Patrol Force, reputedly the toughest and most elite unit of the New York City police force.

Faced with this situation, Katara members abandoned an earlier plan to concentrate on the third floor of the center and moved to the first floor, where they were in a somewhat better position to keep in touch with what was going on outside the building. The students decided that no resistance would be offered to the police. They would prepare themselves in an orderly fashion and would leave as soon as requested to do so. However, this stance was unknown at the time to those outside, almost all of whom believed that Katara was determined to stay in the building and to have a police bust.

Outside the Student Center, as the time came for breakfast to be served in the center's cafeteria, a potentially ugly situation arose. There was a growing inclination among several students outside, "especially among those denied access to their breakfast, to go in by force and throw Katara out" (Haines Commission Report, 1968:6).[25] Fearing a nasty confrontation between students, Professor Lewis and Assistant Provost Hirsch at the rear door, along with Kurt Mann at the front of the Student Center, persuaded these students to disperse. Hirsch got the staff in one of the dormitory dining halls to open it as a cafeteria for breakfast.

Meanwhile, the likelihood grew of a confrontation between students and police and a repetition of the Columbia experience. As police assembled opposite the main gate to the campus, only yards from the Student Center, groups of students and faculty members assembled at the gate as well, their numbers growing along with those of the police. Even though they did not necessarily agree with Katara, a great many were resolved, like their counterparts in other colleges, that the police would not enter the campus. Also in this assembly were students who wanted the police to empty the buildings, as well as students who were simply onlookers. Thus, all the ingredients were present for a situation in which students would battle the police and each other, the police would engage any and all students, regardless of their reason for being there, and many people would get hurt.

The failure of the negotiations that were simultaneously taking place with black students inside the Student Center made a bust seem increasingly likely. The students were willing to talk, but their basic demand, that Stone be reinstated, could be met only by authorities at Washington Square. At about 9:30 A.M. Todd Little met with Provost Neal at a back door to the center to ask him not to initiate police action until Little could read a formal statement to those outside at 10:00. This was to coincide with the presentation of a similar statement to the central administration by black students downtown. (Unknown to Little and black students at the Heights, the statement presented downtown was rather different from that agreed to the night before and from the one Katara presented. Also unknown to Katara, or anyone in the College, was the fact that black students downtown were at this point already negotiating directly with President Hester.)

Though he had earlier denied such a request, the provost now agreed because he knew that the police would not be ready until 10:30. Little emerged from the front door, read his statement asking for Stone's rehiring, and then re-entered the building.

Expecting the police at any time, Katara sent out word asking students at the main gate not to block police entry and indicating their desire for a non-violent, non-confrontational arrest process. From that point on the organization was silent, waiting more or less calmly for the police action that all its members expected.

> Professor [Lewis], believing police action to be imminent and feeling that faculty presence might help protect the students from an excess of police zeal, gained entrance to the building through a second story window with the help of several students. No one was on the second floor. He found Katara in orderly rows, four abreast, in the stairwell and lobby. Although the students first ignored him, he sensed that they were glad to have a faculty member there. (Haines Commission Report, 1968:6)

It was now 10:15 A.M. Todd Little's statement had indicated that Katara was not going to leave voluntarily, and hence neither would SDS.

> At this time it was known that SDS was anxious to avoid any violence in their confrontation with the police. . . . Through Prof. [Nicholas] they had informed the Provost and Dean [George] that if the police entered the building peaceably, they would not resist. Of the 90 students then in the library, 15 wished to walk out without arrest, 12 would come out only if carried (but otherwise would not resist), and the rest were willing to walk

out peacefully under arrest. These three groups had separated themselves physically, and [a member of the faculty] had been authorized to indicate to the police which were which. This attitude had been communicated to the police officers, who agreed that they also wished to avoid violence and that if the SDS students did act in this way, no violence or unnecessary force would be used. (Haines Commission Report, 1968:7)

SDS shared Katara's fears. Its members had reached much the same conclusions about how to react to police actions, with the difference that SDS members were willing to be arrested peaceably and Katara members preferred to leave before arrest. The two groups were not in direct contact at this point. The administration felt very strongly that Katara would not resist arrest.

The police, on their part, had been instructed to keep force to an absolute minimum. It was clear from earlier talks with [Todd Little] that the students were very fearful of police brutality; they had on several occasions asked for a promise from the Provost that the police would use restraint. It is significant that both Katara and the police requested that when the moment of confrontation actually occurred, representatives of the press, both photographers and reporters, should be present to "report it like it is." Katara in addition asked for faculty to be present. This desire for impartial observers strikes the commission as strong evidence that both sides fully intended to act in as restrained and responsible a manner as possible. (Haines Commission Report, 1968:7)

Thus, by 10:15 the stage was set for what looked like inevitable police action. No one knew if the students at the main gate would let the police enter the campus unopposed; no one knew if the police would control both the crowd at the gate, which outnumbered them, and themselves. No one could guarantee that the police would not use force in the buildings, even if the students did not resist. Nor could the peaceful non-resistance of the students themselves be guaranteed when they were actually faced with the presence of police in the building. Many students and faculty members felt that the provost was determined to have a bust. They objected strongly both to the decision to call in the police and to the manner in which it had been made. They were determined that police action should not take place, or should be severely circumscribed.

The faculty, with the Columbia bust of the previous spring very clearly in mind, made one last effort to avoid police action.

At the urging of their colleagues two professors pleaded with the Provost to postpone calling the police on campus until either an ad hoc faculty meeting or the regular meeting scheduled for 1:00 that afternoon could be held. The Provost, however, felt that "delay could do nothing but exacerbate the situation which had already caused the faculty to divide severely, and no one suggested any possible outcome of the meeting which would change the situation and make it more tolerable than the one that existed at 10:15 A.M." He felt that the responsibility for calling the police, being essentially an administrative one, was and must be his alone and that the faculty's feelings in this matter were not relevant to the needs of the moment. (Haines Commission Report, 1968:7)

It was now nearly 10:30, the time set for action to remove the students from the buildings, beginning with Katara in the Student Center. "'Accordingly,' reported the Provost, 'I determined that the time had come to enter the building and this I proceeded to do in the company of about eight people, including Dean [George], [Morris Grinnell], [Arnold Hirsch], the locksmith and others'" (Haines Commission Report, 1968:7). The others included two representatives from the news media, invited by the provost, and two police officers. The officers entered the building with the provost but remained in the Playhouse rather than going on to the lobby, where black students had assembled. "The Provost asked [the students] to leave so that he would not have to call in the police. "When it became clear that they would not leave in response to my request, I retired down the hall to summon the police officers and to arrange our next steps carefully'" (Haines Commisssion Report, 1968:8).

Though the stage was fully set for police action at this point, *no bust occurred*. Largely because of the procedures followed by the College and the time needed for their mobilization, the actual entrance of the police was delayed long enough for President Hester to get a phone call through to Provost Neal in the Student Center (at approximately 10:30) and another one to Todd Little immediately afterward. The call to Little came not a moment too soon: another five minutes and the provost would have summoned the police into the building. Instead, at 10:30, black students voluntarily left the building, summoned SDS out of the library, and with SDS members went on to a "victory" celebration in the lounge of Silver Hall, a dormitory. Hester's call ended the occupation, but it ultimately prolonged and intensified the conflict between black students and the institution, engendering much bitterness and misunderstanding.

Throughout the morning, unbeknownst to black students at the Heights, intensive negotiations had been going on at Washington Square between the president, the chancellor, and the vice-president of the University and black student leaders at the Square, notably Charlton Stevens and Tom Wilson. Very early that morning, even before

Todd Little read Katara's formal statement at 10:00 A.M., black students at the Square had presented to President Hester a letter signed by every black student organization in the University, including Katara, the organizations of black law students and black social workers, and those of African, Haitian, and West Indian students. The letter included the following demands and statements:

1. Brother [James P. Stone] be financially sustained, for the rest of the year.
2. Seeing that in our original demands we called for a DEAN OF BLACK STUDENT AFFAIRS, we now APPOINT Brother [Stone] to that position.
3. We demand that the Administration rent us or in some way provide office space for the Black Allied Student Association to use to house our new Dean.
4. Dean [Stone] will concern himself directly and indirectly with matters affecting Black students.

> We consider a Deanship of Black Affairs as being a function *not* governed by existing criteria.
> Brother [Stone], as Dean, will immediately address himself to the social, economic, and cultural welfare of the black students on New York University campus. He will have no ties, nor will he take any orders from, anyone at New York University except the Black students.

Though listed as one of the signers, Katara was not consulted, or even informed, about the letter's content or wording. Further, the demands presented in this letter differ from those presented in the joint resolution of black and white students the day before, which called for Stone's full reinstatement, and also from those embodied in the formal statement read by Todd Little that morning. Katara had called for Stone's reinstatement in the University, at least until the charges against him were clearly specified and black students had taken part in the decision-making process regarding his future in the University.

Equally important, by no longer calling for Stone's reinstatement, the letter's demands, deliberately or not, were framed in such a way that the University could accept them without compromising or changing its position—which is precisely what the administration proceeded to do. The first step was to communicate news of the settlement:

> The President, responding to the concern of the black students over their inability to communicate with their colleagues at the Heights, called the student center, spoke to the Provost, and then spoke to [Todd Little]. He read the . . . letter verbatim and indicated that the administration was

ready to accept these demands. [Todd Little] then called the secretary of
BASA and was told that she thought that an agreement had in fact been
reached. [Todd Little] then rejoined the members of Katara in the lobby
and announced that Mr. [Stone] had been appointed Dean of Black
student affairs. (Haines Commission Report, 1968:9)

Katara received the news joyfully and with immense relief. As noted
above, members left the occupied buildings, together with SDS, and
held a victory celebration on the Mall. Thus, by noon on Friday, 11
October, the crisis that had begun the previous day seemed to have been
resolved to the satisfaction of all contenders. Part of the compromise
ostensibly resolving this crisis was agreement by the University that no
disciplinary or legal action would be taken against the students who
occupied the buildings. Significantly, no disciplinary action was ever
taken against the protesting students, black or white, then or later.

By the middle of that Friday afternoon, Todd Little and the Katara
membership learned that the various black student organizations at the
Square did *not* accept the compromise. Further, they had not only
rejected the compromise but repudiated and withdrawn the letter originally sent to Hester. Now they were demanding the full reinstatement
of Stone as director. Once again Katara found itself out of step with and
isolated from BASA.[26]

This news hit black students in the College with tremendous force. In
a moment their joy and triumph turned to fury and outraged frustration. All felt that they had been used, manipulated, co-opted, tricked
into leaving the building before anything was accomplished. More
important, Todd Little and other black students felt that he had been
deliberately deceived by the president. Katara now immediately rejected the compromise also and denounced the administration for
double dealing. The anger and confusion of black students was so great
at this point that for the rest of that day and through Saturday, 12
October, virtually no communication or contact existed between
Katara and the College administration. At the same time, Katara took
no organized, coherent protest action beyond rejecting the compromise, demanding reinstatement, and terminating contact with the College
authorities. This is all the more noteworthy because at this point the
potential certainly existed for even more extensive and violent protest. I
think the absence of organized protest in these two days was due to
several factors.

This situation represented a significant crisis for the black student
movement in University College.[27] It was the first time since Katara's
inception that the organization and its leaders had not been successful,
had not been able to claim a victory; it was, in effect, the first real failure

of the movement. More important, it was a failure that followed the most extreme and psychologically demanding action yet undertaken by black students at the Heights. Hence, in contemplating further collective action, the leaders of Katara were faced with a situation in which black students were definitely angry and frustrated, but also uncertain about what should be done next. They had already taken more drastic action than ever before, and it was more than many students were comfortable with. Several members were demoralized and perhaps psychologically unprepared for some of the possible options.

At this point the preponderance of freshmen in the black student population began to be a major factor in events. For most black students, the Stone affair was a totally new experience. Most of these students had not been involved in Stone's appointment, and many had no previous knowledge of prior negotiations or agreements regarding Stone. Moreover, the College itself was a new experience for them. Having just arrived, they were still to some extent isolated from the campus, though with high expectations. In the fight over Stone, they were suddenly confronted with apparently thwarted expectations and the need to make critical decisions and take serious actions—all without any previous experience or precedents and with little guide to predicting University responses. Added to this were the uncertainties that many freshmen ordinarily feel about themselves and the world.

It is little wonder that despite intense anger and frustration, Katara did not develop any coherent, organized collective action through Friday and Saturday. The confusion, uncertainty, demoralization— perhaps even the trauma for some students—were simply too great. As one student put it: "A lot of people were really hurt. A lot of people were really stunned. People were crying, people couldn't study. People even started talking about leaving this fucking place" (Student Interview no. 18). These morale and cohesion problems had to be dealt with before further action could be undertaken.

Equally important, the events of the preceding days and hours had made clear to Katara the extent of its isolation from black students downtown. In this instance, isolation from BASA also meant isolation from participation in substantive decision making or negotiation, since the Stone crisis could only be resolved by the central administration. As long as this isolation continued, Katara always ran the risk of "co-optation" or manipulation by the University on any issue that transcended the College or was unresolvable locally. Thus, before taking action, Katara wanted to be quite certain of the positions and actions of black students at the Square.[28] Over the weekend there was much debate within black organizations downtown. As a result, Katara's action was further delayed by uncertainty over the ultimate position of BASA and the other black student groups at the Square.

In short, the movement at the Heights did not become more radicalized at this point—although emotions were intense enough—because factors creating a crisis in the movement had a more immediate priority. Katara handled this crisis by trying to maintain and reinforce internal consensus and commitment and establish external coordination with black students downtown. Late Saturday afternoon, Katara and BASA issued a joint call for a strike to begin Monday (14 October) if Stone had not been reinstated by that time. On both campuses white student supporters joined the call for a class boycott.

Throughout the weekend interpersonal and interracial tensions created by the controversies over Stone's appointment and dismissal were heightened tremendously by black students' new bitterness, frustration, and anger toward the University, the College, and whites in general in the wake of the ending of the building occupation. The campus was polarized and remained so over the next months. A number of clashes between black and white students were reported, as well as a number of incidents of vandalism in College buildings and property. Many on campus believed that black students were responsible for the acts of vandalism, but no evidence was ever presented to connect them with these acts. Such suspicions, however, did little to relieve campus tensions.

Indeed, both at the Square and at the Heights, bitterness, recriminations, and anger had reached such a state by Saturday that President Hester felt compelled to issue an open letter on Sunday morning to "the New York University Community" providing "information about the Stone matter" and justifying Stone's dismissal. Stone was dismissed, according to this statement, because it was no longer possible to defend him. His "insensitivity to his role as part of the university administration" and his highly controversial public statements reduced his effectiveness and "encouraged suspicion and distrust" between groups. There were fundamental "inconsistencies between his attitudes and university policies." More particularly, he was dismissed because of his failure to perceive his accountability to more than just "the particular group of black students that nominated him for his position." The president went on to point out that even though it was "not a customary procedure," the recommendation for Stone's dismissal was discussed fully with the University Senate at a meeting where Stone and three black students were given an opportunity to state their views.

President Hester acknowledged receipt of the letter from black students on the morning of 11 October and indicated that in his reply, delivered to students downtown but not to Katara that same morning, the University had agreed to four major points, covering the demands of black students: Stone's salary for 1968–69 would be paid as separation pay; black student organizations could designate Stone as their representative and give him any title they wished, though he would be no longer in any way an official part of the University; the University would rent office space to the organizations because they were officially recognized and registered campus organizations; and henceforth Stone's activities (and his pay after 1968–69) would be their responsibility, not the University's. Thus, the president argued, the University had met black students' conditions "responsively and quickly," and even though black students had rescinded their earlier position, he remained open to further communication.

The president's letter did not address directly the charges of bad faith and lack of candor agitating Katara and others, nor did it relieve their alienation. The same Sunday morning Stone announced that he would not compromise with the University, putting a damper on hopes that students would eventually accept the 11 October compromise that they had already rejected.

The faculties at the Heights (those of University College and the School of Engineering) met continuously for almost all of that day in joint session, attempting to understand the actions of students in occupying buildings and to arrive at some resolution of the issue that was dividing the campus. About halfway through the meeting, two representatives from Katara, Todd Little and Harry Woodruff, joined it. Little announced that neither Katara nor Stone would compromise on reinstatement. He then announced that Stone was guiding Katara during the present controversy and that Katara would act in support of any demand presented by Stone. From here on, Katara demanded to talk with the men who made decisions, not middlemen—with the central administration, not College authorities. Little urged the faculty to continue trying to create dialogue between black and white elements in the University. Katara wanted a dialogue, even if Hester and others from the Square could not attend. He then announced that henceforth there would be no discrepancy between the demands of BASA and Katara.

At this point Provost Neal suggested that Katara allow BASA to act as its agent in dealing with the central administration and promised to set up discussions with senior administrators. Though welcoming such a meeting, neither Little nor Woodruff was willing to accept BASA as agent or to delegate the kind of power such an arrangement implied. After a short discussion, the Katara representatives left. Little's statements indicate Katara's feeling of isolation and its determination to end it—its desire to keep all communications open.

With the end of the faculty meeting, there were no further efforts to resolve the crisis and prevent the student strike scheduled for the following day. Monday morning Katara put out a position paper urging support of the strike, reiterating its demands for full reinstatement, formally rejecting the appointment of Stone as unofficial black dean, and vowing continued protest. An article by Todd Little in that afternoon's special edition of HDN (14 October) publicly claimed that Hester had lied to him on the phone, telling him that BASA had accepted the compromise when it had not. The first day of the strike tensions and feelings ran high. The class boycott was about 60 percent effective at the Heights.

In the 15 October HDN, President Hester responded to Little's charge that the president had lied. As quoted by HDN, Hester denied that he had deceived Little. He argued that he had told Little that BASA and the administration were still negotiating and that nothing was settled. He claimed that he had never told Little that the compromise had been accepted by BASA. The president concluded by apologizing for any misunderstanding and expressing the hope that the conflict could be resolved amicably soon. This response did not ease tensions or reduce students' bitterness.

This was the second day of the strike and the fifth since Stone's dismissal. At Washington Square elevators in classroom buildings were blocked as part of the strike. At the Heights, the conflict continued at least in part as a result of actions by separate groups of white students. One group, which included SDS members, working with Professor Rob Nicholas, drew up a statement and presented a list of demands Tuesday morning. Though these demands supported Katara's (e.g., calling for Stone's reinstatement), they represented independent action and included demands that concerned student power issues.[29] For example, the statement demanded that Provost Neal be dismissed because he had been appointed against the "unanimous dissent" of students; that all standing committees at the Heights be reorganized to have "50% student and 50% faculty composition"; that the current governance structures of NYU be replaced by a new governing body, half student and half faculty, with major decision-making power; and that the administration serve only as an instrument to implement that body's decisions while possessing no veto power over it.

On the same morning a very different group also became active. The Majority Coalition of Students (MCS)—a coalition of the Young Republican Society, the Young Americans for Freedom, and others—announced its formation and issued a call for punishment of the protesters, support for Stone's dismissal, an end to the strike, and a return to the traditional values of the University. Thus, the campus was polarized not only between black and white, but also within the white student population.

That same day the strike committee, composed of black and radical white students, held the first of a series of rallies. In this rally, and in those to follow over the next several days, a constant stream of speakers—faculty members and administrators as well as students—spoke about racism and for and against Stone's dismissal, the strike, and the University.

Later that afternoon the College's student government took a public stand on the Stone controversy with the release of an official statement by SGB. While supporting the University's position that any official administrator must have primary allegiance to the administration rather than to any particular constituent group in the University, SGB criticized the University for breaking the precedents and rules it had itself established in hiring Stone. By first allowing black students full participation in hiring Stone, "the University granted *de facto* the principle that black students have a right to choose their own leaders." Because black students were not consulted and had no voice in his dismissal, the University had violated its own principle. Further, the dismissal was unfair because Stone had not had time to prove his effectiveness in the job. Moreover, the dismissal violated all students' rights to be represented in decision making, particularly in making those decisions directly affecting them. Finally, "in a signed statement President Hester guaranteed Mr. Stone his right of free speech."

In effect, SGB accused the University of having caused its own difficulties, which it now had to solve without sacrificing either the needs of black students or its own responsibility to meet those needs. These needs focused most immediately on having a black director of the MLK Student Center. SGB proposed that Stone be retained as ombudsman for black students, paid and given facilities by the University, but not responsible to it. A second black should then be appointed director of the center. Though neither of these proposals was taken up by black students, they, along with HDN's earlier editorial position, indicate continuing support for black students by significant organs of the student body.

Because of continuing tensions on campus, a meeting was held at the Heights later that evening between black students, administrative officials from the College, and representatives of the central administration to discuss the crisis and to try to reach a solution. This was the first meaningful, serious contact between authorities and black students since the Sunday faculty meeting. No resolution was reached; polarization and protest continued.

Indeed, the following day (16 October the third day of the strike and the sixth of protest), the University College protest escalated slightly.[30] A boycott of the cafeteria and a sit-in by black and white students were begun in Gould Student Center. Fraternity members presented a statement announcing their opposition to the protest and the protesters, their tactics, and their goals and demanding that the University take prompt action against them. This statement exacerbated the interracial tensions plaguing the campus. More rallies and demonstrations were held on the Mall, while negotiations and talks continued between the administration and black students at the Heights and at the Square, with little or no progress.

The next day, Thursday, 17 October, rallies and demonstrations on the Mall continued, as did the boycott of the cafeteria and the sit-in at Gould Student Center. The strike, however, was called off at the Heights because of declining participation and effectiveness. Downtown at Washington Square, Kimball Hall, a classroom building, was declared "liberated" by black students who for a time blocked entrances and elevators and shut down the movement of people within the building.

At this critical juncture, BASA shifted leaders. The shift was in large part the result of internal dissensions that apparently had been building since the previous Friday. Charlton Stevens, head of BASA, and Tom Wilson, head of the Black American Law Students Association, were both removed by their constituents from leadership positions. Stevens and Wilson, it will be remembered, were the prime student negotiators in the ill-fated 11 October compromise rejected a few hours after its announcement by BASA and other groups.

This leadership shift delayed further talks between black students and the administration: both the change of leaders and the factionalism it implied were seen as imperiling talks and any progress that might be made. The new leadership was unknown, both by name and in the sense that the administration had had no previous contact with them. As one administrator put it, "More extreme elements have taken over, they will take only reinstatement" (HDN, 18 Oct.).

Tensions, polarization, and vandalism at the Heights had reached such a state that Katara was impelled on Friday, 18 October (the eighth day of protest), to issue a formal statement in HDN condemning all acts of violence and vandalism and warning that black students were ready and able to defend themselves from insult and injury on campus. (Only a few months later, in the spring of 1969, black students at Cornell would arm themselves because of their perceived need for self-defense.) In Katara's view, self-defense was necessary because neither the College nor the University seemed concerned with the severely strained relations between black and white students.

College authorities were in fact aware of and concerned about these tensions, but there seems to have been little they could do about them; at least no conspicuous official steps to deal with them were taken. As bad as tensions were, they could have been worse. At least one administrator suggests that it was largely the publicly sympathetic stance of student government and the student newspaper toward black students' positions that helped prevent violence: "I think our student government essentially sympathized with them very much in feeling they hadn't been dealt with fairly. They were anti-establishment, too. And that perhaps helped prevent any kind of really violent conflict" (Administrative/Faculty Interview no. 6).

At both campuses talks between students and the administration showed no progress toward resolution of the crisis. The sit-in at Gould Student Center continued, as did rallies and demonstrations on the Mall. During the course of one rally I attended (on 18 October), a black student presenting the case for Stone indicated the feelings of black students:

> We are fighting for a change: a change that may sweep the entire administration and all administrations in the country. If we let things drop, we will have to put up with the same crap that has been going on for years. We have the administration pretty much where we want it and we won't bend now. We must keep an eye on the administration and pin them down at every available opportunity.

A second black student summed up student sentiment and determination by declaring, "This place has gotta change. It won't do it by itself so we have to force these racist bastards to do what is right. We have to change it ourselves." Positions had hardened on both sides, and black students were in no mood for compromise.

Protest continued. The next day (Saturday, 19 October), Dean George appeared at an afternoon rally and reviewed the actions the College had taken in the past to meet the needs of black students. He pointed out that the class of 1972 had the largest number of blacks in the College's history and that educational support programs had already begun to help at least twenty-two of them. He went on to note that even before the expanded admission of black students, courses on the black experience had already begun and that the faculty had just voted in its last meeting to expand curricular offerings in this area. He then announced the appointment of a black assistant dean in the College who would also be director of both the MLK Scholars program and the College's educational support programs.

Though this new appointment was greeted with enthusiasm, the rest of the dean's statement was received politely but had little impact, at least on the black students who were there. They wanted to know what the administration was going to do now and in the future, not to hear a recital of past accomplishments, however important those might be.

Speaking after the dean, Todd Little, referring to Stone's dismissal, declared, "If he leaves, we leave." Further, he announced, "We are now declaring a legal state of war with the University administration," which had fired Stone illegally, since "no list of formal charges had ever been brought" (HDN, 21 Oct.). Despite this declaration of war, Little indicated that talks with the administration were continuing. Black student groups in the University had just submitted a new proposal to the administration that Stone make a token return as director of the MLK Student Center and then be reassigned as executive director, a position in which he would be responsible only to black students. What, if any, future connection Stone would have with the University was unspecified.

That evening the speaker scheduled by Katara in its regular program did not appear, and the session was turned over to an impromptu discussion on the Stone affair. This led students to an intensive analysis of past events, the current situation, and steps that could or should be taken next. There was no question of discontinuing the fight to retain Stone, and the meeting produced a reaffirmation of the decision to maintain the protest.

Monday, 21 October (the eleventh day of protest), came with no resolution of the conflict and no reduction in campus tensions. Talks continued between students and the administration, but with no break in the deadlock. HDN came out with an editorial condemning many of the rallies and demonstrations of the previous week for having a too-festive air. Nevertheless, these and other protest activities continued.[31]

For the next three days, 22–24 October, organized protest declined while interpersonal racial tensions remained high. The decline in protest was not accompanied by any progress in negotiations. Indeed, President Hester was moved by 24 October to note publicly that no talks at all were then in progress and to imply that students were holding private discussions among themselves and with various faculty members. Continuing factionalism and the effects of the leadership shift within BASA and other black students groups downtown were also partly responsible for the temporary break-off of negotiations. In Katara's case, however, there was a much more critical reason for the break-down.

Sometime between 21 and 24 October, Katara secretly held a meeting with Stone. Black students entered this crucial meeting with their faith in Stone undiminished, prepared to continue their struggle to retain him and expecting encouragement and advice on the next stage of the fight. They came out of the meeting with very different feelings indeed.

In this meeting Stone allegedly gave them some thanks for their efforts on his behalf (Student Interviews nos. 3, 6, 12, 14, 18). However, he is reported to have informed them that he had other irons in the fire. He had received another job offer and was going to take it; he was no longer interested in the position at NYU, did not need it, and thought that there was no point in continuing their fight. If they wanted to, however, that was their affair.

This meeting had a tremendous, almost catastrophic, effect on black students in University College; in some ways it was even more traumatic than the ending of the occupation. The man they had supported so ardently was rejecting their actions. Their efforts, their emotions, their energy, all had been for naught. They were stunned and shocked. Many were deeply hurt. Their anger, their frustration, and especially their disillusionment were intense. In the words of one student who attended the meeting: "We all felt like fools. Lots of us said never again—I know I did. Over one man it's ridiculous. You don't squabble and fight the university over one man. He just had all this charisma. Everybody thought he was such a together black man. We fell in love with [Stone] and he let us down" (Student Interview no. 3).

For all intents and purposes, after this meeting Stone ceased to be a protest issue for black students in University College (though this was unknown at the time to the rest of the campus). Although some previously scheduled activities had been continued during the protest,

Katara's efforts, time, and energy had been concentrated on retaining Stone. It was no longer possible to accept that focus.

This meeting produced the second major crisis in the black student movement. For a short while, the movement foundered (though this, too, was unknown to the campus). The disenchantment and anger engendered during this period left a legacy of bitterness and disaffection that would plague Katara in the months and years to come. However, the immediate task faced by Katara leaders was to relieve the widespread sense of angry disillusionment and discouragement, to find a renewed basis for solidarity and action, new directions and worthwhile activities. It was this situation that, at least for black students in University College, accounts for the decline in protest and the near cessation of negotiations that began 22 October and lasted to the end of the month.

On Tuesday, 29 October, President Hester issued a call for a resumption of positive relations between black students and the University. He emphasized his desire to have the University recognize black students' needs and help their careers, particularly on campus. Though none of the parties provided any indication of this, intensive negotiations between the administration and black students at the Square resumed about this time. On Friday, 1 November, three weeks after the first protest over Stone, Hester announced a settlement of the conflict.

Significantly, the solution reached was one in which neither the director *nor* the center would be officially part of NYU. This was perhaps not surprising, given the very different views of the administration and black students on the functions of the center and the role of the director. These views, as SGB had noted in its statement some time earlier, were essentially incompatible. Stone's place in such a center was not specified. He was never mentioned by name. Given his unavailability for the job, this is hardly surprising. However, the lack of official University sanction and support for the center and its director implied serious problems for their long-term future.

In announcing the settlement, President Hester also issued a general statement about the crisis and the deliberations involved. In it he acknowledged that Stone was hired because of black students' expressed desires and fired without their consultation. He conceded that this lack of consultation had been insulting to black students and that in view of the procedures followed in his hiring, consultation before Stone's dismissal would have been desirable. In the future the University intended to provide for adequate "consultation about terminating" administrative appointments in which students had initially been consulted. Further, he recognized the "unique problems" of black students in white universities, and the need for substantial measures to be taken to meet their interests and needs. Black students thus won at least a symbolic victory.

The president went on to pledge that it would be the University's objective to make necessary "structural improvements as soon as they can be worked out." Students would be given more opportunity to participate in the "improvement of the educational programs of the University." And more efforts would be made to increase the recruitment of and scholarship aid to minority students. Sympathetic statements, in other words, were to be followed sometime in the future by concrete accomplishments.

Finally, he announced that the University would financially assist the MLK Afro-American Student Center for the rest of the year, though it would be run by an independent board. An anonymous donor had already funded it for the following year. Thus, the controversy over Stone had, in the end, cost black students not only a director but, more important, a black student center clearly integrated into the University.

## CHAPTER V

# "Nobody Said It Would Be Easy"

*T**he key challenge confronting insurgents . . . is to devise some way to overcome the basic powerlessness that has confined them to a position of institutionalized political impotence.*——Doug McAdam (1983:735)

In the preceding two chapters we have looked at the emergence of the black movement and its most dramatic protest actions. This chapter examines phases four through six of the movement's activism and looks at its ultimate fate in University College. Phase four, directly influenced by the Stone affair, presented the movement and Katara with two basic challenges: to produce successful changes in the College and to cope with the internal difficulties caused by the failures and crises of the Stone affair. In this phase we see the movement returning to a programmatic and local focus and, despite rhetoric to the contrary, acting essentially alone. Phase five finds the movement largely stalled. There is continued, though reduced, activism, still with a programmatic focus. During this period, however, the movement faces its third major crisis, while problems of member cohesion and mobilization become critical.

In phase six the movement faces major problems of organizational maintenance and internal dissension. Paradoxically, the limited activism of which the movement is still capable produces some programmatic success and some limited institutionalization. This is the only period in which black students attempt to form a coalition with other students. Finally, we shall see the movement becalmed and Katara a mere shell of its former self. This chapter and the preceding one illustrate a history of important early successes followed by increasing difficulty in achieving goals and maintaining momentum, significant failures, and near disintegration.

## PHASE 4: NOVEMBER 1968 TO JANUARY 1969

On Friday, 1 November, President Hester announced the terms of the settlement that resolved the Stone crisis. BASA and black students at Washington Square accepted promptly, but Todd Little and Katara made no comment. Throughout the weekend Katara's acceptance of the settlement remained uncertain.

On Monday, 4 November, the editors of HDN proposed that a branch of the MLK Student Center or an entirely separate center be established at the Heights, thus resurrecting an idea briefly contemplated before the Stone controversy. They urged the college to consider the appointment of a black ombudsman for the Heights.[1] The editorial noted that as of press time, Katara still had not made clear its acceptance of the settlement announced earlier; at the same time, the editorial indicated that at some point during the previous weekend, Katara had been in communication with the College administration and, apparently not receiving satisfactory responses, had broken off contact. The editorial did not expand on this point, and Katara itself remained silent.

Katara ended the suspense about its intentions on Wednesday. In an official statement it categorically rejected the "Hester settlement" and presented a list of fifteen demands. Thus, Katara gave the clearest possible indication that the resolution reached downtown did not mean the end of black student activism in University College. Black students there still had many grievances: they would continue to engage the College until it acted on them. So began the third phase of activism by the black student movement in University College in less than a year. This was the first action by Katara completely on its own, without BASA, SDS, or other allies.

The Stone crisis created the context and preconditions for this renewed protest. The secret meeting with Stone and the 1 November announcement of the settlement may both be seen as precipitating further action: the former because it jolted black students at the Heights into a re-examination of their position and aims; the latter because it signaled an opportune moment for renewed attempts to achieve College-oriented goals. As Todd Little said in a subsequent interview:

> We knew that changing NYU would be hard. We knew it was going to be hard, and that it was going to be a long fight. We couldn't give up the fight just because we were frustrated. We still had things to accomplish and we couldn't let the University think we were beaten. Nobody said it would be easy.

Between its meeting with Stone and the president's announcement, Katara spent two weeks not only dealing with its internal problems, but also taking stock of itself, what it had accomplished, and what it felt still needed to be done. By taking the time to establish new directions and a new consensus, Katara prepared for the next phase of activism. By 1 November it had apparently dealt with its internal difficulties and the lessons it had learned, had prepared its new agenda, and was simply waiting for the Stone crisis to be resolved in some fashion in order to renew its own activities. The announcement of a resolution was the signal. With the Stone affair resolved, there would be no distractions for College authorities, yet the momentum generated by that controversy would not be completely lost. Katara apparently believed that the administration would be more receptive to demands centered on issues that the College could resolve locally. Moreover, the authorities would want to avoid further protest, which could exacerbate the still-high tensions on campus. Katara's policy was thus to strike while the iron was hot.

Since Katara had not participated directly in the negotiations that produced the settlement of the Stone crisis, its own position had not been "compromised" or limited. It was not bound to honor either the settlement or the implied cessation of activities that went with it. Equally important, if group commitment, consensus, and organizational loyalty were to be retained among black students, Katara needed to show some independent political success, some concrete positive results of its own. And it needed to show them fairly quickly if its internal problems were to be fully resolved, rather than simply papered over.

Its actions between 1 November and its 6 November statement show that Katara carefully considered its strategy for this round of activism. Though the exact time of contact is not entirely clear, either the day of the settlement or the following day, Katara leaders had a private, unpublicized meeting with College officials. The lack of publicity was apparently at Katara's request.[2]

Katara presented its demands at this meeting and, according to those present, indicated that its acceptance of the Stone settlement was tied to positive action on its demands. In effect, Katara proposed a kind of *quid pro quo* with an implied ultimatum, which, however quietly presented, however restrained the language, gave the College the choice of changing or facing continued protest.

Early in the meeting it became apparent that the administration was not prepared to act then and there on the demands. Realizing this, Katara leaders left the meeting after some discussion, indicating their willingness to wait a short while for a positive response. After that, if there was still no favorable action, black students would take whatever further steps they felt were necessary to accomplish their goals. The administration refused to take action under such circumstances. Thus it was that Katara issued its official statement on 6 November.

Katara's renewed activity caught many on the campus by surprise, especially those who had identified black student concerns exclusively with Stone. In so doing, they failed to recognize black students' interest in other issues and goals. That Katara had other concerns had been demonstrated by the general activities it kept going during the Stone crisis—demonstrations, rallies, sit-ins, negotiations, and internal meetings. At several of these events black students had expressed themselves strongly on a number of other issues.

Katara's statement rejecting the settlement and presenting a list of demands was accompanied by a separate statement from Katara's president, Todd Little. Both were quoted in the 7 November HDN. Little indicated that the fifteen demands would have been presented earlier had not the Stone affair come up. He noted that an MLK student center would be established at the Heights; that is, the idea had already been accepted by College authorities, though it was unclear whether this was to be a branch of the downtown center or entirely separate. The College would supply rooms and equipment, but the center would be responsible only to black students and faculty members. Finally, Little emphasized that from now on Katara would insist on signed statements when agreements were reached between black students and the College: it could no longer put its faith in verbal agreements. This demand indicates the legacy of bitterness from the student center occupation, though there is no evidence that this procedure was ever carried out. Further, he stressed that Katara now had better coordination with black students downtown; from now on black action would be more unified.

Katara's list called for: (1) the hiring of more black faculty members in all departments; (2) a similar increase in the number of black administrators, including the appointment at the Heights of a black assistant chancellor, an ombudsman with voting power in all faculty and administrative committees; (3) the formation of a committee (50 percent black students, 50 percent faculty and administrators) to review potential black faculty members and administrators; (4) a major expansion of the curriculum to include many courses "relevant to black students," and the immediate investigation of the feasibility of a black studies major; (5) the immediate expansion of the library's holdings in black literature and history and increased accessibility of such materials; (6) the establishment in the next year of an exchange program between University College and black colleges; (7) the adoption by the College of a more active role in community affairs; and (8) the issuance of a monthly report on the progress of the MLK scholarship fund and the MLK Institute, along with "biweekly reports to the student body on progress to meet these demands."[3]

At the end of the statement the College was informed that it had until 11 November to reply outlining its intentions. Though it did not specify what would happen if the administration failed to do so, Katara seems to have felt (or hoped) that the administration *would* make a positive reply by the deadline, thereby avoiding the necessity for confrontation.

The first public response of the administration came from the provost. Noting that the statement of demands had been unsigned, Neal asserted that an "anonymous" paper did not reflect the true opinion of the majority of black students (HDN, 7 Nov.). In addition to ringing one more change on the old refrain, "it's only a small group of malcontents," the provost's response indicated continuing resistance on the part of the administration to meeting the demands, especially under the pressure of a deadline.

Katara made no public response to the provost's comments. Monday, 11 November, came without any official or public response from the administration. However, an HDN editorial that day endorsed the substance and goals of Katara's demands while deploring the method of their presentation.[4]

The administration responded through Provost Neal on 12 November, one day after the deadline. In a letter to Todd Little, the provost indicated that positive action, by appropriate groups and individuals, was possible on some of the fifteen demands (those having to do with black faculty, curricular expansion, library acquisitions, the exchange program, and community involvement). The other demands were deemed by the provost either to require action by the central administration or to be too radical; or they were simply ignored.

At least in the short run, therefore, Katara won a positive response on many of its demands. Negotiations began almost immediately, on both the demands that the administration viewed favorably and those that it had, in effect, rejected.[5] These talks continued for the rest of the semester, with varying degrees of success. For example, sufficient progress was made on the student center for HDN to announce on 19 November that the elections for the board of trustees of the Heights Afro-American Student Center would soon be held. It should be remembered, however, that the creation of the center was *not* one of Katara's demands and seems to have been an idea resurrected by others on campus.[6]

The following week, on 20 November, the dean of University College, Wright George, also responded favorably to Katara's demands, particularly to those concerned with bringing more blacks to campus at all levels, although he opposed the demand for a black assistant chancellor. He also responded favorably to the idea of a student–faculty-administration committee to review the appointment of black faculty members and administrators. His response is in contrast to the strong administrative resistance that greeted the idea of a similarly constituted committee with similar function proposed some months earlier.

In the next weeks talks produced few concrete results. During this time significant *white* student protest developed in University College over the recruitment activities of the Dow Chemical Company. Students demonstrated on the Mall and in front of Gould Student Center, and four white students were disciplined for their part in these actions. Almost simultaneously, long-simmering discontent over living conditions in a newly opened dormitory broke into the open, with sit-ins and other demonstrations.

On 9 December the names of the seven black students elected to the board of the new student center were announced. Significantly, the announcement indicated that the center was not yet organized or in operation, though it was expected to be soon. (The name was the Malcolm X Student Center, rather than the Martin Luther King Center, as originally.) The student members of the board held immediate meetings with Provost Neal and the director of student affairs to discuss its formation and function; they were particularly interested in gaining the University's aid in organizing a corporation to run the center, since it was to be independent of the University. According to the director of student affairs, the University would try to meet these requests and would "be happy to give" as much assistance as it could (HDN, 10 Dec.).

Whether because of a break-down in talks, the upcoming Christmas vacation, or end-of-semester examinations, there was little further negotiation between black students and the administration for the rest of the semester. Certainly no concrete progress was made on any of the demands except in the case of College involvement with the nearby Davidson Avenue community center, where the College began a program training community residents in bookkeeping and accounting.

In general, this phase of black student activism was not markedly successful. The administration seems to have talked it to death. The movement continued to be norm-oriented, despite the provocation that lack of tangible results might seem to have provided. One reason was the persistence of internal problems of disillusion and disaffection. Though these problems had been submerged in the excitement of renewed action, they did not entirely disappear.[7] And the longer success eluded the movement, the more likely they were to re-emerge.

## PHASE 5: SPRING SEMESTER 1969

At the end of the first semester of 1968–69, Katara's efforts had borne little fruit. The movement appeared to be stalled, a situation potentially disarming and subverting of the movement and its efforts to achieve change on campus. Hence, starting as the semester ended and continuing into February, Katara held a series of meetings to decide what to do to get things off dead center. The major step agreed upon was to establish an order of priority for its demands: which were to be pushed for first and hardest in the new semester.

At the top of this priority list was implementation of a black studies program. This decision was not unanimous. Todd Little, for one, was apparently unenthusiastic about the decision, feeling that other goals were more important (for example, bringing more black faculty and administrators to campus, or gaining the right to participate meaningfully in decisions affecting black students). Despite his reservations Little was in the forefront of efforts to get a black studies program, but this lack of unanimity, and Little's reservations, would later prove crucial in the history of Katara and of the movement.

During this same period the College, perhaps equally mindful of the perceived lack of progress, held a meeting with black students and concerned faculty members to apprise them of the advances made. In this meeting, held 5 February, the dean noted that the College had had great difficulty in recruiting black faculty, largely because of an apparent dearth of available candidates. He emphasized, however, that the College intended to pursue the task vigorously and called on students and faculty members to aid in the search (HDN, 5 Feb.).

In mid-February an ad hoc committee was formed to consider the institution of a black studies program. Composed of several faculty members and the single black member of the College administration, the committee apparently was formed on the initiative of several white faculty members (a number of whom earlier in the year had submitted a proposal for such a program completely independent of black students' actions, though perhaps influenced by them).

One of the committee's first steps was to form a student-faculty subcommittee whose primary function would be to draw up a specific proposal for a black studies program. By the beginning of March, the subcommittee, composed of four black students, including Todd Little, and two faculty members, one black and one white, had begun its work. It continued with discussions and meetings through the rest of March.

Meanwhile, Katara continued its regular schedule of meetings, concerts, and lectures. At Washington Square, the Martin Luther King, Jr., Afro-American Student Center officially opened on 23 March, independent of the University and with an ambitious program of functions and activities planned.

March was also the month during which the Taylor affair began. An extended series of protests by white students started in reaction to the denial of tenure to a popular teacher, Dr. Lawrence Taylor of the English department, and escalated through March and April, lasting into May. This episode of student protest involved serious actions— occupation of buildings, demonstrations, sit-ins, the employment of court injunctions by College authorities, and the firebombing of two college buildings.[8] Thus, through most of the second semester College authorities were confronted with white student protest of serious dimensions over significant and fundamental institutional issues. It was in this context that black students took further action.

At least some of the issues involved in the Taylor affair directly affected black students and their interests. Even though they were not intimately involved, they had to decide if, and how, the affair might affect their own efforts. No official support for or alliance with white students, and no actions on their behalf, were ever forthcoming from Katara. In contrast to the response of SDS during the Stone controversy, Katara seems to have decided that its political interests were best served by *not* taking an official or active part in the protest. Once more the asymmetrical nature of relations and alliances between black and white students in University College was underscored.[9]

Despite the distraction of the Taylor affair, by the middle of March the subcommittee on black studies had developed a detailed proposal for what was to be called the African and Afro-American Studies Program. The proposal was then sent to the Educational Policy and Planning Committee (EPPC), the relevant policy committee of the faculty. For the rest of the year, Katara's activist efforts focused almost exclusively on the implementation of this program.[11]

The most distinctive feature of the program was that although it would be administered by a coordinator who would teach in the program and hold faculty rank analogous to that of department chairman, control would reside ultimately in a joint arrangement involving the coordinator and a student/faculty coordinating committee. The coordinator would act in concert with the coordinating committee and would be chosen by the faculty/student coordinating committee, as the original proposal put it (New York University, 1969b). The coordinating committee would be composed of two members of Katara, two students majoring in black studies, and two faculty members teaching in the program.

On 19 March the EPPC responded favorably to the proposal, expressing reservations primarily about the roles of the coordinator and the coordinating committee and the composition of the latter. Discussions between the EPPC and the subcommittee that drew up the proposal began immediately.

On 14 April the EPPC gave formal approval to the establishment of an African and Afro-American Studies Program in a form close to that originally proposed, except that the program was to be based in a new, interdisciplinary department instead of a black studies center with academic and community outreach functions. The EPPC accepted as proposed the description of the coordinator and coordinating committee. The proposal was then sent to the faculty for its approval. Black students at this point were understandably pleased and expectant. It seemed that they were about to achieve a double victory in getting the program and in winning acceptance of the principle of student control in the administration and running of a regular part of the academic program. Approval of a program by the EPPC was usually followed by faculty approval, and, indeed, the faculty did approve the black studies program. It did so, however, by only two votes in what was by all reports a tense and emotional meeting. By accepting a student-dominated administrative arrangement, the faculty granted a significant concession to the student-power aims of black students at a time when there was great resistance to the similar aims of white students.

However, this program was never to be implemented. Almost simultaneously with EPPC and faculty approval, the College administration voiced strong opposition to the idea of a student-dominated academic committee and program.[11] Katara's response was strong. Relations between the College and black students were immediately soured.

The next weeks marked the highest level of tension between black students and the administration since the Stone affair. Many of those most strongly in favor of the original proposal were ready to man the barricades once more.[12] Only the efforts of Little and other leaders seem to have prevented full-fledged protest actions, though such efforts themselves contributed to dissension within the organization. As one student recalled:

> I could understand why [Todd] didn't want us to protest, I guess. He wanted us to resort to stronger steps only after every other choice was gone. We might be more effective then and could argue we had right on our side. But I really wanted to let those racist bastards have it right then and there. Some of us never really forgave [Todd] for not being willing to fight harder then. (Student Interview no. 11)

During the next weeks Katara and the administration held a number of intensive negotiating sessions to try to resolve the impasse. Katara continued to insist on a coordinating committee with four students and two faculty members; the administration on four faculty members and two students. At least one faculty member party to the negotiations attributes the administration's intransigence to Dean George's and Provost Neal's insensitivity to black students. In his opinion their dislike of black students was the primary determinant of administrative reactions to the students' requests.[13] As he put it, "Both the provost and the dean felt these students were ungrateful militants whose only concern was making trouble and whose admission to the College had probably been a terrible mistake" (Administrative/Faculty Interview no. 7).

Black students' hostility and anger were very real, stemming from their frustrated expectations. At the same time, not all of their hostile outbursts and walk-outs were entirely spontaneous. The students, especially those involved in the actual negotiating sessions, carefully considered their actions. As session after session went on, it was clear that neither side was willing to compromise. In an effort to reach a resolution, other persons, primarily from the faculty, joined the talks at different points. President Hester himself participated on more than one occasion, recognizing the potential for the eruption of serious black protest in the midst of an already intense white protest. In one of these sessions the president suggested a compromise for the coordinating committee: three students and three faculty members. This was at that point rejected by both sides.

There was for some time little awareness of this confrontation on campus. On 30 April the struggle between Katara and the administration became public with the appearance in HDN of an article describing both the genesis of the conflict and the issues involved. The article presented Todd Little's outline of Katara's position and Dean George's outline of the administration's. Little emphasized that Katara had worked long and hard for a black studies program and had come up with one that was intellectually strong, educationally innovative, and designed to meet the needs and interests of black students. They would not see it "emasculated" and would boycott any program not conforming in every particular to the proposal submitted to the EPPC and already accepted by the faculty. Dean George presented, with what he considered to be great reasonableness, his view that things really were not so serious. The program and curriculum for the black studies program were "pretty clear" and perfectly acceptable. Only the working out of the budget and its administration stood in the way of final approval. The two statements made it apparent that basic differences still remained.

Negotiations continued. Finally, on 6 May, it was announced that the budget, curriculum, and administrative arrangements for the program had been approved by the College administration. A compromise had been reached: the coordinating committee would be composed of three students and three faculty members. The announcement did not say whether the function and authority of this committee would remain as proposed originally, but the fact that it also indicated that the committee would be formed immediately and tackle as its first task the recruitment and nomination of a black coordinator seemed to imply that they would.

Ostensibly, the conflict between black students and the administration had been resolved. Black students had achieved a concrete goal—a black studies program of breadth and depth that would become a viable and permanent feature of the College. Once again, however, this bright prospect was never fulfilled. Before the term ended, the compromise worked out so laboriously broke down. It was rejected by the Katara membership.

Why did Katara reject the compromise, without which the entire black studies program was jeopardized? One reason was the internal dissension created during the Stone affair and continuing through the second semester, exacerbated, perhaps, by the absence of unanimity in the decision to push for black studies. A more militant faction in Katara refused to accept anything less than the program outlined in the original proposal. One of the students involved in negotiation for the black studies program argued, "Some people couldn't see that we had achieved something real. They felt that any compromise with the University was like selling your soul or something. If you gave in on one thing, you'd have to give in to everything. We couldn't change their minds" (Student Interview no. 11).

This rejection and the leadership confusion it created in Katara prevented the final resolution of the black studies conflict. With only two weeks left in the year and with final examinations imminent, there was little time or energy left for negotiations, and there were few black students with whom the administration could negotiate. As a result of this failure, no separate black studies program was ever established in University College. Thus ended the efforts of the black student movement for 1968–69.

That academic year witnessed the most extensive protest and activism by black students in the College's history, yet the accomplishments of the movement were comparatively few. The library began a serious program of acquiring works of all kinds on black life and culture. Some courses in the area of black studies were offered (mainly in African history, Caribbean cultures, and Afro-American history and literature). The College took steps to increase its involvement in the surrounding community, largely through its support for the nearby Davidson Avenue Community Center. Only one black administrator was hired, and the attempt to recruit more blacks into the faculty was not fruitful. There were never more than five or six black faculty members in the College at any one time. Negotiations were begun on a black student center at the Heights, but by the end of the year there was still no center. Most of Katara's other suggestions or demands were left unmet. And despite the movement's efforts, Stone was not retained and the black studies program was not established.

The latter failure in many respects represents the third major crisis in the movement, and the third within the same school year. Yet because of the effect of these crises on morale, cohesion, and willingness to protest, and because of the College's actions and control strategies (as well as other factors already noted), the movement did not become value-oriented. Despite a number of shifts and potentially radicalizing forces, the black student movement ended the year as it began it: essentially a norm-oriented movement.

Equally important, Katara was never able to recapture the cohesion and the sense of purpose and shared belief it possessed in the weeks before the Stone crisis. It failed to eliminate the hostility and bitterness within the black student population that resulted from these crises. One result was a decline in the active membership of Katara during the second semester. The fight for black studies and the dissension it created in Katara, both at the start of the struggle and at its resolution, served to heighten the group's internal difficulties. The failure of the black studies program served, in effect, to increase the division and centrifugal tendencies already present among black students.

It is in this regard that the third crisis was particularly important. The movement's ability to resolve the disaffection and internal division would directly determine its future. As we shall see, the movement would be less successful in resolving this internal crisis than the first two. Nevertheless, some of its most important efforts would come in the next two years.

## PHASE 6: SEPTEMBER 1969– MAY 1970

Approximately fifty black students entered with the freshman class in the fall of 1969, as compared to seventy in 1968. The proportion entering on MLK scholarship aid seems to have been about the same, or perhaps slightly lower.[14]

As the new school year opened, some conditions from the previous spring persisted. The Committee for Improved Educational Values and other activist white student groups gave every indication of intending to continue to pursue most of their various concerns. A series of antiwar rallies and demonstrations was planned for October. The social rift between black and white (especially Jewish) students remained and was to continue throughout the year.

As for Katara, the frustrations and bitterness of the previous year continued, though somewhat muted. The split between Katara members and non-member black students that had developed the year before continued. As a result, Katara opened the year with fewer active members than at any point during 1968–69. Todd Little was replaced by Paul Hunter as president of Katara. A much less charismatic figure, his presidency had great, and negative, influence on the movement. (This leadership change is consistent with the observations of Weber, among others, on the problem of succession crises.) Hunter was not the kind of leader most needed by Katara at this point in its history. From all evidence he seems to have been much more effective in mobilizing students for already agreed-upon action on behalf of already agreed-upon issues than in articulating issues and strategies himself, more effective as an enthusiast in the midst of protest than as the person responsible for meeting the diverse needs of students outside crisis situations.

Further, he did not have the kind of active support from other important or influential black students that would have supplemented his own leadership deficiencies. Todd Little, for example, was less involved in the organization this year, largely because he now faced the pressures of senior year, and also because he had become the target of hostility and resentment from many black students as a result of the kind of "failed faith" and scapegoating that the failures of the movement the year before might be expected to produce.

Perhaps the most important reason for the weakness of Hunter's presidency was the growing suspicion among black students that he was dealing in drugs. His dealing allegedly occurred not only in the surrounding community but also on campus and involved black as well as white students. There are few activities less acceptable to many black students (or for that matter many other blacks) than drug pushing, particularly if it involves black pushers selling to black people. For many black students this was one action that could be neither forgiven nor tolerated.

As these suspicions became more widespread, the divisions within the black student community became even greater. Some students continued to support Hunter, who remained president for the entire year; others simply could not, and refused to be involved in Katara activities as long as he remained part of the group. Thus, the dissension of the previous year was heightened in 1969–70. Katara never fully recovered, and the movement was crippled.

However, the consequences of the Hunter presidency were not immediately apparent as the school year began. What seemed more important to many black students was the fact that the question of black studies was still unresolved. Katara and the administration were still unable to formulate a mutually acceptable administrative arrangement for the program. Katara still insisted on a committee of four students and two faculty members. The administration would not accept more than three students. Despite this continuing impasse, the new dean of the College, Martin Seligman, announced on 18 September that a black studies major *would* begin that fall, with the full program to be implemented in the spring. In making this announcement, Dean Seligman emphasized that this step was intended merely to get things going. It was not in any way an attempt by the administration unilaterally to organize the program or to impose one from above, and the program was not a substitute for Katara's original proposal. The dean declared himself "eager" to work with black and Puerto Rican students to make their careers at University College "more satisfying" (HDN, 18 Sept.).

Despite the dean's statement, the stalemate continued well into October, while the status of the program remained unsettled. Finally, on 17 October HDN reported that Dean Seligman and Dr. Harold A. Allen (the black director of the Martin Luther King, Jr., Institute for Afro-American Affairs downtown) would meet and issue a joint report on the status of black studies in University College.

The entry of Harold Allen into the black studies impasse is important for several reasons. First, it represented, at least in part, a sincere attempt to break the deadlock on black studies and to get a viable program started. At the same time, it demonstrates that a purely local resolution of the problem apparently seemed to the participants to be unlikely. Third, it was another example of the long-established tendency for problems in the College to be referred to or assumed by administrators downtown.[15] Fourth, black students were rarely invited to participate in the talks, nor did they have a direct role in writing the report. Thus, there was a fear that there would be, after all, an administration-arranged or imposed program.

Given their distrust of the institution, many black students were skeptical of both the report and the program that might result from it. While the Allen-Seligman report was awaited, black student discontent simmered. Meanwhile, other, more immediate developments posed direct and serious threats to Katara.

On 20 October the budget and finance committee of the Student Senate granted Katara $700, substantially less than the $3,106 requested. This grant, which contrasts strongly with the relatively generous allowance for 1968–69, required extensive cuts in the varied program of activities Katara had planned. Once again, Katara found itself in a conflict with the primary student funding organ. After an emergency meeting, Katara announced the next day that it would appeal the budget cut to the Committee on Student Affairs.[16] As Paul Hunter noted, a resolution of this problem and the full amount of the requested monies were needed to plan the year's activities with "a firm knowledge of our operating expenses" and to carry out the full program planned by the organization (HDN, 22 Oct.).

Before this meeting could be held and its appeal formally presented,

Katara suffered another blow. On 23 October the Student Senate withdrew official recognition of Katara as a campus organization. Katara's credentials as a recognized student group were suspended because it had been discovered that its president, Paul Hunter, was not a registered student at NYU.

A precondition for any student organization desiring official recognition and funding from the Student Senate was that all members and officers must be registered, enrolled students in good standing in University College. Although Hunter had been registered the year before, and would be the following year, for unknown reasons he did not register for the fall semester of 1969. He had not informed black students of this fact. Though Katara rallied to his defense, many students were annoyed at "such a dumb move," as one put it. Moreover, some were angry that the organization was forced to rally around an issue and an individual many considered highly dubious. Several felt that this situation only served to dissipate organizational energies and needlessly damage its standing on campus. Naturally, this increased Katara's internal difficulties.

The senate informed Katara that this suspension would remain in effect until a new, properly qualified president was chosen and a full list of Katara's members and officers submitted. Further, until that time, no funding of any kind would be granted and the budget question would not be decided.

Katara's budgetary request had already promised to be a source of contention; with the suspension, the senate presented an even greater threat to the continued effective functioning of the organization. This was the first time such a threat had come from the actions of other students. Not surprisingly, the senate's action did not help relieve the separation and distrust between black and white students.

For some days there was much tension between Katara and the Student Senate. Finally, on the evening of Wednesday, 29 October, members of Katara entered and addressed a meeting of the Student Senate (whether they had been invited is not clear). After these addresses and some additional discussion, the senate voted to revoke Katara's suspension, thereby contravening its own rules. This action was vigorously opposed by many white students, in and out of the Student Senate—so much so that the executive committee of the senate agreed to meet the next afternoon to reconsider the revocation.

No further public action was taken by the senate or by Katara the next day. The revocation of the suspension was allowed to stand, and Katara was once more a recognized campus organization. This, however, did not solve the issue of money. The problem was finally resolved in subsequent private talks between the senate and Katara, with the final sum awarded being very close to the $700 first recommended. In a sense, therefore, Katara had once more failed to accomplish its aims in a confrontation with authority, though it had argued its way back to the former status quo.

The matter ended on 5 November when the Student Senate passed a resolution clearly establishing a policy prohibiting non-students from membership and office in any student organization with official senate recognition. There was some opposition to this position from various student groups, including HDN, which argued in an editorial on 7 November that a complete ban on non-students was unwarranted. Groups not funded by the senate should be under no obligation to comply with its requirements for membership or office holding. However, most students, black and white, seem to have accepted this restatement of policy without too much protest and even with some indifference.

Anti-war rallies and demonstrations on campus, which began in October, continued throughout November and into the second semester. In addition to the activist groups formed the previous spring, new ones appeared, including the Progressive Action Committee (a radical splinter of CIEV), a campus chapter of the Jewish Defense League, and El Grito Borenqueno, the organization of Puerto Rican students. In short, the campus clearly had not returned to the traditional academic atmosphere of the pre-1968 period.

The status of black studies remained in doubt. The Allen-Seligman report was still unfinished, with no indication of when it might be completed. As a result, the spring implementation of the program promised by the dean appeared increasingly unlikely. The longer the program was delayed, the greater was the likelihood that it might never be started. Increasingly it appeared that Katara's rejection of the compromise on the coordinating committee the previous spring had inadvertently doomed the program. Growing recognition of this possibility did not help problems of morale and consensus among black students.

A possible sign of some small movement on black studies was reported in HDN on 18 November: Harold Allen announced that he was assuming the initiative in drawing up the report and was at that moment determining the best way to proceed. In this endeavor he planned to meet and work closely with black students in University College. Dean Seligman, quoted in the same issue of HDN, hoped that the report would be the basic guide for the future of black studies in University College. He looked to the MLK Institute to take the lead "in getting a program acceptable to the student body and faculty."

The following day HDN announced that President Hester, Chancellor Cartter, Provost Neal, and Harold Allen would meet privately with Katara in an effort to resolve the question of black studies and perhaps the persisting discontent among black students over continued failure to start the program. At least one such meeting was held. However, the first semester ended without any substantial progress toward instituting the program. This continuing failure to implement the full black studies program took a heavy toll in black students' trust in the College, further damaged organizational cohesion and commitment to the movement, and increased the frustration and disillusionment of black students.

The second semester began with no black studies program, though a few isolated courses in the area were offered. Some talks were held throughout February, but with little progress. The stalemate continued. In February the College suspended SDS from the use of campus facilities because of its disruption of recruitment efforts by General Electric. This move, along with the black studies stalemate, suggested that both black and white students had reached the margins of patience of College authorities. In the same month, notices of Katara meetings were carried for three weeks in a row in the "Noteboard" of HDN.[17] The reason for the frequent meetings was the attempt to resolve the black studies issue. Deliberations focused on possible next moves.

By the beginning of March, there was still no agreement on a course of action. Reporting on the issue, HDN on 3 March noted that the development of a comprehensive program was now in the hands of a committee of students appointed by Harold Allen. When this committee was appointed is unclear. In many ways, however, the problem had come full circle. It was a group of students, along with some faculty members, who had first presented the proposal for a black studies program a year earlier. Now they were being asked to do precisely the same thing all over again.

Despite their eagerness to achieve a black studies program, many black students were not pleased with this turn of events. Nor were they happy with Harold Allen for his part in the situation. For one thing, he had announced in November that he was assuming the initiative for producing the black studies report; it was now March, and Allen had not yet produced it. The formation of the committee of students may well have seemed to black students a kind of abdication of responsibility and final evidence of his lack of any real concern for the black studies program or them. As one student put it, "We didn't know him. We didn't choose him. We never trusted him, and he proved we were right" (Student Interview no. 12).

The formation of this committee was the last important attempt to establish a formal black studies program. The committee produced no report and disbanded shortly after its formation because of an inability to come to any agreement and because of the general doubt among black students about whether it was really worthwhile to keep pushing for the program. For by this time, some shift of interest among black students had begun. Many had come to see the primary value of black studies basically as enrichment and to accept the idea that perhaps it ought to complement traditional disciplines rather than become a separate program or major. For others, who still wanted black studies but saw no possibility of a full program, such a view represented a compromise position. Others increasingly felt the whole effort to be futile. These views combined to prevent any further collective push for black studies for the rest of the term. Despite a number of efforts, the year would close without the establishment of a black studies program in University College.

As black studies was moving toward its final failure, a proposal for another program was in preparation, largely as a result of the initiatives of Todd Little and another black student leader, Al Chambers.[18] The proposal for the Educational Development and Community Enrollment Program (EDCEP) was presented to the administration and the College community on 10 March and immediately gained the attention of the campus.

The EDCEP proposal was *not* made by Katara as an organization; rather, it was drawn up and presented by a committee of fifteen black and Puerto Rican students.[19] This was the first time black and Puerto Rican students worked together on a major academic project. The basic purpose behind EDCEP was the achievement of real diversity in the student body (i.e., more black, Puerto Rican, and non-middle-class students) and increased "relevance" to the surrounding communities. It was in substance a proposal for a kind of open admissions program in University College.

EDCEP called for the Bronx to be divided into five educational areas or districts. Over a period of five to seven years, the College would admit all the interested graduates of all public high schools in the Bronx, rotating districts yearly so that over the five-year period each district would be served equally. In addition, the proposal called for establishing an associate degree program in the College for these (and other) students—in effect, a junior college within University College. Credits from this program could be transferred toward the B.A. or B.S. degrees. Graduates of the associate degree program, whether Bronx high school graduates or not, would be granted automatic admission to either the College or the School of Engineering. Finally, this would be a joint program with the other major colleges in the Bronx, thus ensuring that the Bronx was fully served while avoiding unmanageable pressures on any one college.[20]

Strongly supported by black and Puerto Rican students, as well as some white students, the EDCEP proposal set off wide discussion within the College. The Student Senate, acting as a body, immediately gave its approval to the proposal. However, this action was clearly not unanimous, for three days later the president of the senate released a statement opposing the concept of open admissions in general and the EDCEP proposal in particular.

On 16 March HDN, which usually supported the substance of black students' proposals, came out with an editorial emphatically rejecting the concept of open admissions. Its opposition and that of the senate president were based on two grounds. First, NYU as a private insitution did not have the same public obligations as public institutions. Second, the University could not afford open admissions. These arguments, along with fears of lowered academic standards, formed the basis of most student and faculty opposition to EDCEP.

For the next two weeks there was much discussion of the EDCEP proposal. At no point did the proponents of EDCEP "demand" immediate action on it. Instead, their strategy was to strive for the widest possible discussion of the proposal while gathering support. Their basic approach emphasized reasonableness, discussion, and negotiation, relying on persuasion and the moral strength of the proposal.

On Monday, 30 March, the fifteen original sponsors of EDCEP held the first of several forums "to justify and elucidate" their proposal (HDN, 31 March). Following this forum, at which Todd Little was the principal speaker, another forum was announced for Friday, 3 April. Among those who attended the April forum were President Hester, Provost Neal, and the superintendent of the local school board in the Ocean Hill–Brownsville district of Brooklyn.

During the forum Professor Richard Keller, ombudsman in University College for 1969–70, announced his support for EDCEP. Though the purpose of the meeting was to discuss community admissions and the EDCEP proposal, much of the time was spent in grilling Hester on matters other than EDCEP or curricular issues. This student response suggests the activist mood still prominent on campus, extending beyond black studies, to such issues as student power, and opposition to the Vietnam War.

On Tuesday, 7 April, the EDCEP committee formally asked the administration for its support for the proposal. The committee stressed that it needed the administration's help in working out the details of the original plan. The committee was at this point engaged in trying to gain the support of Bronx communities and high schools for the program, even though it had yet to be approved.[21]

After two weeks of formal consideration, on 14 April, the faculty took affirmative action on the EDCEP plan, accepting and approving it "in principle." Both the speed and the consensus with which the faculty acted took most observers by surprise. The discussions in this faculty meeting centered on two arguments for the program:

1) the moral necessity for NYU to admit more students from the Bronx.

2) the advantage NYU would derive from having a more heterogeneous student body. (HDN, 15 Apr.)

In accepting the plan, the faculty charged the administration "to proceed with its implementation" as soon as possible (HDN, 15 Apr). The committee of fifteen and members of the faculty and administration immediately began a series of discussions on various parts of the proposal. Their basic aim was to produce a workable plan for implementing EDCEP by September 1970. Thus, an important effort by black and Puerto Rican students seemed well on the way to success.

Black students during March and April were active on a number of other fronts as well, in part in an effort to offset the black studies failure. One effort centered on student elections. March and April are traditionally the months when candidates for student government posts begin preparing and running for office. In the spring of 1970, Katara put up candidates for almost every student government post. However, just before the final balloting, the black candidates withdrew. The indications are that they made a deal with the candidate for Student Senate president who seemed to have the best chance to win: they withdrew their candidates in return for the promise of favorable treatment by student government. (This willingness to engage in traditional politics is further indication of the movement's norm-oriented character at this point, and, as we shall discuss later, the results of the deal provide evidence that the movement was to some extent institutionalized.)

Katara also resumed the long-dormant push for a black student center, largely abandoned as organizational energies focused on black studies. Negotiations on the center continued for the rest of the term. The summer programs for neighborhood youth, so successful the previous two years, seemed in April to be in jeopardy. The problem was a projected lack of funding. Black students blamed this situation squarely on the University. In their view, it had not provided adequate funds for the programs in the beginning and had consistently resisted providing adequate funds once they had begun. Katara launched a number of efforts to keep the summer programs at their previous level.

In short, by the end of April, black students of diverse affiliations were active on several fronts: student government politics, a black student center, the continuation of the summer programs. The push for black studies was gradually abandoned, but the efforts to implement EDCEP were proceeding.

On 4 May 1970 South Vietnamese troops and American "advisors" invaded Cambodia. From this point until the end of the semester, normal academic functioning in University College came to a halt, as it did in colleges and universities across the country. On 7 May, following the deaths of students at Kent State and Jackson State universities, classes were officially cancelled in the University. They would not be resumed until summer sessions began.

In University College normal activity was replaced by a student strike, demonstrations, teach-ins, workshops, and lectures by invited speakers and faculty members. In the midst of all this, on 8 May, Puerto Rican students initiated their first independent action, issuing demands for: (1) the end of domestic repression; (2) the withdrawal of all U.S. troops from Indo-China; (3) a complete end to University complicity in the war effort; (4) the freeing of all political prisoners, most especially Bobby Seale and the Panthers then on trial in New Haven; and (5) immediate implementation of EDCEP.

Despite this "Cambodian spring," discussions of EDCEP continued. By mid-May it was clear that a joint EDCEP program involving other colleges and universities in the Bronx could not be implemented; there were too many difficulties and unequal enthusiasm among the various institutions. It was equally evident that the College could not carry out the proposed program by itself. As a result, a joint student-faculty committee was formed to work over the summer to produce a plan for the implementation of EDCEP by University College alone.

Thus the year ended. By the end of June this committee (composed of three black students, one white faculty member, and the associate provost) was already hard at work. Black student efforts to save the summer programs had been successful. They were once more in operation, though somewhat reduced as a result of the College's financial crisis. Moreover, the negotiations for a black student center now appeared to have reached a successful conclusion. The College agreed to provide a house it owned near the campus for such a center.

In terms of its external goals, therefore, Katara had a mixed year in 1969–70. The goal most vigorously sought, a black studies program, was not achieved and was Katara's clearest failure. The organization had not pushed for any new programs or goals. The summer programs, the student center, black studies—all were carry-overs from previous years. The one really new proposal in 1969–70, EDCEP, was the work of individual students, not the organization.

Many of the interpersonal and organizational problems among black students were still not resolved. Dissension and disaffection, though somewhat reduced by second semester activities, persisted. As one former student describes it, "We just seemed to unravel in Katara that year. Several students stopped coming to meetings. There was a lot of backbiting going on" (Student Interview no. 21). Katara lost the impetus and momentum from earlier years. The old cohesion was gone; it was less politically and socially effective. By the end of the year, it appeared, despite a flurry of activity, to be marking time, trying to consolidate gains, prevent further dissension, and contain the erosion of its position and achievements.

The movement in 1969–70 might be described as in a "stable" phase (cf. Cameron, 1966; King, 1961), even if it was also precarious. There was some activism, but not the pronounced activity of the previous year; some success, but more important failures. The movement continued, concentrating essentially on reformist efforts via "reasonable" tactics. The fate of the organization paralleled the history of the movement.

Movement stability implies institutionalization. One development in the late spring of 1970 should be noted in this regard. This was the creation of a Black Affairs Committee as an integral, official part of the Student Senate and its committee structure. Though the creation of this committee *may* have been the result of black student activism, it was never one of their demands, never the focus of any public action. Rather, it was created by the senate, apparently on its own initiative— but an initiative with roots in the deal Katara made during student elections with the successful candidate for senate president. This committee, scheduled to begin operating the coming fall, was created despite black students' tendency—except where Katara's budget was concerned—to bypass student government in trying to gain their objectives.

As *Palisades* (the Heights student handbook) described it, the function of this committee was to act "as a liason for the black student community and as an agent in relating the black experience to the University Heights Center" (*Palisades*, 1970–71:47). One of the more intriguing features of this committee was its composition: "two students with either a Black Studies or African Studies major/minor, *chosen by Katara;* two other students *chosen by Katara;* two members of the Faculty associated with the Black Studies program" (*Palisades*, 1970–71:48; my emphasis). The faculty members could be expected to be at least sympathetic to black students' concerns or desires. Thus, despite the ex officio membership of the president and vice-president of the senate, this committee was to be controlled or dominated by Katara.

Both the existence and the composition of the committee lay outside the electoral process, with no public accountability or responsibility to anyone other than black students. Since black students could still also run for Student Senate positions, their *potential* power vis-à-vis student government was markedly increased by the formation of this committee. This potential power was never realized, however, for three reasons. First, the black studies program never materialized. Second, black students persisted in their belief that real power and the authority to achieve their objectives lay elsewhere. Third, continuing internal dissension made it difficult to find enough students sufficiently interested and sufficiently trusted by other black students to run for senator or to serve on the committee.

## THE DECLINE OF KATARA AND THE MOVEMENT: 1970–71

When school opened in September 1970, the committee formed to consider the implementation of the EDCEP proposal was not quite ready with its report; it promised, having worked through the summer, that a final report would be presented to the faculty by October.

The long-sought student center opened as school began. The official name was completely different from any proposed during the two-year effort to get such a center. The name—the Minority Group Seminar House—reflected its official purpose. From the point of view of the College administration, the House was to serve the needs of *all* minority students (not just blacks) for meeting space, a social center, and a place for counseling, tutoring, and similar activities. Thus, its official identity was markedly different from that envisioned by black students.[22]

From the day it opened, however, the center was unofficially known as the Black House. In practice, it served primarily the needs of black students, especially Katara members; Puerto Rican students and El Grito used it occasionally for meetings, and it was used for a few joint activities by the general campus community. The black student monopoly remained a permanent and accepted characteristic of the House from the time it opened. Though ultimately it fell under College authority (and thus was not politically and financially independent of the College, as was the downtown student center proposed earlier), in practice black students were responsible for its upkeep. The result was double funding for Katara. As a student organization Katara was funded by the student government; the House was funded by the provost's office. Because it controlled the House, Katara received and utilized the funds for it. Whether or not this is evidence of Katara's political acuity, it does represent a kind of partial institutionalization of the movement.

The freshman class that entered in the fall of 1970 showed another decline in the number of black students.[23] There were no more than forty blacks in this class, with fewer receiving MLK aid (proportionately and absolutely) than in previous years.

Katara opened the year with a new president, Geoffrey Brook. However, it had no new programs (other than the House) and no new initiatives. The momentum developed in earlier years had virtually dissipated by 1970–71. Moreover, the group's internal problems persisted. The number of active members was the lowest ever. One black student expressed the feeling of many when she said, "I decided I just didn't want to deal any more with the hassles, the disappointments, and the you-better-be-black games people played" (Student Interview no. 10).

As the semester began, Dean Seligman informed the College that the report on EDCEP, due in October, would *not* call for an open-admissions program. Rather, the committee's proposal would call for a two-year program for students who could not meet the College's regular admission requirements. Students would have to complete the two years before they could enter the College. The dean stressed that the program would successfully answer the fears of lowered academic quality in the College and objections based on the University's financial crisis.

In addition, the administration announced that as of that September, the Higher Educational Opportunities Program (a program funded by New York State) would be expanded to the Heights. With the added funds provided by HEOP, additional counseling would be available for minority students in the College. The space problem created by the presence of additional counselors would be solved by having them operate out of the Black House.

Significantly, this use of the House did not last out the year and was never reinstituted. For one thing, Katara was opposed to such use of the House. In addition, some black students were reluctant to go to the Black House for fear of unpleasant encounters or a less than warm welcome by Katara members, a further reflection of relations within the black student community at this point and Katara's difficulties in gaining the adherence of many black students.

By mid-October the report on EDCEP was still not quite ready, but the administration and the EDCEP committee indicated that the report would be presented to the faculty at its November meeting. During October the NYU Liberation Front and the Contact Action Forum (coalitions of white student activists) held a number of protest rallies to demand an end to University complicity in the war effort, the release of political prisoners, and the implementation of EDCEP.

On 15 October the University announced that the Root-Tilden scholarships (an important endowed source of financial aid) would be cut. This was the first indication that the worsening financial crisis would directly and adversely affect scholarship and financial aid. It was also the first major cut in a series of cuts or rumored cuts in aid that increasingly troubled black students during the year.

A special Black Affairs Department page appeared in HDN on 23 October. It highlighted the continuing existence and functioning of the Opportunities Program, centered at Washington Square, and instituted as one of the University's responses (though less publicized at the Heights) to Martin Luther King's death.[24] However, the greater significance of this page is its strong emphasis on the unity of black and Puerto Rican students, of Katara and El Grito. This was the first time that Katara specifically, officially, and publicly sought an alliance with another student group. Faced with continuing division and disaffection, Katara tried to emphasize its unity with others, to seek allies and fellow partisans outside the black student community, to establish its connection with a wider group. Katara's attempt to ally with others in the face of internal and external threats is typical of protest groups and social movement organizations.[25] It was also a response to increased numbers of Puerto Rican students on campus.

On 30 October the report on the implementation of EDCEP was finally released to the faculty. The proposal called for a two-year Educational Support Program (ESP), which would have departmental status, would be funded by the College, and would be a precursor to the implementation of the original EDCEP plan. In ESP students would take a variety of courses, substantive in content and focus, but also designed to develop college-level skills. Tutorials, workshops, counseling, and other educational support efforts would be available. Up to twelve of the forty-eight required course credits could be in remedial courses.

Faculty and administrators of the program would, as much as possible, be black and Puerto Rican like the expected students. Student advisors (as teaching assistants, counseling assistants, and tutors) would be an important, integral part of the program. At the end of two years, students would receive an "ESP Arts" or an "ESP Science" diploma, one year's academic credit in the regular College or School of Engineering programs, and admission to the degree programs of the Heights College or other institutions.

Generally, the ESP curriculum would be separate from that of the College, though it might employ some of the College faculty. One hundred Bronx high school graduates would be enrolled in the program each year, with recruiting for the fall of 1971 to begin immediately. To qualify for the program, students had to meet certain requirements: they were to be unable to meet normal NYU entrance requirements and among those deemed hardest to educate; not admitted anywhere else; unlikely to succeed in any other educational support program; highly motivated; residents of the Bronx; and graduates of Bronx high schools.

The first four requirements represent the most significant aspect of ESP, for they indicate a willingness to take a far greater gamble on disadvantaged students than most four-year institutions have. At least in its admissions requirements, the ESP plan was a fundamental departure for NYU's efforts to increase the diversity of the student population.

During the next days the ESP proposal was a subject for much discussion in the College. On 4 November the Student Senate voted its support of the ESP report and proposal. This favorable response was indicative of the general campus attitude. The faculty met on 6 November and, after much debate, sent them to the Educational Policy and Planning and Curriculum committees for further study because of their concern that a realistic and solid program be established and certain details in the report be resolved; some members of the faculty still had not received a copy of the report.

On 11 November the first Sickle Cell Anemia Symposium was held on campus for students and residents of the Bronx communities. Significantly, it was sponsored by the newly formed Heights chapter of the Sickle Cell Anemia Association (SCAA). This was a group of black students separate from Katara, though some Katara members seem to have been involved. It was, in effect, a new black student organization, different from Katara in membership, aims, and actions.

In former years, such an event would likely have been presented by Katara. The fact that it was presented by a new group shows how far Katara had declined as the central organization for black students and its failure to serve the interests of some segments of the black student community.[26]

On 16 November another special Black Affairs Department page appeared in HDN. The most important article on this page, written by an active Katara member, deplored the lack of unity between black and Puerto Rican students on campus. He roundly condemned what black students saw as the principal reason for the lack of unity: the prejudices of Puerto Ricans against blacks. The article ended with a renewed call for "Third World Unity." Katara's drive to find renewed cohesion and purpose through alliance with Puerto Rican students was not making much headway so far.

On this same day, many students received an unpleasant surprise. Without warning, the Student Senate suspended twenty-three student organizations and cut off their funds because they had not submitted the required lists of members and officers. Among the groups suspended were the Chinese Students Society, the Jewish Defense League, the Newman Club, the Young Americans for Freedom, SDS, and Katara. Although the same action had once produced a confrontation between Katara and the Student Senate, no such reaction occurred this time. Instead, after a rather perfunctory and almost completely symbolic resistance, Katara gave in and submitted the required list.

Another special Black Affairs Department page appeared on 23 November and provided additional information on the "state of existence of Katara and developments within the black student community." First, great attention was given to a just-concluded meeting between black, Puerto Rican, and Oriental students and faculty members. The apparent purpose of this meeting was to increase the awareness of the need for unified actions and stances and enhance the prospects for them. This meeting was held at the initiative of black students. Attention was also given to the "hospitality" that the Minority Group

Seminar House offered to *all* minority students. At least for this page in HDN, the Black House had been unofficially renamed Unity House.

The second development highlighted by the page was the appearance of still more black student organizations, each of which was represented by a separate article written by one of its members. Most notable in this regard were the black pre-law society, the pre-med society, and the Black Engineers, the first successful organization of the least politically active black students at the Heights.[27]

At its 4 December meeting, the faculty passed a resolution requiring the EPPC to present a full set of recommendations on ESP for the faculty to vote on near the end of January so that ESP could be initiated in September. Although the passage of this resolution indicated the faculty's general approval of ESP, the fact that it passed by only three votes suggests serious continuing reservations.

Another special Black Affairs Department page appeared in HDN on 7 December. Katara and El Grito had finally achieved some kind of united position (at least rhetorically), a development much applauded by the black student writers for the page. Actual physical unity was not achieved; however, they agreed to work together to develop programs on campus and in the community. Thus, Katara's objective seemed to have been gained. Though it did not restore the lost cohesion and effectiveness of the organization, it may have kept it from disappearing altogether.

The first semester ended without any further important development. The EPPC presented its final report on ESP to the faculty's 5 February 1971 meeting. The faculty voted acceptance without amendment or modification. Thus, ESP was formally created, and though not the original EDCEP program, it was consistent with many of its essential aims and ideas. A student-faculty advisory committee would help with faculty appointments to the program. Though members would be appointed by the dean and the director of ESP (who would officially be a member of the dean's office), there was no mention of the proportion of students and faculty on the committee. The issue that wrecked the black studies program was effectively sidestepped.

The only remained obstacle to full implementation of the ESP plan was the acquisition of funding. Assistant Chancellor Lane Green, the highest-ranking black general officer of the University, was put in charge of funding efforts on 9 February.

March and April passed while Green and other administrators, at the Heights and downtown, sought funding. The New York State Education Department expressed some interest in the program, but had strong reservations about the admission requirements and the kind of students the program would bring to the College. ESP remained stalled while funds were sought. Finally, on 21 April, Green announced that no recruiting for ESP students could be undertaken before summer because of the funding delay. At the same time he indicated that he was sanguine about the prospect of obtaining state approval and funding, probably in June, and expressed the hope that despite these delays the program would be able to meet its planned fall starting date.

While these developments took place, other important events occurred in March and April. Black and Puerto Rican students, at the Heights and at the Square, had become increasingly concerned over what they perceived as a University move to cut back the amount of financial aid given to *new* minority students, including cuts in the MLK program. Moreover, they saw it moving to cut financial aid *already* held by black and Puerto Rican students. These fears were reinforced— indeed, created—by the University's open acknowledgment throughout the year of its grave financial crisis, the near-exhaustion of its scholarship funds, and the need for economy and cutbacks in all areas of its operations (the Root-Tilden scholarships, as already noted, had been cut the previous fall). At the same time, tuition increases appeared very likely.

Though Chancellor Cartter continually insisted that no cuts would be made in the aid or scholarship packages received by students already in the University, or in the number of MLK grants, many black and Puerto Rican students did not believe his repeated assurances. As discontent rose during late March and April, the University held a number of meetings between administrators and black and Puerto Rican students.

Frustration and anger among students had reached such a pitch that the last meeting, held with Chancellor Cartter and the University's director of financial aid on 27 April, was for many the last straw, the precipitating event for open protest. Just hours after this meeting, on 28 April, the largest and most intense black and Puerto Rican student protest of the year took place at the Washington Square campus. This was a joint protest involving black student groups at the Square, Puerto Rican students from the Heights and the Square, and black students from the Heights protesting as individuals, *not* as the organization Katara.[28]

Early on the morning of 28 April, a large number of black and Puerto Rican students occupied Vanderbilt Hall, the main administration building at Washington Square. This occupation was meant not only to express student discontent over financial aid cuts and increased tuition, but also to emphasize the five demands simultaneously presented to the administration:

1) that all present scholarships held by Third World students remain at the 1970–71 level and that new scholarships reflect tuition, room and board increases;

2) that no Third World student's summer earnings be figured into their scholarship package;

3) that the number of incoming MLK freshmen be maintained at the level for 1970–71;

4) that all Third World students wishing to return to NYU from other schools, leaves of absences, etc., be given their previous scholarships in total;

5) that the decision-making over MLK scholarships be taken away from the All-University Director of Financial Aid and be put in the hands of a committee composed of Third World administrators, faculty and graduate students. (Broadside handed out at Washington Square, 28 April 1971)

The University's immediate response was that none of these demands or any other matter of substance could be discussed until the students left the building. The students, not unexpectedly, refused to leave until their demands had been met. Further attempts to end the occupation on its first day were not successful.

Realizing that the students were unlikely to leave of their own accord and desirous of ending the occupation quickly, the University called in the police on the morning of 29 April. The actions of both police and demonstrators were peaceful as the building was cleared. Forty-six students were arrested and charged with criminal trespass. Thus, twenty-two hours after it began, the occupation ended.

Black and other minority students were outraged by the arrests. They immediately began a series of rallies and strikes protesting against the police action and the arrests, supporting the five demands, calling for financial support for the defense of the "NYU 46," and demanding that they receive neither University nor criminal punishment.[29] Reactions to the arrests and to the rallies that followed were mixed. The NYU Black Faculty Association, the *Washington Square Journal*, the student newspaper, and students in an undergraduate residence hall at the Square called for amnesty and supported the protesting students. Despite their efforts, the University Senate refused to grant amnesty.

On 3 May at least one hundred black and Puerto Rican students marched on Vanderbilt Hall. They were met by Chancellor Cartter, who again denied that there had been a cutback in aid, saying "there is a scare over a program that is not in jeopardy" (HDN, 4 May). In the view of many black students, this statement did not truly represent the University's intentions.

> According to a statement released by Chancellor Allan Cartter on May 3, 1971, the administration has no intention of maintaining the "official" level of 250 new MLK grant-students this coming year. According to the figures, the number of students on MLK grants will go up from 892 to 1,015, an increase of 123 [but] a drop of 127 from the 250 goal. Also, we know that it is normal bureaucratic procedure in this situation to overestimate rather than under-estimate, so one might also safely assume that [even] an increase of 123 is an inflated figure. . . .
>
> Black and Puerto Rican student representatives have found the university's position unacceptable due to the fact that "scholarship package" is interpreted by the administration to mean that the student's MLK grant supplemented by various loans is a "scholarship." Thus, they can cut $1,000 from a student's "scholarship" and then inform him that he must take out loans to make up the difference. Thus, his "package" remains the same or is adjusted to meet rising costs, but he foots much more of the bill, either immediately or in the future when he tries to pay back the loans. (Sojourner, June 1971)

In short, in the view of protesting students, the University had already admitted that it was cutting financial aid and was simply manipulating the figures for cosmetic purposes.

On 5 May, as protest rallies continued, Chancellor Cartter met with student representatives in order to negotiate a solution. These efforts proved unfruitful, and students stuck to their demands. Efforts to negotiate an end to the protests persisted through May. Black students continued to reject the University's position and offers on the five demands, while the University continued to resist the demands and to insist that there would be no cutbacks in financial aid.

The school year ended with the impasse unresolved. Black and Puerto Rican students still did not believe University assurances that aid would not be cut. Some cuts in aid had already been made; continued administrative pronouncements about the University's financial crisis tended to undermine assurances about financial aid, especially in the context of annual tuition increases. Students feared that unless aid was actually raised each year, they would be priced out of NYU entirely. Any threat to scholarship aid represented for many black students a threat to their continuing in college and hence to their futures, and this issue was therefore of more immediate concern than most other University actions or policies.

A solution to the conflict was not found until well into the summer, and then it was an administrative solution, not a negotiated one, and left many black students discontented. The University conceded little; most of the demands were rejected, though a committee to oversee the MLK program was established in University College. It lasted a few months.

It is clear in retrospect that 1970–71 marked the lowest point yet in the fortunes of the black student movement. Katara, which began the year with a diminished membership, ended it with an even smaller one. The internal divisions created in the previous year persisted and increased. By the end of the year these divisions had helped to create a number of new organizations, rivals of Katara for the loyalty and energies of black students.

Katara's program of social and cultural activities was much curtailed in both scope and attendance. By the end of the year, Katara was much more like a small, ineffective sect than the center of a vital social movement. Complete disintegration seems to have been avoided only through an alliance with other student groups. Though alliance produced no reversal in Katara's fortunes, it seems, along with the double funding noted earlier, to have provided a necessary prop.

As Katara disintegrated, the movement declined. There was not a single protest incident initiated by black students in University College during the entire school year. The movement was well on its way to becoming becalmed (cf. Zald and Ash, 1966). The one event that ran counter to this trend, the April protest over financial aid, did not take place at the Heights and involved black students from University College largely because the issue represented a direct personal threat to so many of them.

What about the accomplishments of the movement—new policies or programs that resulted from black students' efforts? There were not many, and these were not the result of any new initiatives: there *were* no new initiatives during the year. The opening of the Black House was essentially achieved the year before after two years of efforts. Moreover, at least officially, it opened under rather different auspices and circumstances than originally planned. Not only was the push for black studies completely abandoned, but the year brought a decline in enrollment and student interest in the few courses in the black studies area still being offered. This decline occurred among both white and black students (among the latter perhaps attributable to persisting dissension, and the tendency at this point for black students to reassert or retreat to careerist concerns). The effort to reach out to and ally with other student groups ran a rocky course. The small success it achieved was as much rhetorical as substantial.

As for the successful effort to get the EDCEP plan started via ESP, this too had begun the year before. Its acceptance was largely in the hands of the faculty once the summer committee had delivered the ESP report. Moreover, the whole effort for EDCEP/ESP was the work of a small group of individual students, not Katara.

In short, in 1970–71 the movement declined and the organization disintegrated significantly.


## THE FINAL YEAR: 1971–72

*Black News,* a newsletter put out by Katara in September 1971, provides pertinent information about developments in the last years of the black student movement in University College. Reviewing the accomplishments of Katara and its various presidents, the newsletter acknowledged that the organization and black students themselves had lost much of their former impetus, and provided some indication of why that was so.

> In the past, Katara has had to deal with a division among Black students caused by cliques, repressive attitudes, the middle and upper class beliefs of many Black students with interests other than the welfare of their own people, the failure of other minority students' groups to band together and work with Katara towards similar goals, and even more recently, the nationwide crackdown on Black education now that the threat of fire and rebellion has died down.

The newsletter goes on to emphasize the necessity for Katara's existence and outlines its plans for a resurgence in 1971–72.

> KATARA has served the minority students well, and should not be written off as past the age of usefulness. On the contrary, the older KATARA gets, the more imbedded in our minds should be its ideals!
>
> Now we look to the future. Under [the current president, Katara] regained much of its lost impetus. He has designed a program for KATARA based on the education of Black students through participation, community involvement, and self-help.

This analysis was in fact a little premature, since this presidency only began in September 1971.

Despite these hopes, by June 1972 revitalization had not been achieved. The alliance with Puerto Rican students, shaky to begin with, was now non-existent. Active membership in Katara declined until by spring no more than twenty black students could be said to be members in any sense.

As the year progressed Katara held fewer and fewer meetings, largely because not enough people were interested in coming to them. Its program of social and cultural activities was greatly reduced. The Black Week-End held in the spring of 1972 was not a success, losing several thousand dollars, according to a member of the student affairs office, despite the presumed draw of some big-name entertainment.

Several factors combined to bring Katara to the nadir of its existence in 1971–72: (1) the bitterness and dissension engendered among black students over the previous years, which had not healed; (2) disenchantment with Katara as a result of such feelings and the various failures of the organization over the years; (3) students' desire to avoid these problems and potentially painful intramural encounters; (4) the essentially careerist orientation prevalent among black students, and the desire of many to graduate from college with a minimum of entanglements and difficulties. Even incoming ESP students in 1971–72 seemed to have little or no interest in Katara, as those active in the organization noted with disappointment. A black student then in the College put it succinctly: "There were those of us who felt we simply couldn't go through that anymore. We had worked so hard and what did we end up with? A lot of hurt feelings and a lot of tired heads. Some of us flunked out. Some of us lost good friends we couldn't agree with. It cost too much to struggle" (Student Interview no. 23).

Aside from the functions Katara served for its few active members, in the view of its leaders, its only function of any importance in 1971–72 was to act as a kind of umbrella for other black student organizations, such as the Sickle Cell Anemia Association, the Black Engineers, and the black pre-med group. It provided meeting space in the House, information sources and services, and some funding. In a sense, it was serving a largely custodial function.

In sum, for a variety of reasons, in 1971–72 Katara barely managed to maintain its existence and an extremely modest program of activities. It engaged in no political efforts of any kind and had difficulty attracting people even to its purely social and cultural activities. As for the movement, the absence of activist or political efforts and the disintegration of the organization indicate its becalmed state and incomplete institutionalization.

After 1971–72 University College moved back to Washington

Square as part of the general organizational restructuring undertaken by NYU in response to its financial crisis. The University Heights campus was sold (to the City University of New York, to become the campus of Bronx Community College); the School of Engineering was severed from the University and merged with Brooklyn Polytechnic Institute, while University College, in moving to Washington Square, merged with Washington Square College to form the University's single undergraduate liberal arts college. By September of 1973 University College no longer existed as a separate entity. Katara had begun to merge with the black student groups at the Square. It, too, had effectively disappeared.

# CHAPTER VI
# "We Gave It Our Best Shot"

*S*ocial movements may falter on par-
*tial success, winning small victories which, while leaving basic dissatisfaction*
*untouched, hamper the members in their ability to mobilize resources for*
*further influence.*——William A. Gamson (1968:114–15)

How do we measure the success or failure of the black student movement at University College? The answer is complicated by the need to
determine how much change is the result of black student actions, how
much the result of "white liberal guilt," deliberate pre-emptive action
by authorities, or unrelated decisions.

Several broad indices can be used: the principal goals of black students, the extent to which they were achieved, and the extent to which
those achieved were implemented—that is, how *much* change resulted
and how *permanent* it was; the indirect or unanticipated consequences,
positive and negative, of black student efforts; the subjective views of
black student success held by students themselves and others within and
outside the College.

Black student goals focused on six areas: (1) increased black representation on campus—as students, faculty members, and administrators—along with its corollaries (financial aid, special recruiting, etc.);
(2) an expanded and/or changed curriculum, most frequently involving the creation of some form of black studies program; (3) expanded
or alternative on-campus cultural and educational resources and activities emphasizing the black experience: visiting speakers and cultural
groups, library holdings, centers and institutes for specialized study;
(4) the formation of all-black social centers, most often in separate
houses or buildings and, in some places, all-black residences;
(5) autonomy for and/or black control over these new activities and

programs; and (6) greater service by the college or university to the off-campus black community.

The effects of the movement at University College were felt at both the institutional and the personal level. Let us consider some of these effects.

## GENERAL POLICIES AND ORIENTATIONS

Several of the changes in University College policy or practice sought by the movement were not implemented or were implemented in only a limited way. In a sense these were failures for the movement. Yet through its very existence the movement had consequences in the College and brought about changes that might not otherwise have happened. The black student movement made an impact not least because in University College racial protest was of some duration and at times significantly interrupted normal activities, as it did in many other colleges (see e.g., Astin, Astin, et al., 1975).

According to one senior administrator, an important consequence of the movement (though one not specifically sought by it) was greater sensitivity to student problems, academic and non-academic: more attention to the importance of advising and counseling and increased acceptance of them as a central function of the institution. (This effect was apparently common in white colleges and universities; see, e.g., Boyd, 1974b.) More counselors were hired and counseling was upgraded.

The same administrator, expressing the consensus among faculty members and administrators interviewed, argued that a further consequence of black (and white) student activism was a redefinition of faculty and administrative roles and functions vis-à-vis students. This tended to produce "new" administrators, both in the sense that different persons occupied administrative posts and in the sense that they were less traditional and more flexible in their approach to students. There were attempts to include students in decision making, particularly in those areas of College life most directly affecting them, though always without granting students authority to make fundamental institutional decisions. Again, this was true not only in University College but on a number of other campuses as well (Astin, Astin, et al., 1975).

Another administrator noted the creation in the College of "greater sensitivity to our surrounding community's existence and to our role in it, to the fact that it did exist and the possibility that we could be of some direct benefit to it, and perhaps ought to be" (Administrative/Faculty Interview no. 6). To the extent that black students had such an impact, they filled the same social conscience role in the University as blacks often have in the larger society. The administrator's remark suggests that black students were partially successful in achieving their goal of increased College concern for the off-campus community. However, one can legitimately ask how deep was such concern, how long did it last, and, most crucially, what kinds of policies were implemented as a result.

The answers to these questions are not as positive as black students hoped. Concern for the surrounding communities, as expressed in material terms, did not last more than a year or two, nor did it involve more than a small portion of the College community or affect many in the off-campus community. Indeed, by the end of the 1969–70 school year, such outreach efforts had been abandoned except for the summer recreational programs for neighborhood children.[1] These were saved, on a much reduced scale, only after intensive effort by black students.

Thus, black students' attempt to broaden the institution's mandate to serve the community through the implementation of community outreach programs was only a symbolic success. On reflection, this is hardly surprising. Student demands for community service and outreach are, in effect, directed at making organizational boundaries more permeable, while simultaneously including new members or clients in the organization. The organization that is the college has little control or influence over these potential members or their life-situations. Their loyalty to the organization is problematic, and it has few resources for ensuring either their loyalty or their compliance. Further, these potential new clients do not fall within the organization's traditional mandate. This can be a special problem for private colleges and universities, since in many instances their guiding tradition is that they exist to serve society in general (or particular, largely elite, groups in society), not the immediate local community, which has been considered more properly the responsibility of public colleges and universities. This tradition has been especially strong at the more elite private institutions.

Moreover, the benefit these new clients bring to the organization is also, from the point of view of the college administration, likely to be problematic, particularly in terms of the costs—social and political as well as financial—they may create. Their inclusion could result in opening the door to all sorts of demands from all sorts of external groups, as well as to internal and external conflict. Problems of academic and institutional freedom might be vastly complicated.

It was almost inevitable that University College (like others) resisted most of these demands and let the few programs it initially implemented lapse, particularly in a time of steeply rising costs. It has, after all, often taken outside political activity—for example, the nineteenth-century Morrill acts establishing land-grant colleges and universities—to get American higher education to broaden its service mandate and become more inclusive. Thus, it is not surprising that the most lasting result of black student efforts in this regard has probably been the creation of administrators or offices responsible for "community affairs." This accomplishment is not unimportant, but it is rather less than black students sought.

## INTERPERSONAL RELATIONS ON CAMPUS

Many faculty members and administrators felt that the increased enrollment of black students helped produce a more diversified and enriched student body. If enrichment comes simply from the simultaneous physical presence of different groups in the same place, then University College was clearly "enriched" to a limited extent. However, if enrichment means social interaction, free exchange of ideas and experiences, and learning to understand others and see the world from their perspective, this seems not to have happened on a large scale. While such interchange certainly took place between individuals, the racial polarization that occurred in 1967–68 and subsequently hindered the development of these exchanges.

Black student opinion on this issue differed from that of the faculty and administrators. Students interviewed did not feel that their presence produced much diversity in the College, partly because there were too few of them, and partly because they often tended to perceive the rest of the campus rather monolithically in ethnic and class terms (i.e., as predominantly Jewish and middlclass). Many did not feel that *they* had been enriched much by being in the College, nor that they had much enriched the College, partly because there were fewer black students than hoped for, partly because many of their goals were unmet, and partly because they believed that the College did not really want them there and did not want to be "enriched" by their presence. As one student put it, "NYU is really hypocritical. They tell you how much they want you and how much they want blacks before you get here, and then when you're here you find that nobody really cares about you. And they sure as hell don't care about anything black" (Student Interview no. 7).

Yet some faculty members and administrators believed, on the contrary, that the movement sensitized the campus to blacks and the black experience. To quote a faculty member intimately involved in all the issues and events discussed here, the black student movement

> proved that [black students] weren't so marginal as students. It demonstrated that students could participate responsibly in College affairs and decision making to the benefit of the College. It made the campus aware that there was something real called the black experience. Their presence has been vital and very, very helpful. (Administrative/Faculty Interview no. 6)

That is, the presence of black students helped dispel at least some stereotypes about blacks and black students.

On the other hand, a kind of negative sensitization to blacks indicated by the polarization on campus also followed the activities of the movement. Further, many white faculty members and students continued to see black students as marginal, unprepared academically, and present in the College only because of special efforts and perhaps lowered standards. Others came to define the black experience and students in terms of new stereotypes: marked by urban ghetto origins, poor, militant, separatist, perhaps dangerous. In spite of the black student movement and in some ways because of it, the patronization, condescension, less than full acceptance, and polarization typical of the black student experience in white colleges persisted in University College, even if it was less overt than in earlier times. In short, the diversification of the student body was neither as extensive, as enriching, as positive, or as unambiguous as some believed.

An especially interesting consequence of the black student movement in University College was the apparent radicalization of a number of white students and the proliferation of radical white groups. The movement helped to politicize such students and encouraged their protest activities on a wide range of issues, including student power. In addition to reinforcing the radicalism and legitimizing the protest of other students, the movement served as a model for tactics and strategy on campuses nationwide (see Donadio, 1968a; Flacks, 1971b), Columbia and San Francisco State being only two of the more visible examples. Like the activism of black students in the South in the early 1960s, that of black students on white campuses in the late 1960s illustrates the vanguard role played by black students and the larger civil right movement in political activism in the United States during the last three decades.

The movement also helped to intensify the division between radical white students and white students with opposing views and created significant interracial tensions, particularly during and after the Stone controversy. These tensions produced a separation between black and white students—partly self-imposed—that lasted well beyond the movement's most active phase. This polarization made difficult the development of individual black-white relationships.

Given black students' beliefs, objectives, and self-images on the one hand, and white students' fears, anxieties, and conscious and unconscious expressions of racism on the other, tension and polarization seem a "natural," perhaps inevitable, consequence of the movement. Many students, black and white, openly expressed their resentment and hostility toward the other group. The polarization between the black and Jewish communities in New York City, as well as the racial situation in society at large, reinforced these tensions. Polarization was important in itself and indicated a tear in the social fabric of the College community that was difficult to repair.

## SPECIFIC PROGRAMS AND POLICIES

Two goals seem to have been especially important to black students in University College: a full-fledged black studies program and more black students, faculty members, and administrators. Students experienced some limited success in the latter case, primarily in the area of student enrollment; they failed to get a coherent, coordinated black studies program, as opposed to isolated courses intermittently offered by individual departments.

As in other areas there was some divergence of opinion about the movement's success. Almost all the faculty members and administrators interviewed were much more positive than students were. For example, many felt that the movement had enriched and improved the flexibility of the College's curriculum, despite the failure to establish a formal black studies program. In their view the movement made people aware that important areas of knowledge were absent from the curriculum and that knowledge might be acquired and transmitted in ways other than the traditionally academic ones.

Not surprisingly, black students disagreed with this assessment. As one put it: "Some of us worked awfully hard for a black studies program. But we just couldn't make it happen. We couldn't keep our act together, and the institution never really wanted it to happen"

(Student Interview no. 20). At no point were there more than a small number of courses that could be seen as part of a black studies program. Their number declined significantly after the 1969–70 academic year, so that by 1972 at most four or five courses in disparate departments were still being offered. No formal, integrated black studies program was ever implemented.

It is useful to compare the situation in other colleges and universities. By the end of the peak period of black student activism (1968–71), excluding predominantly black institutions, approximately 1,300 schools in the United States had at least one black studies course in their curricula; 500 had instituted formal black studies programs (Allen, 1974). If all Third World and ethnic studies programs are included along with separate black studies programs, 62 percent of American colleges and universities had such offerings by 1971–72 (Bayer and Astin, 1971). Thus, at least in the short run, black student activism had a measurable curricular impact on American higher education.

At the same time, there are over three thousand colleges and universities (including branch campuses) in the United States. Even if we exclude predominantly black and technical or other specialized institutions, a great many colleges and universities did *not* implement formal black studies programs; some did not, and do not now, offer even a single course. Indeed, in a large-scale national survey, Astin, Astin, et al. (1975) found that 20 percent of the four-year institutions surveyed still had not instituted *any* kind of ethnic studies program several years after the major student efforts to establish them.

By 1974, according to one estimate, the number of schools offering formal B.A. programs in black studies had declined to 200 (Allen, 1974). Considering that there were virtually *no* such programs in white colleges and universities prior to the late 1960s, this is still a real accomplishment. However, it suggests that the failure of the movement in University College to establish a program was not unique.

Those black studies programs that survived through the 1970s appear to be doing well (Hechinger, 1980; Obatala, 1974; Wilkins, 1975), though the economic difficulties of years of the early 1980s have caused some to be eliminated or downgraded (see, e.g., Afro-American Studies and Research Program, 1982; Bailey, 1984; Fiske, 1983). The Afro-American Studies Program at NYU today offers an interdisciplinary undergraduate major in Afro-American Studies consisting of courses drawn from several departments and clustered in a coherent way. In effect, this is a double major program, since students are required to major simultaneously in another department or program.

All students majoring in the program take a required introductory course and then choose at least eight courses in at least four different areas to fulfill the major's requirements.

Nationally, there are approximately 525 black studies programs, of which 150 are housed in full-scale departments (National Council on Black Studies, 1983); many are non-degree programs. Colleges and universities in thirty-four states, the District of Columbia, American Samoa, and the U.S. Virgin Islands provide some sort of black studies offering. Excluding the historically black institutions, as of 1981–82 bachelor's degrees were offered by eighty-two public and seventy-two private colleges and universities. At least sixteen universities offer black studies graduate degrees, including Yale, Boston University, the University of California at Los Angeles, Cornell, Ohio State University, and the universities of Iowa, Michigan, North Carolina (Chapel Hill), Pennsylvania, and Wisconsin (Madison) (Afro-American Studies and Research Program, 1982). Major Afro-American studies research centers have been established at Harvard, Cornell, NYU, and the universities of Texas, Virginia, Michigan, and California (Los Angeles). In general, the most successful and stable programs are housed in leading research universities, elite private universities, flagship state universities, and the strongest four-year colleges.

Few have the kind of full autonomy that black students in University College and elsewhere sought (see Miles, 1971; Obatala, 1974). NYU's program, for example, is run by an interdepartmental advisory committee. Black studies departments have more autonomy than interdisciplinary programs (which draw faculty from other departments, usually have a director or chairperson, and are often run by an interdepartmental committee) or "catalog" programs (which consist of a listing and clustering of courses drawn from a variety of departments, but usually have few courses and faculty or staff members of their own). Indeed, in a recent survey of 968 colleges and universities, Daniel and Zike (1983) found that 775 had never offered a black studies program with a formal administrative structure of any kind.

Thus, the failure to gain a fully autonomous black studies program that allowed students real power and participation in decision making was more the rule than the exception. As Miles (1971:244) argues, "In the case of the demand for autonomy . . . there were no major successes, although participation schemes were often devised. The demand for "self-determination" was the sticking point, and on that issue, university administrations did not compromise."

The second major goal of black students was to increase black representation in the College and the University at all levels. Once again some divergence of opinion about the movement's success should be noted. Faculty and administrators tended to perceive a greater increase in the number of black students than did black students, or than actually occurred.

There was, indeed, an increase in the number of black students, at least for a time. However, as we have seen, the important increase achieved in 1968–69 was not maintained. Various explanations might be suggested: lessened or less successful recruitment efforts; lessened pressure for black admissions as the movement faltered; and competition for finite financial aid resources by other minority students. Whatever the reasons, the decline in black admissions and enrollment was not reversed, even with implementation of the Educational Support Program plan.[2]

Black students were well aware of the decline. Many of those I interviewed agreed with the sentiment expressed by the student who said: "I think after a while they didn't care very much about getting more black students. That may not be fair to say, but that's how I feel. I think the University felt we were too much trouble" (Student Interview no. 18).

Gains in black enrollment in white colleges and universities have been significant. In 1964 no more than 2 or 3 percent of college students were black. At present, three-quarters of all black students are enrolled in predominantly white institutions, though the historically black colleges continue to award approximately 40 percent of the baccalaureate degrees received by black students (Exum, 1983; National Center for Education Statistics, 1984).[3] As of 1982, 10.4 percent of total college enrollment was black (1,133,000 black students). These numbers have been relatively unchanged over the past several years (Gerald and Weinberg, 1984; National Center for Education Statistics, 1984). This suggests that the marked increase in black student enrollment that characterized the late 1960s and continued into the mid-1970s has leveled off. The picture is considerably less positive when one turns to black graduate enrollment, where there have been significant declines in recent years (see, e.g., National Center for Education Statistics, 1983). Moreover, although nationally black enrollment has been maintained at levels much higher than in the years before 1968, in many schools absolute declines have occurred. NYU's University College is one example.

Furthermore, a much smaller percentage of blacks in the 16-to-34 age group enroll in post-secondary education than do whites (Institute for the Study of Educational Policy, 1975; U.S. Office for Civil Rights, 1978). There is a continuing high concentration of black students in two-year institutions, and the greatest growth in black enrollment has been in these schools (U.S. Department of H.E.W., 1979; U.S. Office of Civil Rights, 1978). Indeed, in 1980–81, of 1,104,750 black college students, 472,451 (or approximately 43 percent) were enrolled in two-year institutions (Grant and Snyder, 1984). The situation is even more skewed in particular states. In Illinois, for example, a state with large black enrollment, in 1981 fully 65 percent of black students were in two-year colleges (Bailey, 1984).

Overall, the picture of black college enrollment continues to be a mixed one: real advances on some dimensions; a leveling off of enrollment in recent years; great variability from one institution to another. Black enrollment gains have been greatest in two-year institutions, public institutions, and in less expensive, less selective institutions without major graduate or research programs. Unfortunately, the black drop-out rate is highest in these institutions (Grant and Snyder, 1984; Institute for the Study of Educational Policy, 1975; U.S. Department of H.E.W., 1979; U.S. Office for Civil Rights, 1978). American higher education is still, in many ways, "the white sea" (Egerton, 1971:37), and is likely to remain so as attacks on special admissions and other programs for minorities mount, both from within and outside academia (see, e.g., Lavin, Alba, and Silberstein, 1981), and as federal financial aid programs are cut back or face a period of little or no growth.

The movement was not very successful in expanding black representation in the faculty and administration. Not only did it fail to secure the retention of a major black administrator, but the College hired only a few black faculty members and two black administrators (an assistant dean and a director of admissions) during the period under study. This failure is related to the failure to establish the black studies program, in that such a program would have employed a good portion of the potential black staff. It also reflects the difficulties of recruiting "qualified" black personnel, as defined in traditional terms by the College, given the historically (and currently) small pool of such persons. And it suggests an indifference, if not resistance, to such hiring by various academic departments and administrative offices in the College—a resistance that current attacks on affirmative action and similar programs demonstrate was not unique to University College.

Nationally, the picture is only slightly better. While there have been real gains in the numbers of black (and other minority) faculty members in predominantly white colleges and universities, they continue to account for less than 5 percent of total faculty members. The percentage is even smaller when predominantly black institutions are excluded (Exum, 1983a). There is some variation from institution to institution: a significant growth in numbers in some schools, modest growth in others, and stasis or a decline in others. Black teachers are found disproportionately in less prestigious colleges and universities though they are still underrepresented in these and in the two-year colleges that enroll a disproportionate share of black college students. They are least well represented in the major, elite institutions (Exum, 1983a). Indeed, the situation appears to be worsening: small numbers are getting smaller (see, e.g., Mackay-Smith, 1984).

A number of factors are responsible for creating or contributing to this situation. These include the legacy and continuing experience of economic and educational disadvantage; historic and continuing racism and discrimination in higher education; ambivalent commitment to affirmative action on the part of institutions; declining black enrollment in the kind of graduate programs that provide entry into faculty ranks; the concentration of black Ph.D.s in education as opposed to other fields; and the nature of the academic market. (For extended discussions of these issues, see Exum, 1983a; Exum, 1984; Exum et al., 1984; Menges and Exum, 1983; Staples, 1984). In terms of faculty, too, American higher education remains pretty much a "white sea."

Black students at University College did achieve two goals: the library expanded its holdings of materials pertaining to the black experience, whether in the United States or in other parts of the world, particularly Africa, the Caribbean, and Latin America, and they obtained a separate social center, though, as we have seen, long after it was originally proposed and with a different name and function. Although the center almost immediately came to be known as the Black House, in the administration's view its purpose was to serve all minority students on campus. This administrative resistance to the idea of an all-black student facility was mirrored in a number of colleges and universities (see Astin, Astin et al., 1975). On some other campuses black social centers were formally established. At University College the situation was tacitly accepted by the administration.

Thus, the movement's successes in changing policies, programs, practices, and personnel in the College were real and measurable but more limited and more temporary than black students' original goals. In some instances (e.g., the case of black studies), students in University

College were less successful than those in other white colleges and universities.

Astin, Astin, et al. (1975:69) demonstrate in their study of 1960s student protests that of all black student efforts examined, "80 percent were successful in effecting institutional change"; however, as in University College, "the changes were more likely to be partial than complete." Administrations, they note, "accede to partial change largely in response to the pressure of events" and tend to act on those demands deemed acceptable with the hope of thereby defusing protest and more radical demands. The experience of the movement at University College supports their conclusion that universities and large institutions were rather more reluctant and slower to change their racial policies and practices than other kinds of institutions (Astin, Astin, et al., 1975:151).

Faculty members and administrators in University College tended to see the movement's impact as more extensive and, often, more positive than did black students. They seem also to have perceived the movement differently from other whites on campus, seeing it as less radical, more "rational," and more positive. Such perceptions help to explain a seeming paradox: the tendency of College authorities when dealing with the black student movement (except during the Stone affair) to use control methods likely to encourage it to remain moderate and norm-oriented, while many others on campus perceived the movement as radical and value-oriented.[4] Such methods—negotiation, discussion, concession—were pragmatic responses appropriate for authorities in normative organizations, as colleges and universities are (cf. Etzioni, 1961a). The choice of control methods was also influenced by the authorities' implicit recognition of the movement's radicalizing and polarizing potential and the desire to avoid more radical actions by black students.

Some of those who saw the movement as radical, threatening, and value-oriented were members of key power groups and constituencies within the university, and therefore their views were of concern to authorities. These perceptions are a principal factor in the success or failure of black student activists. In the case of University College, for example, we have seen the pressures on University authorities to remove Stone, even before his fateful speech, and the initial opposition to EDCEP, which was partly responsible for important modifications in the original plan.

The perception of the black student movement as radical, shared by many in University College, is not hard to understand. One reason for it was the widespread fear that increased numbers of black students would alter the composition of the student body so that its elite character would be changed and academic standards lowered (see, e.g., Lavin, Alba, and Silberstein, 1981). The fact that black students during this period engaged in activism in a style that many found difficult to accept, while entering in apparently increasing numbers, reinforced such fears, even though underneath the rhetoric and activist style, the tactics, strategies, and goals of black students were often not fundamentally radical.

Moreover, black students frequently seemed to resist or avoid working through normal channels and modes of procedure. Many times they appeared to get more satisfactory results by ignoring the established channels available to students. Naturally, this occasioned in others envy, resentment, and the perception of black students as a threat and their actions as illegitimate. Some believed that this behavior was accompanied by a willingness to use coercive tactics and combined with rhetoric that others found disturbing, irritating, or unacceptable.

Furthermore, in this period the College's self-image as a harmonious, close community was already being questioned by white students. At the same time, its self-image as a socially and academically elite institution was being undermined within the University by the rise of Washington Square College and the College's feeling of being a second-class citizen. It faced increased competition for students and faculty from other colleges. Add to this a growing institutional financial crisis, and members of the College may at this point have been rather insecure about its continuance as the kind of institution it had for so long been. In this context the black student movement was especially threatening to some and therefore likely to be perceived as value-oriented.

Put simply, the black student movement in University College had important effects on the College, though not always those for which it aimed. At the same time, it was misperceived by many as being more fundamentally threatening than it actually was. Black students themselves, not surprisingly, often had different views of their movement, and its impact did not always leave them feeling good about the movement, or the College.

## BLACK STUDENTS

In University College the movement's record on achieving its internal goals—cohesion, solidarity, and mutual support among black students—was as mixed as its record on external goals. The movement seems to have had the paradoxical long-term effect of helping to increase alienation and lack of community among black students.

The result was the malaise noted among black students in the College by 1971–72. This alienated withdrawal, in University College and other schools, characterizes the attitudes of many black students toward the white college and the black student movement alike after 1971–72 (Boyd, 1974b; Newsweek, 1983; Walters, 1974; Willie, 1981; Yankelovich, 1972; see Etzioni, 1968a, for a more extended theoretical discussion of the passively alienated).

Two of the students I interviewed expressed these feelings of frustration, alienation, and psychic withdrawal very clearly. Although both acknowledged the positive consequences of the movement and the need for it, both also felt spent and let down and believed that the movement had ultimately failed. Their sentiments were echoed in varying degrees by nearly all the black students interviewed. As one put it: "We gave it our best shot, but we didn't really make it, at least not the way we wanted to. This place is more racist than we really could imagine, and at a much deeper level. Trying to fight it is just like punching a pillow. You can't make any kind of lasting dent" (Student Interview no. 14). Another student agreed, arguing that

> the university is more a political arena than any other thing, and people in it act on that basis, not on whether they really care about you. We're in it but not of it at the same time. The purpose of the university in the United States is to turn everybody into members of the white middle-class, not to do anything different. . . . In that regard we're completely out of it. Aside from certain practical things it can give us—how to do our income taxes, some skills, etc.—it is wholly irrelevant because we live in a totally different world. And always will . . . at this point I'm rather like a spectator [vis-à-vis] the University. I expect a lot and I expect nothing. . . . Their greatest concern is institutional self-perpetuation, not what happens to us. All I want to do now is to get out of here. This place is too draining to deal with every day. (Student Interview no. 11)

These comments indicate cynicism and a kind of strategic withdrawal from active engagement with the College, which was replaced by a strictly limited instrumental relation to the institution. They also suggest the great difference between the black student's world and that of white students, on campus as well as off. Such differences produced the black student movement and continue to determine the experiences of black students in white colleges and universities.[5]

Withdrawal into privatism was a principal reason for the falling off in overt political activity after 1971 by black students and what Daniel (1973) and Napper (1973) term their "get in, get over, and get out" attitude. Indeed, by 1972 a sympathetic observer, looking at the national scene, argued that card playing, partying, and hanging out in the cafeteria or student lounge had completely taken the place of politics among black students. They seemed, in Obatala's (1972:272) view, more and more to be engaging in escapism rather than activism; many black student unions were "withering away," and the "stagnant, almost impotent posture of those which managed to survive" was quite apparent. Many had become nothing more than "negotiating committees."

It does seem to be the case that by 1972 several black student unions had disappeared, become fragmented and apolitical (as in the case of Katara), or become simply one more student social organization on campus. And the decline of the movement followed that of the union.

It would be incorrect, however, to conclude that black student activism is moribund or even non-existent. As I shall argue later, this was not completely true in 1972 and is not necessarily the case even now. To put that discussion in context, some further explanation of the varied outcomes and impacts of the movement is in order. This is the task to which we turn in the following chapter.

## CHAPTER VII

# The World Without and the World Within

*T*he life cycle of a social movement *shows the ever-present impact of the outside world. . . . To survive, a social movement must be compounded of whatever proportions of conventionality and uniqueness the world demands at the time. It must maintain identity through self-segregation, but it cannot do so to the point of making the world within more frustrating than the world without. It must serve as an instrument for persons alienated from the world but still usually part of it.*——Hans Toch (1965:227)

How can the black student movement be explained sociologically? What factors are responsible for the ebb and flow of its activity, the shifts in goals and tactics, its transformation through time, and the near-disintegration of Katara, the black student organization?

The assassination of Martin Luther King, Jr., and particularly the dismissal of James Stone had great radicalizing potential. Indeed, they were the precipitants of black students' most intense activism in 1968. Yet even then the movement in University College was not as "radical" as that in other universities during the same period. How can we explain what might be termed the incomplete radicalization of the movement, despite highly provocative events?

## RADICALIZING FORCES

The prolonged protest and intense black student disaffection that followed the dismissal of James Stone can be understood as resulting from the combination of several factors: (1) rising black student expectations; (2) the inherent conflict of interest between the organizational needs and interests of the University, on the one hand, and of Katara on the other; (3) blocked communication; (4) black students' collective inexperience in dealing with the University; and (5) their beliefs, perceptions, and emotions.

### Raised Expectations and Deprivation

Revolutionary actions appear to result from the frustration of raised expectations—sharp, often sudden, setbacks after a period of rapid progress by an oppressed or relatively powerless group (Brinton, 1965; Davies, 1962; Flacks, 1971b; Gurr, 1970; Runciman, 1966; Tocqueville, 1955; Useem, 1973).

The prevailing social construction of reality is primarily determined by the actions and interests of authorities, elites, or ruling groups (cf. Berger and Luckmann, 1966). Changes in such construction occur when ruling groups (for whatever reason) begin to make changes in policies, practices, or social structure. These changes can lead to a realization on the part of the ruled of their own relative deprivation and of the possibility for positive changes in their situation (Runciman, 1966). They may be led not only to expect, but even to demand, that change continue and perhaps be expanded and accelerated. Such demands are especially likely where rising expectations are accompanied by increased political awareness and sophistication as well as greater resentment of deprivation.[1]

As long as ruling groups continue to meet these expectations or demands, the ruled tend to stay within legitimate channels. However, when their expectations are unfulfilled or their demands refused, particularly if this is seen as a sudden, unexpected reversal after a period of progress, then drastic protest behavior is likely.

This is what happened in University College. Even before King's assassination, the College had made a number of internal changes affecting students, including some directly relevant to black students. Moreover, students' social concerns and political activity were accepted if not actively encouraged by the College. As Walter Metzger has pointed out:

> A University already tempered by equalities tends to incite a yet more thorough egalitarianism. When the rate of admission is high, then the expectation of admission is also high, and the underrepresentedness of any group (blacks matriculate only a quarter of their age-eligible) can more easily be laid to discrimination. When the curriculum is notoriously eclectic, any subject absent from its listings . . . will seem maliciously debarred. (Metzger, 1970:584)

The growing politicization of black students and the King assassination provoked demands for further changes. The swift response by the University and the College to King's death significantly raised expectations of *continued* positive changes and responses.

At the same time, perhaps paradoxically, the assassination confirmed for many black students the feeling that desired changes were not necessarily going to be voluntary. As one student active on campus in 1967–68 put it, "Even before they killed King we knew we couldn't wait for the University to act. We knew we would have to take steps on our own" (Student Interview no. 9). Black students' participation in implementing new programs and policies following King's death further served to bolster their expectations and their sense of collective competence. At the same time, it reinforced the importance, perhaps the necessity, of their own role in changing the College's social construction of reality.

These expectations were nowhere more important, nowhere focused more strongly, than in the efforts to launch the MLK Student Center at Washington Square and to find a director for it. In the words of one student, "We worked damn hard to get [Stone] and we, or at least I, finally felt that real things were finally going to happen" (Student Interview no. 21).

It was in this context that Stone was dismissed. His firing dashed students' hopes. It created great mistrust of the administration and of whites in general. Students immediately mobilized their resources.[2] The result was militant and extended protest. The denial of students' expectations and the subsequent delegitimation of University authorities were major elements in the radicalizing impact of the Stone affair.

### Conflicts of Interest

Just as important was the conflict of interest between the University and black students, which was brought to the fore by the Stone controversy.[3] This conflict had up to that point been masked by institutional responsiveness. At some stage, however, its exposure was inevitable.[4]

Essentially, this conflict of interest arises out of the organizational nature of colleges and universities. All organizations, including colleges and universities, function to enhance their own survival and to optimize their own interests. Because of the University's "white liberal" orientation, it was willing to accede to black students' demands, but *only* so long as its basic interests were not threatened, including its ability to retain the support of a variety of internal and external interest groups.

The Stone controversy clearly threatened the University's basic interests. Alumni contributions, vital to all private colleges, dried up during the controversy, as did the private funding of the MLK scholarship program. After Stone's 8 October speech, the university was censured by the *New York Times*. Stone's appointment and retention had offended important ethnic groups associated with the University, particularly Jews. There was widespread and intense opposition to him *within* the University, in all divisions and at all levels. Further, it seemed clear to many that not only had his appointment caused great internal dissension within the University but that it would only increase if he were kept on, quite possibly causing irreparable harm to the social fabric of the University community and making governance of the University more difficult.

Faced with this situation, the University acted pragmatically to protect itself and its interests. In this sense, Stone's dismissal was a rational decision. It seemed, however, like hypocrisy to black students, a final confirmation of the institution's inherent racism.[5]

Just as the University acted pragmatically to protect its organizational interests, so, too, did Katara. Katara's organizational interests may be summed up simply. One was to maintain its political effectiveness in gaining changes in the College and altering the social construction of reality on campus. Moreover, Katara had been so successful in gaining at least the nominal adherence of black students that by the time of the Stone controversy almost all black students on campus belonged to it. Much of Katara's on-campus status derived from the appearance that it represented a solidary black student community. Hence, it had a vested interest in maintaining social and political cohesion among black students.

If Stone's removal went unprotested, Katara would have been compromised in the eyes of others on campus, members and non-members alike. Its prestige would have been undermined and the ability of black students to gain their objectives jeopardized. The University would have learned (or been allowed to feel) that it did not have to consider black students in matters directly affecting them, that it did not have to respect their wishes, consider their needs, or accede to their demands.

Throughout the preceding year, both on and off campus, black students had constantly emphasized the necessity for universal black solidarity. This, plus their identification with Stone, placed them under a kind of obligation to stand up for a "brother" in a fight with "whitey." This feeling may have been all the stronger because that brother had come to the University as a result of their efforts, articulated many of their own beliefs, and identified himself with them rather than with the institution. He could not be abandoned when the going got tough.

As the central organ of the movement and the guardian of the ideological purity of black students on campus, this obligation weighed heavily on the organization. Meeting it became one of Katara's organizational objectives. What would its reputation have been—among its own members or others—if black students at the Heights had not protested Stone's dismissal vigorously—particularly when national events had made such action the appropriate—indeed, the expected—response of students in such circumstances? Failure to protest might well have led to the disaffection of many of its members and to a loss of prestige in the eyes of others.

In short, Stone's dismissal represented a threat to the power and prestige of the organization, to its continued effectiveness, and to the cohesion of the black student group. These interests, necessarily in conflict with those of the University, were a principal factor in the radicalization of the movement. Thus, despite the high emotion involved, black student actions were also a pragmatic and instrumental response.[6]

### Blocked Communication

Another factor in the radicalization of the movement was blocked or faulty communications between the administration and black students. In the words of the Haines Commission Report (1969:22), Stone's firing galvanized black students into action because, among other reasons,

> it closed what was to them the last channel of legitimate communication. They therefore felt there was nothing left but extreme action to reopen this channel.
> Katara has said that it did not want this kind of extreme action but that it was a last resort when they felt all other channels had been closed. Their action did in fact open these channels again.

The communication problems stemmed in part from the structure of the University at the time, which permitted little direct access by either black or white students to the University's highest administrators and virtually no participation by them in the decisions that were these administrators' province. The University had made a clear but temporary exception to this when it allowed black students a voice in Stone's selection and appointment.

There was also the perennial problem of communication between Washington Square and the Heights. More important, although some white administrators had worked with black students in various capacities, most still did not know them very well or adequately appreciate their views and interests. One result was their apparent failure to anticipate a strong reaction to Stone's removal.

### Student Inexperience

A further factor in the radicalization of the movement was black students' relative political and sociological inexperience in the organizational setting of the College and University. Black students suffered what Stinchcombe (1965:148) has termed "the liabilities of newness" in at least two senses.

First, they had not been in the University long enough to fully comprehend its character as a formal organization. Its earlier positive responses had tended to obscure the essential conflict between the University's interests and their own. They had not fully grasped the fact that the University would always act to optimize and protect its own interests whenever threatened, even though their political beliefs predicted this. Such beliefs attributed this self-interest to racism per se, not to the structural character and imperatives of any complex organization. Failing to appreciate the organizational character of the University, they were forced to interpret and react to Stone's dismissal in terms of their political beliefs and interests, which required strong protest.[7]

There is a second, closely related sense in which inexperience was a radicalizing factor. Black students were relatively unused to bureaucratic procedures, the mode by which universities principally get their work done. They had little access to such procedures and few resources to make them work for them. As one faculty member suggested: "My experience during the period is that they viewed administrative procedures with suspicion if not outright hostility. In part this was because, perhaps rightly, they saw it as a trap, but also because they had no experience with such techniques" (Administrative/Faculty Interview no. 4).

Some black students, in fact, saw bureacratic procedures as simply a mechanism by which white institutions avoided meeting black needs. Given their inexperience, they acted on the view that it was in their interest *not* to use bureaucratic procedures in reacting to Stone's removal. To have done so, even if they had access to such channels, could have put them in the position of playing according to the University's rules, thereby allowing the University a greater opportunity for successful resistance while minimizing their own chances for success. One student leader answered forcefully when asked why they did not negotiate as black students had downtown: "Hell, we couldn't do that. They were experts at that talking and discussing shit. That's just what they wanted us to do. We would just have gotten the run-around, wasted a lot of time, and Stone would still have been kicked out. We knew our only chance was to do what they didn't want us to do" (Student Interview no. 10).

Inexperience of the organizational realities and bureaucratic procedures of the University was a factor in radicalization not least because it made student political beliefs more important in providing a rationale for drastic action. This, of course, is not to deny the possibility that students were correct and that *only* protest offered a chance, however slim, of having Stone retained.

### Student Perceptions and Beliefs

The "filter" through which all these forces were experienced, and which ultimately focused them and impelled students to action, was a certain set of beliefs and perceptions. Principal among these were (1) a feeling of betrayed trust and symbolic rejection by the University; (2) frustration and a sense of imperiled progress; (3) anger; and (4) the political beliefs that channeled these feelings and provided a rationale for action.

For black students, in removing Stone the University broke an unwritten covenant to take them seriously and to work for their on-campus welfare: hence Todd Little's denunciation of the University, on the night following the dismissal, for having lied to black students and thereby proved its untrustworthiness. Their sense of betrayal was heightened by the fact that after they had participated in the decision to appoint Stone, he was dismissed without any prior discussions or consultation with them: the University, knowing how much Stone meant to them, still got rid of him and did so without consulting them, violating both their trust and its own precedent.

Further, the University had dismissed a man whose primary identification seemed to be with blacks and black students, rather than whites and the white University. As Todd Little put it, Stone was "for us 100 percent." Hence, his removal was taken by some black students as a symbolic rejection of *them* and their beliefs, values, and objectives. In their view the University had shown itself to be indifferent to their concerns and needs. This was one of the reasons Katara was willing to take the serious step of occupying a building, running the risk of academic and possibly civil or criminal sanctions. Even if they had to leave the University as a result of their actions, separation from an irrelevant institution was equally irrelevant. For many the loss of trust was complete. Loss of trust is a critical variable in political action (see, e.g., Coser, 1967; Flacks, 1970, 1971b; and Gamson, 1975) and was certainly a factor in the radicalization of the movement in University College.

Frustration was also intense. A great deal of energy and effort had gone into Stone's appointment. After his dismissal the efforts appeared to have been for naught and the expectations to have been unwarranted and unwise. In addition, the dismissal did not bode well for future progress or past gains. There was no indication whether, when, or by whom Stone would be replaced. This meant that the MLK Student Center might be without direction for some time. The dismissal represented for black students a deflection of their progress at the very moment that an important part of their program was to be realized.

The president's insistence that Stone was fired because he had failed to facilitate harmony between the University's various religious, ethnic, and racial groups seemed particularly unfair to black students as it referred to the University's interests, not their own. Three years later, reflecting on the Stone episode and on University responses before and after, a senior put it this way:

> NYU is responsive in a curious way. They are quite willing to talk, even occasionally to do things; but you find unless you're constantly alert that over a period of time things you fought for, changes, etc., gradually fade out or disappear. The University gradually closes them out, so you end up with the same nothing. (Student Interview no. 14)

A natural result of this sense of betrayed trust and frustration was rage. Black students were furious at Stone's dismissal. That this anger was not expressed in a random, haphazard, or spontaneous fashion was, of course, due in part to the prior existence of organization among black students. More important, however, were their political beliefs about white institutions and effective political action.

Basically these beliefs emphasized black solidarity and collective consciousness. Indeed, under conditions of white intransigence and a critical issue, collective protest is not only legitimate but necessary. A popular slogan held that blacks were justified in using "any means necessary" to achieve their goals. Given these views and the belief that Stone's retention was a critical issue, the natural response to his dismissal was highly organized collective protest.

Why was protest more militant at the Heights than at the Square, where the MLK Student Center was located? Katara may have felt partly responsible for Stone's fate: it was after his 8 October appearance at the Heights that he was dismissed. Further, black students downtown were at the center of the University, where negotiations and talks could begin almost immediately. Katara, at the Heights, was isolated from these negotiations and regular channels of communication.

Third, mobilization was easier at the Heights than at the Square. Only one black student organization existed there, not the several found downtown, among whom relations were not always intimate. There were fewer organizational interests to reconcile, fewer students to contact and mobilize, and a higher percentage living on campus and therefore available than there were at Washington Square.

Fourth, the smaller student body at the Heights also made mobilization and occupation easier. There were fewer student adversaries to contend with inside or outside the building, so that entrance and egress were easier to control, thereby facilitating control of the building. And there were fewer security precautions and guards in the Heights buildings than at the Square, which is much less isolated from the surrounding city.

Fifth, the high proportion of black freshmen in University College was significant. Katara leaders had made great efforts to depict the College and the University to freshmen as a reasonable, responsive place. Stone's dismissal was a severe test of member commitment, as well as of leaders' influence and effectiveness. Just as freshmen may have been easier to mobilize, they were also, for many of the same reasons, more subject to quick disillusionment and disenchantment (and thereby disaffection) in the face of failure.[8] Since they were the majority of the black student population, their disaffection could spell ruin for Katara and the black student movement. Thus, organizational cohesion, power, and prestige (as well as individual status or prestige) were on the line more significantly in University College than downtown.

When one looks back over the development of the Stone affair and the radicalization of the black student movement in University College, it seems clear that social and structural conditions, along with student perception and beliefs, played the central part in pushing the movement toward becoming value-oriented. Generalizing from the Stone affair, one might predict that black student protest is likely to occur in white colleges whenever the following conditions are present: a college action or change in policy that seems to black students both unjust and adversely affecting (organizationally and individually), that produces a sense of betrayal, and that occurs in a context where legitimate channels for communication and/or the expression of grievances are closed.

To generalize even further, protest seems especially likely in an organizational setting that strives to engender members' trust in it, but that ignores or takes for granted such trust, and the compliance it implies, when it acts to optimize its own organizational interests; that prides itself on its responsiveness to all members' concerns, but that responds to discontent or disagreement by informing them that "the matter is settled," "such action was necessary and is not reversible," or "there is no need for further discussion."

As Etzioni (1968a) suggests, such arrangements are by definition inauthentic. Inauthentic conditions in organizations are predisposing to political protest when negative perceptions of the situation are shared by members with important social ties to each other and some degree of organization among themselves, and when common political beliefs prescribing remedying action are at the same time held by these members. The white university often provides such a setting for black students.

## MODERATING FACTORS

These radicalizing forces were neutralized by moderating factors, both internal and external. The University's control methods kept the movement norm-oriented, both during the Stone affair and afterward. Even more crucial were the movement's internal problems. Chief among these were: (1) the heterogeneity of the black student population on campus and within Katara; (2) the failure of the occupation; (3) conflict between Katara and BASA; and (4) the "betrayal" by Stone.

### The Control Methods

A critical factor in the history of a movement is the effort exercised by the relevant authorities to contain or control it (cf. Mauss, 1971).

Control efforts are themselves influenced by a number of variables. As I have earlier argued, colleges and universities are normative organizations (see Etzioni, 1961a, for a discussion of such organizations), so that authorities in them must depend upon normative means and socialization to obtain compliance from members. Thus, they tend to emphasize normative control methods; the use—indeed, the availability—of coercive control is severely limited. This is why they must sometimes call in outside agencies—the police, for example—when forceful action is required. The danger is that to do so in a sense doubly violates member expectations: coercion is employed when it is not expected, and is employed by those who are not members of the campus "community."[9]

As normative organizations relying on normative compliance and stressing a self-image as a community, colleges and universities tend to allow a fairly wide degree of freedom of action to members, including students (see Barzun, 1968; Kerr, 1970a, 1970b; Newcomb and Wilson, 1966; Otten, 1970; Scott, 1965; Trow, 1970). This latitude is an important factor in control efforts directed toward student protest.

Control efforts are also influenced by the fact that students traditionally have not been regular participants in university decision making, at least partly because normative organizations tend to rely on leadership rather than participation for compliance (Etzioni, 1964). Administrators and faculty members find student activists and their efforts a phenomenon for which the standard operating procedures are not readily congruent or fitted. This is likely to be even more the case with black students, who are significantly different in many respects from other students and student activists (see Bowles and DeCosta, 1971).

Moreover, in an organization in which power, authority, and leadership are seen as resting on a base of normative consensus, authorities may not be able to act solely by decree, and the university often finds it difficult to take rapid, decisive actions based on a solid consensus of those with authority and power—precisely the kind of action that may be called for in responding to students (Gusfield, 1971; Heyns, 1968; Kerr, 1970a).

Finally, efforts to control student movements are affected by the fact that authorities in the university, like those in other organizations, almost always act to maximize or protect organizational interests and to maintain normal operations and procedures as much as possible.[10] Further, the university or college must continue to try to satisfy the often conflicting interests and expectations of its many constituencies. Hence, it will meet the demands of students only so long and so far as its basic interests, or the interests and expectations of critical constituencies, are not significantly threatened or compromised.

We have seen how the conflict of interest between the University and black students led to Stone's dismissal and the radicalization of the movement. At the same time, certain administrative social control actions were factors in the movement's remaining norm-oriented. The most important of these were: (1) the absence of actual and potentially violent police action; (2) the failure to invoke academic sanctions; and (3) the University's efforts to maintain constant negotiations and open communications once protest began.[11]

As noted earlier, authorities apparently failed to anticipate protest over Stone's firing. At the Heights, this fact, plus College authorities' inability to reinstate Stone, limited the options available to them when faced with the building occupations. The decision to call the police was one result. This step, which had potentially radicalizing consequences, was essentially the decision of the provost. It was clearly within his province, but neither the Haines Commission nor a great many others in the College were happy with the decision or with his mode of operation during the crisis, not least because it violated the need for a normative consensus among faculty and administrators that many perceived as necessary in any formal response to students.

Because of the phone call from President Hester to Todd Little, however, police action was avoided by the narrowest of margins. A "bust" might well have radicalized both the black student movement and the campus in general.[12] In addition, as we have seen, at no point were sanctions invoked against student protestors in University College. This in itself helped moderate the movement's actions.

Since no police action took place, and no court injunction was sought, the absence of civil or criminal sanctions is easily explained. But why were no academic sanctions invoked against the student occupiers, even though protesters fully expected them and University policy specifically called for them in such circumstances?

Because of the non-destructive and disciplined character of the protest by Katara and sDS, there was little disposition on the part of the College administration or faculty to impose academic sanctions after the buildings were evacuated. Academic sanctions were not invoked *during* the occupations, however, because of the action, or rather inaction, of key administrators. The provost failed to invoke them because, as he reported to the Haines Commission, he forgot them.

The Dean of University College, on the other hand, was well aware at the time that suspension was the next step called for according to the President's formula, but he believed that its invocation would be a mistake under the circumstances because he sensed from the whole atmosphere that Katara would not respond to such a threat. He therefore did not remind the Provost of this agreed-upon step. (Haines Commission Report, 1968:15)

The failure to apply academic sanctions prevented the further embittering of an already tense campus. Sanctions invoked in the face of orderly and non-destructive occupations might have outraged many other students, and it is not clear that the faculty would have upheld them.

The University's strategy centered on opening and sustaining communications, as long and as extensively as possible, to show a willingness to negotiate and to demonstrate the University's sincerity and seriousness. Moreover, while negotiations were in progress black students would be less likely to take extreme action. As Schelling (1956) points out, this is an old bargaining technique, used frequently in labor negotiations and elsewhere. (McGill, 1974, has indicated that he deliberately used this tactic during his tenure as president at Columbia University.)

It was through such intensive discussion and negotiation that the Stone affair was finally settled. These talks occurred in tandem. Black students at the Square negotiated directly with Hester and other senior administrators, while Katara held discussions with College administrators. Katara took little direct part in negotiations downtown, once again displaying its isolation from BASA. Given the centralization of power at Washington Square, as long as the issue remained Stone's tenure, discussions at the Heights served mainly as a means of keeping the campus relatively calm.

The 1 November settlement represented a greater gain for the University than for black students. Though the president acknowledged the validity of black students' complaints that they were ill-used when not consulted in Stone's dismissal, the hard fact was that Stone could remain as director of the MLK Student Center only if neither he nor the center was officially part of the University. While the University would provide support for the rest of the year, it relinquished all responsibility for the center's continuing operation.

Thus, the University protected its interests, made a positive gesture, and got rid of a problem. Students, while they gained autonomy and independent authority for the center, lost the financial support, permanence, and bureaucratic resources that would have come with institutionalization of the center within the University.

The University's emphasis on negotiation and communication once protest began followed rather closely, though probably inadvertently, Smelser's (1963) theoretical prescription for the kinds of control methods authorities can use to keep a movement norm-oriented. These methods continued to be a significant factor in the movement's development.

### Student Heterogeneity

The large number of new black students in September 1968 introduced to the campus a much more heterogeneous population with a great variety of backgrounds, interests, aspirations, and views. Even at the time of the Stone controversy, not all back students belonged to Katara and were active in the movement. Some were not involved in any black student activities, including, perhaps most importantly, West Indian students and engineering students (see Donald, 1970, 1971; Edwards, 1970, 1971; Pugh, 1972; and Willie and McCord, 1972, for evidence that such non-participation was also true elsewhere). Further, the participation of some black students was apparently less than completely voluntary. This meant that the movement could not mobilize all of its potential resources to the fullest extent. Inclusive and voluntary participation by all potential partisans is crucial in effective mobilization and important in sustaining a movement's value-orientation (Gamson, 1968; Smelser, 1963). Hence, heterogeneity in itself was a factor in the movement's not becoming value-oriented; however, it is the combination of heterogeneity with other factors that is most central in this case.

### Failure to Gain Stone's Reinstatement

The failure of the occupation to gain Stone's reinstatement was the first real failure of the movement. Moreover, the occupation itself ended through what many black students felt was a trick. As a result, the commitment and ideological reserves among movement members were severely tested. Many black students were unsure what else they could do, since they had already taken strong action. Katara had no "contingency plans" for further protest action. These strains and the momentary faltering by the organization helped to prevent the radicalization of the movement.

### Lack of Coordination Between Movement Organizations

Even before the Stone crisis, coordination of positions and activities between Katara and BASA had generally been limited at best. The Stone crisis pointed up the lack of coordination. For example, Katara was told just before the occupation that BASA had already occupied buildings downtown. Only later did members learn that BASA had never occupied any building. Friday morning, while Katara was vowing not to leave the Student Center, BASA was already negotiating with the administration. BASA first worked out a compromise and then rejected it, largely as a result of internal politics within BASA. Katara was left out on a limb.

Friday night at a meeting Katara leaders attended downtown, more vigorous action on Stone's behalf was called for; Katara's occupation and events at the Heights during the preceding day were completely ignored. In this meeting a strike was decided upon. It was more successful and lasted longer at the Heights than at the Square, but, again, there seems to have been little acknowledgment of this by blacks elsewhere in the University.

Katara found itself consistently out of step with BASA. (As one student interviewed put it, "We were sold out.") It went farther and did more, earlier and longer, than BASA. Because power in the University was centered at the Square, because its isolation undercut its effectiveness, and because its political beliefs emphasized black solidarity, Katara made efforts to coordinate and bring its own actions into line with those of BASA: thus the various shifts in its demands and goals during the Stone affair.

Since the movement downtown was less radical at this point than Katara, such efforts essentially meant a move away from radicalization. As the split continued, Katara's demands and positions became more reformist and moderate. This tendency was reinforced by hostility toward BASA as the source of the split between campuses and Katara's isolation.

### Stone's Withdrawal

Finally, there was Stone's sudden and unexpected withdrawal. He abandoned the battle, abandoned the black students who had supported him, and took away the protest issue. After his meeting with black students at the Heights, there was no point in continued protest over his dismissal. Again the movement faltered; when it recovered, it had abandoned its more value-oriented tendencies and potential.

### Internal Crises in Katara and the Movement

From the Stone affair Katara learned several lessons that affected the future course of the movement. First, it came face to face with the limited power of College authorities and its own isolation from the center of power. To produce changes in the College, it would be better to focus on issues capable of being solved locally by College authorities.

Second, Katara members learned that they must rely on themselves, not on third parties, and especially not on black students downtown. After the Stone affair, not only did Katara avoid almost all University-wide issues, but it ceased coordinating its activities with BASA almost completely.

Third, it learned the need to choose issues carefully and to make its own evaluations of them. It learned not to become irrevocably committed to persons, positions, or issues about which it had little independent knowledge.

Fourth, it came to a kind of existential recognition of the conflict of interest between the white college and black students (a conflict still defined largely in racial terms) and the unavoidable reality of bureaucratic procedures. Henceforth, it showed greater willingness to work through channels.

The impact of all these lessons on black students was tremendous, producing great disillusionment and bitterness toward the University. Most important, for Katara it produced major problems of morale, cohesion, and commitment, in regard not only to the aims of the movement, but to the organization itself.

Those who had been pressured into participation wondered if it had been worth it and perhaps began to wish they had not given in or to resent those who had pressured them. They would think more than twice before getting involved in such actions again. Many of those who had participated voluntarily also wondered if it had been worth it, and if there was any point in continuing in the face of University resistance and superior strength.

Black students were uncertain, frustrated, and bitter. Not a few began to question the validity, the skills, and the status of Katara. In addition to the problem of maintaining momentum, Katara was faced with potential member withdrawal and disaffection on a scale greater than any in the past.

All of these reactions produced major internal crises, which were most severe in the immediate aftermath of the occupation and the meeting with Stone. Problems of maintaining commitment and morale were at the center of these crises, which kept black students from taking more serious or extended action, despite their greater anger.

Equally important, these crises led to intense hostilities and intramural conflict among black students, especially between those who had participated and those who had not. They produced conflict precisely because black students were much more heterogeneous in background and outlook than they had often admitted to themselves or appeared to be to others in the University. The failures and disillusionments of the Stone crisis not only brought these differences to the fore but intensified and exacerbated them. The result was to add serious problems of cohesion and solidarity to those the movement already faced.

In this regard, the Stone affair was a watershed in the life of the movement. Though Katara managed, in the short term, to handle these problems with some success, their continued existence and cumulative effect created long-run difficulties that kept the movement from continuing extreme action or, indeed, ever again mounting an extensive protest.

## THE TRANSFORMATION OF THE MOVEMENT

The black student movement in University College was never able to regain its pre-Stone momentum, despite the radicalizing potential inherent, for example, in the fight over black studies. Though they continued to present demands, black students at the Heights never again occupied a building or staged protest demonstrations and rallies; the only public meetings they held, the forums on EDCEP, were distinctly moderate. Black students worked consistently to maintain open channels of communication to the administration and faculty and were always willing to negotiate as opposed to engaging in protest. More than once they used the threat of protest in these negotiations, but it was apparently more strategic than real. Even when negotiations became increasingly acrimonious and student discontent rose daily, they did not leave the negotiating table for protest: the fight over black studies is a good example of this. Though they could be quite tough in negotiations, they relied heavily on open communications, bargaining, and persuasion.

Further, in their demands and proposals in the post-Stone period, black students focused on concrete, local issues, generally academic ones, and essentially stressed the reform of specific practices and policies. Essentially, black students were asking the College to live up to its own ideals, not fundamentally to change them; they were not generally concerned with off-campus issues or basic questions about the underlying philosophy and structure of the institution.

In short, despite the clear radicalizing potential of the black studies fight and the value-oriented tendencies of some demands made (e.g., community outreach and the open-admissions plan embodied in EDCEP/ESP), the black student movement continued (perhaps at times involuntarily) to be norm-oriented throughout this period. Hence, we are concerned here with the transformation of a norm-oriented movement.

## Incomplete Movement Institutionalization

In the long run, social movements tend to decline in activity and often become institutionalized or disappear entirely. As Useem (1973:25) indicates, protest movements are mortal and not infrequently undergo a "decay process," in which loss of members, increased factionalism, loss of confidence, and attempts to "reorient the movement's objectives and style" are characteristic. This is a good description of what happened to Katara and the black student movement in University College. Our task is to understand why it happened.

The movement declined to the point that in 1970–71 black students undertook no new initiatives and no activism of any sort in the College. However, the trend of its career led neither to full institutionalization nor to total disappearance. Instead, the movement achieved partial institutionalization and became becalmed rather than disappearing entirely.

Let us look first at "traditional" theoretical expectations for the fate of the movement in University College, and then at some others. One important analysis of institutionalization is that of Hans Toch (1965). His admittedly more psychological conception stresses that institutionalization is a process in which ideology becomes more and more a means to an end: whenever a belief becomes an impediment to public acceptance, it is modified or abandoned (Toch, 1965:215). Toch sees institutionalization as involving a shift by movement members toward pragmatism and expediency in their efforts and away from adherence to predefined values and goals. The focus becomes survival rather than change in the world.

If we conceive the "public" to be all black students at the Heights (most particularly, but not exclusively, activist black students), Toch's general proposition has some relevance to the movement in University College, especially after 1969. The abandonment of the black studies effort, the efforts to save the summer programs and finally to gain the Black House, might be seen as evidence of this kind of shift.

Equally, Katara's attempt during 1970–71 to form an alliance with El Grito and other minority student groups in a kind of Third World coalition, might be seen as an effort at survival through universalism and ideological flexibility and thus seem to conform to Toch's proposition. However, the fact that neither this nor earlier efforts of various kinds, whether change- or survival-oriented, were greatly successful raises a crucial point.

Toch's conception seems to assume success in accomplishing external objectives and maintaining internal cohesion, stability, and commitment. However, the black student movement in the College had a rather checkered record of external success and internal morale. Thus, Toch's conception may not be fully adequate for understanding the movement examined here.[13]

The traditional sociological view of institutionalization presented by Turner and Killian (1972) also seems to assume a successful movement. In their view, as a movement becomes more successful it gains members and power. This leads to a transformation of the movement because increased size "threatens to remove control of the movement from any set group," making both control and policy making more problematic. Hence, those in control will "seek to regularize procedures to support their own power and policies." As a result, there is a transformation of "earlier spontaneous patterns into embryonic traditions governing behavior within the movement" (Turner and Killian, 1972:404). In this sense, it is not always movement survival that is the issue in institutionalization, so much as the survival of those in power.

This kind of success—increased size and power—came to the black student movement primarily in the spring, summer, and early autumn of 1968, rather than later. These were as much the result of the death of Martin Luther King—and the legitimacy that tragedy imparted both to black students and to University responses—as of the movement's own efforts. Further, the increase in membership came not from within the "society" (the College), but from outside as a result of increased black admissions. Though these new members gained entrance to the College through Katara's efforts, they were not entering the movement because of its attractiveness per se, but as a by-product of entry into the College.

Katara's summer and September orientation efforts were intended to deal with increased numbers, insure the continuance of control by those leading the organization, and produce continuity, regularity, and a sense of full participation among movement members and enhance their sense of belonging to a responsible movement. Whatever embryonic traditions may have been in process of development at this stage were aborted, in effect, by the series of events that overtook the movement beginning with the Stone affair.

Basically, Turner and Killian's conception of institutionalization (which follows from the ideas of Weber and others) emphasizes increasing bureaucratization, routinization, and formalization of norms, with consequent increase in rigidity. Such rigidity they tend to equate with stability (unlike Toch, 1965, who seems to equate stability with flexibility and constant adaptation). Because of the press of events, the exigencies of its existence, and its limited success, the black student movement in the College had little chance of achieving this kind of institutionalization after the spring of 1968.

Turner and Killian also suggest that institutionalization involves the movement's being accorded "a recognized position within the larger society" (1972:404). That is, the movement is accepted as having some continuing legitimate function, and certain areas of special competence. Further, institutionalization involves the "establishment of patterns by which the community can deal with the movement" and limits the "scope of a movement that had tended toward a self-definition of universalized competence" (1972:404).

At least in these senses, the black student movement in University College achieved institutionalization. Katara was a recognized and accepted reality in the College. Certain perspectives, interests, and functions were expected or accepted as legitimate for black students; acceptance was formalized, for example, in the Black Affairs Committee of the Student Senate. Activism and protest gave way to an emphasis on maintaining organizational existence and such changes in the College as had been achieved.

Turner and Killian also suggest that institutionalization occurs "through the acquisition of a stabilized body of adherents with stabilized expectations" (1972:405). In this sense, we can only speak of partial institutionalization of the black student movement in University College. Throughout the period from 1969 to 1971–72, Katara lost members, and the remaining members experienced disaffection on a major scale. This aspect of institutionalization, then, eluded the movement in the College.

Finally, Turner and Killian (1972:405) argue that as a movement becomes institutionalized, it offers a greater diversity of rewards to members for participation, including, in particular, societal prestige. Though Katara attempted to diversify movement activities and gratifications (via cultural events, lectures, recreational and social events, educational projects, and so on), it was not always successful. Nor could the movement after 1968 offer much in the way of societal prestige. Prominence in the movement did *not* necessarily mean high prestige on campus. Indeed, such prestige decreased rapidly after 1968.

In short, the history of the black student movement in University

College shows a great decline in movement activity but failure to achieve the kind of institutionalization generally posited for social movements. It is a history of movement glory turning to dissolution and a struggle to maintain a much-diminished existence. Hence, it seems more accurate to speak of partial institutionalization, partial disintegration, and partial collapse—in effect, a movement becalmed.

A more appropriate theoretical explanation for this development is suggested by Zald and Ash (1966). The virtue of their conception is that it looks at both the movement and the movement organization simultaneously and sees the transformation of one in terms of the transformation of the other. This seems to be especially useful in the case of movements, such as the black student movement, in which the fate of the organization is absolutely central in determining the movement's history. Equally important, their view allows for kinds of institutionalization and movement transformation other than the one proposed in what they term the traditional Weber-Michels model (as exemplified, e.g., by Turner and Killian), including the one that I have suggested characterizes the black student movement in University College.

In addition to institutionalization as defined in the traditional model, Zald and Ash suggest a number of possible alternative kinds of transformation: coalition, disappearance, factional splits, and increased rather than decreased radicalism, among others.[14] They argue that the traditional Weber-Michels model fails to account for these alternatives because it assumes that movement organizations are subject to the same conditions and processes as are bureaucracies. Although the two *may* have traits in common, they are significantly different. In the first place, movements "wish to restructure society or individuals, not to provide it or them with a regular service"; and second, in relation to their goals, "movement organizations are characterized by an incentive structure in which purposive incentives predominate" (Zald and Ash, 1966:329), "purposive incentives" being defined as the achievement of goals. Further, solidary incentives (i.e., those enhancing feelings of community, solidarity, etc.) are more important in movements and movement organizations than in bureaucracies.

The black student movement was organized to produce important changes in the college and university. However, as Olson (1965) suggests, given the high potential costs to individuals of participation in group action, in order to attract and retain members a movement organization must use incentives other than those it is organized to seek, and/or it must use coercion. Following their beliefs and values, Katara members employed a wide array of solidary incentives, both as means and as ends in themselves. Equally, they exerted constant pressures for commitment and conformity that were perceived by more than a few members as coercive. However, overreliance on solidary incentives, especially if these involve pressure on movement members without significant external success, may be counterproductive, increasing rather than reducing factionalism (Gamson, 1975; Olson, 1965). This was one of the principal problems faced by the black student movement, and a major element in its fate.

In the light of these ideas and the history of the black student movement in University College, the following proposition may be suggested. The more emphasis a movement gives to solidary incentives, the more likely it is to have difficulty in maintaining its existence over the long run in the face of limited success or failure, and the more likely it is to undergo some transformation other than that suggested by the Weber-Michels model. The ultimate condition of the black student movement in University College is one such outcome.

Zald and Ash indicate several other factors that can lead to alternative movement transformations: organizational responses to the ebb and flow of sentiment in society, within the movement, and within the potential recruit population; the relations of the movement organization with other organizations and groups, especially antagonists and potential allies; and success or failure in achieving goals and objectives.

All these factors operated in the black student movement examined here. The result was, as we have seen, a partially institutionalized and becalmed movement.

> Its goals are still relevant to the society but its chances of success have become dim. . . .
> [A becalmed movement has] been able to build and maintain a support base; they have waged campaigns which have influenced the course of events; and they have gained some positions of power. In short, they have created or found a niche for themselves . . . but their growth has slowed down or ceased. Members do not expect attainment of goals in the near future, and the emotional fervor of the movement is subdued. (Zald and Ash, 1966:333, 334)

The black student movement in University College continued to influence the course of events, even after Stone's withdrawal. The double funding of Katara and the creation of the Black Affairs Committee in the Student Senate are evidence of success in attaining some niches in the College. Yet protest activity ceased, and black student's expectations diminished, as did their emotional fervor.

At the same time, Zald and Ash's description does not completely fit the movement in the College. Although black students built a support base, they were not able to maintain it. Over time, it was eroded by dissension and disaffection among members and potential recruits. Moreover, Zald and Ash argue that a becalmed movement is *most* likely to conform to the Weber-Michels model, largely because lack of major success produces member apathy and increasingly complacent and conservative leaders for whom survival (their own as well as the organization's) becomes paramount. The model predicts a process of oligarchization, increasing conservatism, and rigidity because of the becalmed movement's necessary "dependence on and control of material incentives" (Zald and Ash, 1966:334).

Much of this proposition does not apply to the black student movement examined here. It is true that lack of success produced apathy among black students, but it was a kind of alienated apathy, not simply indifference. Moreover, it was a continuous, growing apathy accompanied by widening dissension.

Leaders did not become complacent; they could not afford to. And if they became more "conservative," it was only in the sense that they discontinued attempts at large-scale or intense activism in the face of mounting internal disaffection, not because of changed evaluation of the white University and its policies, and not because Katara controlled important material rewards or incentives. Leaders in fact had few material rewards in their possession or control. The principal ones the movement offered were successes in bringing about changes in the College. Further, it is by no means certain that the kind of material rewards implied by Zald and Ash would have been valued by black students as a substitute for tangible, meaningful changes in the College. Accepting such substitutes, given black students' political views and values, would have seemed too much like being bought off or co-opted—one of the "primal" fears of many black activists and a very real problem for both black and white activists (see Mauss, 1971). Moreover, the black student movement, based on a commitment to certain kinds of changes and certain ideological beliefs, did not depend upon acquisition and possession of material rewards in the sense and degree stressed by Zald and Ash, though, of course, the ability to provide such rewards would probably have made a difference in its ultimate fate.

Finally, the repeated lack of success encouraged dissension and contributed to the failure, in important senses, of the movement. Thus, though becalmed, it partially collapsed rather than achieving traditional institutionalization.

In short, the career of the black student movement in University College after the Stone affair involved a transformation not easily explained by any one theoretical perspective. Instead, its developmental trend led in the end to a becalmed movement, partially institutionalized and partially collapsed, with much internal fragmentation. It was just the increasing disintegration within the movement's organization, Katara, which helped to determine this trend and to which we now turn. As Nelson (1974:136) notes, "It is schism which sets the stage for differential transformation."

## The Disintegration of Katara

Movement organizations generally play a central role in the life and history of any social movement, and the role of the black student association in the black student movement is critical. Without organization there is no coherent movement or effective activism. The organization is the vehicle of effective protest, the mechanism for setting goals, the organ for enhancing generalized beliefs, and the means for meeting a variety of needs and interests, individual and collective.

In essential respects, what happens to the organization critically affects the movement. The trend in movement transformation after October 1969 was vitally influenced by the growing dissension among black students. How can we explain this dissension and the disintegration of Katara?

Among the variables that might be examined are the effectiveness and competence of the organization's leaders, as Barlow and Shapiro (1971) clearly demonstrate in their discussion of the excellent leadership provided by the San Francisco State University black student union during this period. However, with the exception of Paul Hunter, Katara was fortunate in its leaders. More charisma might have helped, but the forces leading to organizational disintegration were such that it would have been difficult for any leader to overcome them. (See Napper, 1973, for discussion of inherent dissensus factors among black student groups, and Poussaint and McLean, 1968, for a discussion of these problems among black groups in general.)

Two sets of factors seem to me most important in understanding Katara's history. One is the question of cohesion in the organization, and those things that over time severely undermined it. The second is the unavoidable problem of *battle* fatigue. While the latter problem surfaces after a period of movement activity, many of the issues affecting cohesion existed prior to the Stone affair.[15]

As several observers have noted, a critical factor in the success of a movement and in the life of the movement organization is the degree of cohesion the organization can maintain over long periods of time.[16] For this discussion cohesion is defined as "the total field of forces which act on members to remain in the group" (Festinger, Schacter, and Back, 1950:164).

What were the forces supporting cohesion among black students? One, of course, was the fact of shared blackness. Indeed, this was the basis upon which Katara was founded—more, perhaps, the social fact of blackness than the biological. This implies the expectation of a shared social experience based on a shared social and biological fact.

Also encouraging cohesion was the related factor of the shared experience of University College, combined with students' similar responses to that experience. One dimension of this is indicated by the fact that each of my student informants reported one or more personal experience of racism on campus. A third factor was shared general beliefs and values. The greatest consensus was found on beliefs about: (1) what it means to be black in a white society; (2) the white university as an instrument of that society; (3) the need for change in racial policies and practices in the university and the larger world; and (4) the importance of black unity and solidarity.

These basic elements encouraging cohesion were recognized and emphasized by Katara. In the post-Stone period, however, these forces were clearly not sufficient. A number of other factors and counterforces ultimately proved stronger: the particular kind of movement organization Katara was; the heterogeneity of the black student population; constant pressures for conformity and solidarity; lost member commitment; and movement success and failure.

In the long run, a critical factor working against internal cohesion was Katara's character as an exclusive organization. The distinction between inclusive and exclusive movement organizations (Zald and Ash, 1966) reflects differences in membership requirements. Inclusive organizations have few and highly flexible criteria for membership and require a minimum level of initial commitment and a minimum level of continuing commitment and involvement. Exclusive organizations, on the other hand, have rigid criteria for membership and demand a high level of initial commitment, continuing involvement, and ideological conformity. As a result, the exclusive movement organization "more extensively permeates all sections of the member's life, including activities with non-members" (Zald and Ash, (1966:331).[17] In addition, "exclusive organizations are more likely than inclusive organizations to be beset by schism," largely because inclusive organizations have "looser criteria of affiliation and of doctrinal orthodoxy" (Zald and Ash, 1966:337). Nor do they demand constant participation and involvement.

Katara, like most student unions was, or attempted to be, an exclusive organization. The membership requirement of being black was inflexible, though this seems to have been the only formal requirement. So was the expectation that *all* black students should belong; in this Katara was both exclusive and imperialistic. Though a high level of commitment was not always required for entry, particularly in the post-Stone period, such a commitment was expected and continually urged after entry. To the extent that all except the most instrumental social interaction was to be limited to Katara members and other black students, there was some attempt to permeate the life of the member as suggested by Zald and Ash.

In any group pressures for high commitment and ideological and behavioral conformity often lead, in the long run, to discontent and disaffection. This is particularly the case where (1) the group attempts to "run one's life" and be its only focus; and (2) the beliefs or values that led to the acceptance of such a situation have lost their potency or salience. This was the situation that developed in Katara after October 1968.

The tendency to schism inherent in exclusive organizations is enhanced when the population from which members are drawn is highly heterogeneous (Gamson, 1975). This was clearly the case in regard to Katara. What were the elements of this heterogeneity? One was the dramatic increase in the number of black students in University College in the fall of 1968. An important result was an increase in the class and ethnic diversity of the black student population, which brought with it enhanced potential for dissensus.

This increase was sudden.[18] Smelser (1963:301), in noting the importance of sudden change for norm-oriented movements, could almost be describing Katara: "the accumulation of hetereogeneous elements during the . . . phase of phenomenal growth provides the basis for internal wrangling and factionalization." As we have seen, such wrangling began during the Stone affair, only a month after large numbers of black students entered, and continued throughout the period under study. Let us first consider the issue of size apart from that of heterogeneity.

Several observers have noted that the question of numbers has particular importance for cohesion when the group in question is black students on a white campus (e.g., Donald 1970, 1971; Hedegard, 1972; Willie and McCord, 1972). For example, the size of the black student population has a direct bearing on their intraracial social life. Contrary to the hypothesis that "small black student populations foster tightly knit, cohesive black communities on white campuses," Willie and Levy found that this cohesiveness is much more apparent than real, with "*less* cohesion and *more* tension among black students at white colleges where the black student population is relatively small" (1972:52; my emphasis).[19]

Among other things, a small population tends to eliminate anonymity. Thus, the kind of permeation of members' lives characteristic of exclusive organizations may *seem* easier and be attempted more strongly on the one hand, while being resented more by the individual on the other. This may be especially true in heterogeneous populations. The black student group becomes like an extended family. "When this occurs, all relationships, including those that might otherwise be secondary, become intensely personal. The black students who make unlimited claims upon each other find such relationships sometimes supportive, but they also find them stultifying and confining" (Willie and Levy, 1972:52).

A third reason for the fragmenting effect of small numbers is suggested by Peter Blau. Following Simmel, Blau (1974:621) argues that if group barriers are firm and a group is isolated or insulated from other groups, then small size is necessary for, and enhances, within-group solidarity. On the other hand, if group barriers are *not* firm and it is not insulated from other groups, then the small size tends to lead to more outgroup choices by members, perhaps at the expense of internal solidarity.

While it is true that Katara, and most black student unions, have tended to be exclusive organizations, in practice group barriers have been firm for *entrance,* but highly permeable for *exit.* In such a situation, the fragmenting role of small numbers (which implies a strong need for forming intergroup alliances) is likely to be a problem for many student activist groups, including black ones.

The movement also, as we have noted, faced the problem of heterogeneity per se. One component was *class differences.* Class tensions seem to have contributed to the internal wrangling and dissension that overtook Katara at the end of the Stone affair. (Such tensions, it should be noted, are a likely problem in all black student unions, given the

tendency for the most affluent and the least affluent students to participate more than other students; see Boyd, 1974*b*).

Though black students after September 1968 did not, as a group,
conform to the stereotype held of them—that is, that they were all from
"underprivileged" and "disadvantaged" backgrounds—there were sufficient differences, in comparison with the pre-1968 years, to create
difficulties. Despite the growth of the movement, such differences (in
dress, leisure activities, world view, etc.) as can be attributed to class did
not disappear. Indeed, after the Stone affair they seem to have intensified, or at least were seen more critically.

One example of these tensions was the derogatory labeling of two
groups of black students as "the Silver girls" and "the Gould girls"
(after the dorms in which they lived.) This label was attached to them
because as a group they *seemed* to have more money to spend and to
dress more fashionably than other students and to come from more
affluent backgrounds. They *appeared* to have less cognizance of street
language and manners, and to be less militant in their views. They were
apparently less than enthusiastic about the building occupation during
the Stone crisis; a widespread belief that, as a group, they were "not
really black" received greatest emphasis during the occupation, and the
first application of the labels came during its aftermath. Certainly
almost all the students interviewed were aware of these labels and their
negative connotations.

Willie and McCord (1972:3) indicate that it is a rather common
occurrence on white campuses that "black students living in different
dormitories get identified as separate groups, often with social and
political overtones." More important, they suggest that gender can be
an additional element of heterogeneity. Donald (1970, 1971) provides
some empirical evidence that it was a source of heterogeneity and
disunity at Cornell, as does Napper (1973) in the case of Berkeley.

Further, in University College it seems that black women were somewhat more likely to be labeled "bourgeois" and attacked as not militant
or "black" enough than were black men. Such attacks were paralleled
in other colleges and universities. They may be an expression of a
certain kind of sexism. They may also reflect the possibility that "young
men tend to be threatened by and ill at ease with young women who are
more effective academically and socially. One way to deal with this
problem without admitting it is to attack . . . bourgeois blacks" (Boyd,
1974*b*:18–19). The fact that studies show greater conservatism among
black students about gender roles (Yankelovich, 1975) seems to support this interpretation. Gender-based factionalism appeared at Berke-

ley in a male-dominated black student union resented by black women (Napper, 1973), and also at Cornell, where black women objected to the tendency of black male activitists to date white women while pressuring black women *not* to date white men (Donald, 1970, 1971). This double standard was not uncommon among black students in this period (Willie and McCord, 1972).

The reality of class differences was often denied by black students in the College, affluent and nonaffluent alike. Shared beliefs about the negative qualities implied by being middle-class were one important reason. For those from middle-class backgrounds, denial of such backgrounds served the more immediately practical purpose of easing their relations with other black students highly critical of the black middle class, largely because of its reputed "tomming" and lack of "revolutionary consciousness." The same denial of the reality of class, for largely the same reasons, and the same class tensions have been widespread among black students in white colleges (see, e.g., Donald, 1970, 1971; Napper, 1973).

Such denial generally took the form of claiming to be poor and from the ghetto and adopting ghetto fashions, behavior styles, language, and so on. In this way many students from middle-class backgrounds tried to avoid the label of "bourgeois," a term of particular opprobrium among student activists. It was also, perhaps, a way to express solidarity with the masses of the black population. And the "ghetto style" was a way of symbolically proclaiming the correctness of one's views and thus perhaps avoiding hassles and indicating that one belonged to the group.[20] Yet this denial of the reality of class differences was itself a source of fragmentation and dissension. First, it was likely to be resented by at least some of those who *were* from poor, ghetto backgrounds. As one student put it, "it used to burn me up when some of those people with doctors for daddies would pretend they knew all about the ghetto" (Student Interview no. 11).

Second, the tendency for such symbolic identification and rhetoric to take the place of firm commitment and real action was an additional source of resentment and, to both activist students and those from non-middle-class backgrounds, another example of middle-class hypocrisy.

Ethnicity is an additional dimension of heterogeneity. The black student population in University College (and NYU generally) was composed of two major ethnic groups: a majority of North American blacks and a significant minority of blacks of West Indian background.

Though students from both groups often denied it, many felt that there were real differences between the two groups, differences that were rarely bridged adequately during the period examined. Many American blacks believed that the West Indians were not really black, that they snubbed American blacks, that they were too middle-class (or "bour-gee")—in a word, too different.[21] As one student put it, "They were just too uninvolved, too standoffish. We wondered what they had to be so snobby about" (Student Interview no. 23).

Whether such perceived differences were real or not, all the evidence suggests that West Indian students associated more with each other than with American blacks, were more moderate or conservative in their political views, and participated less frequently or wholeheartedly in protest or activism than other Katara members. And a higher proportion did not belong to Katara, both before and after the Stone affair.

Part of the explanation lies in their immigrant status. For immigrants desiring citizenship, activism—or association and identification with activists—may have seemed a dubious enterprise, regardless of personal sympathy. The application of academic and/or civil sanctions during the Stone affair, for example, might have jeopardized their chances for citizenship. Further, recent immigrants had to spend much time and energy getting adjusted to the United States and its racial situation, and to New York City. Given the differences in the educational systems of the West Indies and the United States, these students may have had more difficulty than others adjusting to the College itself.

In addition, there is parental pressure. West Indian parents sometimes *appear* to be more politically conservative and more bourgeois and to have more influence in the lives of their children than American parents. Parental pressures not to get too involved, not to become too "radical," may have played a role in creating some differences between the two ethnic groups. Closely related to family pressure are the high mobility aspirations that seem to be typical of West Indians in the United States (see Cruse, 1967; Epstein, 1973). These aspirations, plus parental pressures, made them perhaps less prone to take the kind of chances with their future that full and constant commitment to the movement and to Katara might entail.[22]

Additionally, as Harold Cruse (1967) points out, in the larger off-campus world, and particularly in New York City, antipathy between West Indian and North American blacks dates at least from the 1920s. Tensions and differences within the black student group in the College, as in the case of those between black and Jewish students, can be seen as mirroring larger processes off campus and provide another indication of the influence of off-campus factors in the experience of the black student movement.

Finally, an obviously significant element in student heterogeneity is the diversity of political views found among black students. Black students differ widely on such matters as identification with the larger black community; acceptance of radical or nationalist ideologies; degree of "militance"; and attention to vocational or other individualistic interests as compared with political activity (Boyd, 1974*b*; Donald, 1970, 1971; Edwards, 1970; Gaier and Watts, 1969; Gurin and Epps, 1975; Napper, 1973; Orum and Cohen, 1973; Pitts, 1975; Trow, 1970; Walters, 1974). This was just as true in University College as in colleges across the country.

Given a heterogeneous population and a movement organization exclusive in character, constant pressure for solidarity and consensus are likely to follow. These in themselves were major factors in the disintegration of Katara, as they have been in other black student unions (cf. Anthony, 1971; Napper, 1973). Building solidarity and consensus was one important function of Katara's summer and fall orientation activities. However, it was during the Stone affair that pressures for solidarity became most divisive. We have already noted the efforts employed to gain the fullest participation in activities during the crisis. In this, Katara was like many movement organizations (cf. Hiller, 1975). These pressures to participate engendered resentment in many black students, particularly in view of the failure of the occupation and Stone's withdrawal.

Indications of the kind of pressure exerted, both before and after the Stone affair, were given by several of the students and former students I interviewed. One senior who had entered as a freshman in 1968 recounted his experience as a freshman and afterward:

> Incoming freshmen were, and are, at a disadvantage because doing anything shaky immediately gets them classified as Toms, etc. All the time people must prove themselves to the members of Katara. If they fail this, they're not ever really given another chance; they become permanent outsiders. People who are naturally loners like me are also in a difficult position, the most immediately prone to being put down and out. (Student Interview no. 28)

These comments indicate the degree to which such pressures may enhance division by a kind of excommunication process and suggest the difficulty of being a freshman (or any ambivalent black student) in such a situation.

Intense, "coercive" pressures for mobilization and constant participation created both manifest and latent alienation from the organization. Some students became disaffected immediately; others did so somewhat later as pressures continued. Moreover, as the goal of mass mobilization and participation seemed hopelessly utopian in retrospect, future mobilization became more difficult. This was a major legacy of the Stone affair. More and more people, faced with a continuation of many of the same conditions, became disenchanted and less ready to become, or remain, active, particularly as activity seemed to bear few fruits.

Pressures for solidarity ignored and foundered on several social realities. In a social movement a major task is the creation of new norms. These may have only a "tenuous claim to legitimacy for the membership"; thus, "the 'compelling nature' of movement order may be considerably weaker than other types of order" (Nelson, 1974:136). Moreover, not all members of politically active groups are equally involved or participate directly (Etzioni, 1968b; Gamson, 1968, 1975).

Further, it is not always easy for individuals to join, or to remain in, groups or movements *seeking* gains and change instead of already providing them (D. E. Morrison, 1973; Olson, 1965). For the individual, participation in group political action may involve costs greater than the costs of non-participation, while concrete gains remain problematic. Thus, even those who are nominally members of the group often do not take part in its activities. In addition, it may well be the case that the individual will benefit from whatever success the group achieves anyway, even if he or she does not directly take part in its activities; this can be an important incentive *not* to participate in "costly" action. This is the "free-rider" problem noted by Gamson (1975) and Olson (1965), one faced by black students as by other activist groups.

For a variety of reasons, therefore, individuals may remain, or become, disengaged from membership in an actively change-seeking political group, before as well as after the emergence of factionalism and dissensus. Black student unions in white colleges, including University College, have constantly faced these problems (Donald, 1970, 1971; Edwards, 1970, 1971; Napper, 1973; Pugh, 1972).

This apparently universal problem of member disengagement is intensified by a tendency among many black students toward individualism, vocationalism, and moderate political views.[23] Such students *need* the university or college to fulfill their interests and goals. In their case, "black militancy is restrained by black aspirations" (Horowitz and Friedland, 1970:199).

It is important to note, however, that Gurin and Epps (1975) have shown that, for black students, commitment to collective identity and political action, and commitment to individual achievement and career success, are not opposite ends of a continuum of possible individual orientations. Rather, "activism and traditional achievement were simply independent of each other" (Gurin and Epps, 1975:350). This appears to be as true for black students in white college as for the students in the black colleges studied by Gurin and Epps. Yet there can still be conflict or tension between individual and collective identities, between individual and collective norms, between individual mobility aspirations and group political goals, and these problems are faced by black students in black colleges as well as in white ones (see Gurin and Epps, 1975). The difficulty is that the insistence on unity treats, or is perceived by black students as treating, individual and collective commitments as if they *were* polarized. As a result, many black students in University College came to feel that Katara was pressuring them to choose a collective, political commitment *instead of* a commitment to individual achievement and interest.

Faced with what they perceived as too costly a choice—particularly in the context of intramural friction, failures, and decline—many students resolved the conflict in favor of their own individual interests by disengaging from active involvement in the black student union and movement, becoming, in effect, "free-riders." In this situation, constant pressures for solidarity can create greater dissension, especially if they are not accompanied by effective means of satisfying individual interests. Thus, "youths who continue to *need* the university (and there are many more who do than will admit it) become increasingly cautious, while others give up in disgust and drop out" (Flacks, 1971b:100; emphasis in original).

Conflict between individual and collective norms and values is often reflected in disagreement over goals. Certainly this was true in Katara and the black student movement examined here, especially after the Stone affair.[24] Where disagreement over goals exists, the constant push for consensus, particularly if perceived by members as coercive, can create frustration and dissensus instead. It is apparent that what Schein (1969) calls a "passion for unanimity" over time created more disaffection than conformity, more fragmentation than solidarity, in Katara and the black student movement in University College.

The critical result was a continual lessening of members' collective commitment after the Stone affair. While many black students shared certain basic political and moral values, these could not, in themselves, override the disagreements and divisions we have seen.[25] As a result, fostering and maintaining collective commitment—that is, realizing its passion for unanimity—was a crucial problem facing Katara.

Turner and Killian (1972:335) suggest that such commitment might be achieved "through esprit de corps; by the provision of secondary rewards for participation; by devices that anchor the individual identity in the movement, often through conversion; and in the case of movements strongly at odds with society, by burning the bridges back to conventional life." Both esprit de corps (a sense of collective identity) and morale (a sense of collective discipline and purpose) are central in fostering commitment. Indeed, Blumer (1951a) argues that morale is the more critical element.[26] Morale determines whether the movement, and the requisite solidarity of its organization, is maintained over the long haul, especially in the face of setbacks and failure. For as Lang and Lang (1970:95) point out, "a group demoralized beyond a certain point becomes unable to pursue any legitimate objective." Esprit de corps is a major factor in recruiting new members and retaining old ones and gives "life, enthusiasm, and vigor to a movement" (Blumer, 1953:208). It often has much to do with mobilization and with the formation of positive rather than negative interpersonal relationships among members.

Katara in the post-Stone period was not able to retain esprit de corps and morale. It tried a number of means of doing so: emphasizing the ingroup-outgroup relation between blacks and whites; holding many purely social and recreational affairs; engaging in collective rituals of various kinds (special handshakes and gestures, observing various black leaders' birthdays, Black Solidarity Days).[27] That is, it tried to utilize a number of solidary incentives and provide a variety of expressive rewards. It was not notably successful with any of these techniques. Further, Katara was unable to provide the kind of secondary or instrumental rewards that would have enhanced commitment.

There are numerous indications that Katara failed to anchor the identity of many black students in the movement and in the organization, as was necessary for the movement's survival (cf. Kanter, 1968; Turner and Killian, 1972). Some never joined Katara. Others did so only because they were expected to, not because they believed in its goals or agreed with other members; their commitment was weak. The individualistic career-orientation of many students militated against a strong and lasting anchoring of identity in the movement. The shocks and disillusionments of the Stone affair loosened the ties of several whose individual identities *had* been so anchored. Continued failures to achieve change and increasing internal division loosened those of others.

Only once, perhaps, did Katara engage in action that could be called bridge burning. This was during the occupation of the Student Center, when Katara members were willing to accept both academic and civil (possibly criminal) sanctions in their fight to retain Stone. As time went on, however, bridge burning might have resulted in Katara's destruction. Hence, this means of cementing commitment was not available.

As Blumer (1953) and Useem (1973) point out, successes of some regularity and dimension are necessary to maintain esprit de corps and morale. Katara's limited successes and important failures were a final factor undermining cohesion and commitment. The failures had a reflexive, mutually reinforcing effect on organizational cohesion and member commitment.

Smelser correctly notes that any movement "which crusades under a fully developed set of generalized beliefs is bound to fail" (1963:305), largely because of its members' exaggerated expectations. Certainly many black students had unreasonable expectations, particularly in regard to internal solidarity.[28] As one student sadly put it: "We came expecting to find real community among black students and in the College. I, for one, didn't find any of these things" (Student Interview no. 16).

As Lipsky (1968:1149) suggests, "cohesion is particularly important when protest leaders bargain directly with target groups." (Provost Neal's initial rejection of Katara's November 1968 demands because he did not believe they represented the views of the majority of black students is a case in point.) And continued failure or delay in achieving external success only worsened the internal situation.

Katara's internal and external failures were disillusioning for many black students. For them, Katara was the "god that failed." Over the long run this produced resentment of Katara leaders, undermined their authority and the compelling power of many of the values espoused by the organization, and severely strained organizational loyalty.

### Social Struggle and Weariness

Movement activists, particularly when they face continued failure or internal difficulties, often experience a kind of battle fatigue. Increasing disaffection is the result. All the high, heroic, and romantic expectations held by members can never be satisfied; hence, interpersonal relations can become embittered, as happened in Katara.

By the spring of 1972, disaffection and weariness may have been greatest for those who started as freshmen in 1968. They had formed the bulk of the troops in the most active period of the movement. After 1968, as both internal and external success continued to elude Katara, it became increasingly difficult to recruit new members among entering freshmen or transfers, or to retain the loyalty and commitment of the decreasing number so recruited. Hence, even greater burdens were placed on those trying to maintain the organization, who were also experiencing the tensions and difficulties faced by black students, even in the best circumstances, in balancing individual and collective commitments.

Though his subject is black students involved in the southern civil rights struggles during the early 1960s, Robert Coles might be describing student activists in University College:

> Struggle to make our world a better one for more people demands effort and commitment, and these are sometimes repaid with exhaustion and despair. . . .
> . . . weariness touches almost all the students who stay in the movement for any significant period of time—that is, long enough to taste its less than quixotic or flashy quality and its hard, grinding daily demands which are not always relieved by spectacular successes and are often encumbered with the new burden of hopes sparked but not realized. . . .
> In many ways these young civil rights workers are in a war and exposed to the stresses of warfare. (Coles, 1964:305, 314, 315)

Weariness develops in students from a variety of class backgrounds and with varying reasons for participating in the movement. Given time and the experiences that developed in the black student movement and Katara—lack of concrete success, intramural friction, a feeling of being able to make it on one's own and of needing to meet individual aspirations—battle fatigue was almost inevitable. The consequence was "exhaustion, weariness, despair, frustration, and rage," all of which "mark a crisis in the lives of those youths who experience them" (Coles, 1964:308). These reactions and the *Weltschmerz* they produce played a significant role in the decline of the movement and the disaffection of its members.

> Depressions occur, loss of sense of purpose, and acceptance of the power of the enemy where before such power was challenged with apparent fearlessness. Sometimes withdrawal from the movement becomes a precursor of the abandonment of a commitment, . . . the advocacy of total, disruptive assault upon the society, or complete,

hateful disengagement from it. In such cases the movement itself may be attacked instead of the segregated society formerly felt to be the enemy.

. . . students may depart the movement, go "back to the world" of schools, job, pursuit of career. . . . Or they may linger on, disabled. Or they may stay on but become troublesome, bitter, and a source of worry. (Coles, 1964:309, 308)

Bitterness, disengagement, and anger were common among black students in University College by the end of the period examined here. Almost all of the students and former students interviewed expressed such sentiments. While often admitting the necessity for continued struggle against the University, just as often they felt that there was little chance for victory or success. And in the face of the institution's powers of resistance, there was little point in wasting one's energies and precious time in futile struggle, particularly when to do so could well jeopardize career goals. Most agreed with the sentiments of the University College student who said, "I just want to get my diploma and get the hell out." To such a state had the black student movement come in University College.

CHAPTER VIII

# Paradoxes of Protest and the Limits of Student Power

*It is rather easier to change the world than to change the university.*——Nathan Glazer (1970a:193)

The black student movement at University College only partially met "the first test of a movement, namely, getting results, and the second test, coping with its own organizational problems" (Rubington, 1973:172). It had real impact but limited success in achieving lasting changes directly benefiting blacks on and off campus and in creating and sustaining a close-knit, supportive community among black students.

The movement's fate highlights the fundamental paradox confronting black student activists: that they have often been utopian groups of limited power using radical tactics to achieve reformist goals in a secular, bureaucratic world that they need for individual mobility, and in which they stay only a short time.

## PARADOXES OF PROTEST

Black students' ideology stressed unity, solidarity and collective action. Collective action is often necessary, and this insistence on collective commitment and action was both inevitable and rational.[1] Yet, as we have seen, one of its results was fragmentation. The failure to resolve this paradox of protest—that the means of achieving internal solidarity and external success were also likely to produce dissensus and disintegration—contributed materially to the movement's fate, especially since black students explicitly rejected one of the means for reducing factionalism, namely, bureaucratization and centralization of power within the union (see Gamson, 1975, on the role of bureaucratization in fighting factionalism).

The union was also caught in a dilemma in which both success and failure contributed to its ultimate decline. The more the union succeeded, the more it eliminated its own raison d'être and raised expectations of continued success. On the other hand, every failure produced disappointment and often disaffection among members; the more failure, the more disaffection—all within the context of an exclusive organization continuing to demand internal solidarity.

Third, members had to reconcile individual, personal interests with the collective interests and goals stressed by the movement. Achieving collective goals *may* enhance and meet individual interests, yet these remain different from group interests and are not always easily reconciled to them. As Gurin and Epps (1975:339) put it: "How can Black students pursue personal predilections, strive to realize their own hopes, and simultaneously work to change the barriers and inequities built into the fabric of the black experience in America?"

Collective interests and personal interests are not at opposite poles, such that giving priority to one necessarily means abandoning the other or relegating it to secondary status. It is not necessarily the case that by opting to stress personal interests when faced with frustration, black students have abandoned or even deemphasized collective commitments. Some merely defer such commitments to a later point in their lives, perhaps having concluded that the university is not the most crucial arena for collective black action.

Of greater importance is evidence that, for black students at least, individual and collective commitment are independent rather than polarized orientations. In their excellent study of the attitudes and values of students in historically black colleges, Gurin and Epps (1975:350) found that

> commitments to individual achievement goals were correlated with traditional indicators of achievement motivation *but not with racial ideology;* commitments to collective action were correlated with racial ideology *but not with traditional achievement motivation.* (Emphasis in original)

I believe this description also characterizes many black students in predominantly white institutions, then and now.

These findings suggest an explanation of how and why many black students shifted allegiance away from the union when it faced internal dissension and frustration. Such a shift, given their dual but independent commitments, was natural, perhaps inevitable, whenever appropriate circumstances developed. But many of the students who became disenchanted and inactive were not, in an important sense, "copping out" or "selling out," although they were often bitterly accused of doing so. Rather, they appear to have acted under the implicit recognition that there are at least two routes to social change for blacks: direct, collective action and individual mobility and success, which, aggregated, produce increased group status. Unfortunately, ideology, the exclusive character of the union, and its political interests all combined to cause other black students to see the disaffected or disengaged as not "truly black." Thus, the union and the movement failed to resolve the paradox of dual and independent commitments.

Fourth, the movement faced the paradox of young bourgeois trying to identify with or prove themselves to the black masses while limiting their actions to the isolated setting of the white college. Except for community outreach efforts (where they occurred), movement demands generally concerned changes that would benefit black students or expand the black bourgeoisie by making individuals economically or socially mobile, not changes that would provide direct, immediate benefit to the black masses. Hence, the movement was limited in its class basis. As a consequence, it might be argued, when black students came to believe in the futility of their efforts, many retreated into privatistic stances typical of a major portion of the black bourgeoisie (see Caplan, 1971; Kauroma, 1971; and Perkins and Higginson, 1971, for development of this kind of argument). This problem was heightened by the heterogeneity of black students in terms of class background, ethnicity, political views, and the degree to which careerist orientations and mobility aspirations took precedence over political beliefs and a willingness to engage in direct on-campus political activism. The romantic identification with the ghetto and its life did not decrease these differences or their impact. Neither denying the reality of such differences, on the one hand, nor castigating those who were considered too "bourgeois," on the other, eliminates the fragmenting potential of heterogeneity or the kind of "blacker-than-thou" competition produced by dissensus.[2]

Finally, the emergence of the black student movement in University College (and elsewhere) presents the apparent paradox of beneficiaries attacking their benefactors while still needing the institution in order to fulfill their individual aspirations for status and social mobility. Thus, we find the rhetoric of demand being used by those heavily dependent on the largesse of the targets of their protest.

One consequence was to limit commitment to the movement and the activist steps many black students were willing to take: the movement could be forced to pull its punches. This may help account for the common view of administrators and faculty members in University College that the movement was "reasonable" and positive, and for the fact that it remained norm-oriented. It probably helped College authorities in their efforts to limit or control the movement.

From available evidence, it seems clear that the black student movement in other colleges and universities was no more successful in resolving these dilemmas (cf. Napper, 1973; Obatala, 1972). Further, fragmentation and decline are not unique to the black student movement but are a fate often shared by student movements generally (see Altbach, 1967, 1974, and Flacks 1971b). Examples can be found in the Vienna student movement of 1848 (Feuer, 1969); the Japanese student movement, the Zengakuren, between 1950 and 1962 (Feuer, 1969); the student movement at the University of Warsaw and Warsaw Polytechnic in 1956 and 1957 (Bereday, 1967); the French-Canadian students' movement at the University of Montreal between 1964 and 1966 (Bereday, 1967); and the student movement at the Free University of Berlin after 1968 (Statera, 1975), to mention only a few cases. The black student movement in University College, like these other examples, demonstrates the truth of Gamson's (1975:99) observation that "internal division is a misery few challenging groups escape completely."

## UNIVERSITY POWER AND STUDENT POWERLESSNESS

The black student movement began in University College with enthusiasm, vigor, and marked impact on the campus. As we have seen, these traits were not maintained over time, the movement declined, and Katara disintegrated. I have suggested some of the forces instrumental in producing this outcome, most crucially failure in achieving major goals, factionalism, and the disaffection of members.

Looked at more broadly, the fate of the movement and black student efforts in University College raises the question of students' power (or lack of it) to produce lasting change in the University. There are several factors that limited students' capacity to achieve their movement and organizational goals. Some of these relate particularly to black students themselves and the way they responded to situations and conditions confronting them. Some are the result of the constraints and role conflicts inherent in the status of student. Still others stem from the organizational character of the University and the social control responses of institutional authorities.

## Resources and Resource Management

One of the critical issues in the history of any social movement, whether it occurs in society or in a large-scale, complex organization like a university, is what kind of resources the movement can claim and how well it mobilizes and manages them (McCarthy and Zald, 1973; Tilly, 1978; Zald and Berger, 1968; and Zald and McCarthy, 1979, provide excellent general discussions of the resource mobilization perspective on social movements.) This was certainly true in the case of the black student movement in University College.

The principal resources potentially available to black students were psychic, social, moral, and political. For a variety of reasons (e.g., their youth, lack of previous experience with the frequent setbacks involved in political activity, the absence of support for movement participation from significant others, and careerist or other nonactivist orientations), many black students did not have sufficient psychic resources to maintain their activity and commitment to the movement when confronted with frustration and dissensus. We have seen how solidarity and cohesion, perhaps the most vital social resources available to black students, were undermined. As for economic resources, most black students did not possess the kind that would maintain them independently of support from family or the college. A significant number received financial aid from the university, aid that they could not replace themselves and whose loss could have prevented them from gaining college educations. Lack of economic resources has also meant that black students could not on their own institute or financially support major new programs or other changes. Nor were they generally, either as students, alumni, or members of families, influential as potential or actual large donors. In short, their economic dependency on the university was an integral part of their relative powerlessness.

Finally, black students were faced with the problem of insufficient political and power resources. They did not have the kind of power that comes from large numbers and the ability to launch a mass movement on campus. Further, as students they had little access to the bureaucratic and organizational channels through which decisions are made and power is exercised in the academic institution.

Of the three kinds of power and power resources commonly noted (cf. Etzioni, 1961a; Gamson, 1968)—that is, normative, utilitarian, and coercive—black students had rather little of the most potent form of utilitarian resources: money. As a result, their principal resources were moral and coercive.

Their moral resources stemmed from being black in a liberal institution at a time when issues of racial deprivation and equity were in the forefront of national concern. Since there are many in universities who oppose the suffering and exploitation of blacks, moral resources have been an important element in black student protest and in negotiation and conflict resolution between black students and white administrators. As Horowitz and Friedland (1970:60) observed in a number of schools:

> The blacks established precedents in bargaining for other student organizations. Until the black confrontations of 1968 university administrators had argued that the established mechanisms of student government provided ample opportunity for the presentation of demands and for effecting change within the normative consensus of the university. The assassination of King not only enhanced the moral position of the blacks, but also undermined the university administrators' insistence on adherence to established mechanisms. At Stanford, for example, the university administration broke precedent by negotiating with the black students in public.

This may explain the apparently greater responsiveness of college and university authorities to black protest than to that of white students (Astin and Bayer, 1971; Urban Research Corporation, 1970) as well as evidence of a willingness on their part to take some limited actions *before* protest. At the same time, if the experience of the movement in University College is in any way indicative, such responsiveness lasted only until black student goals began to impinge on basic College interests. At that point authorities acted to preserve the interests of the institution or key groups within it, not those of black students.

In such a situation, coercive resources can spell the difference between movement success and failure. And it is here, in the long run, that black students' lack of resources and power has been most important. Students can demonstrate, hold rallies, strike, even occupy buildings, with some short-term success. However, such coercive tactics, if tried too often, tend to produce diminishing returns. Mobilizing partisans for such efforts does not necessarily become easier over time—often quite the reverse. And university authorities learned quickly to deal with such tactics, through the use of academic sanctions or court injunctions, for example, without provoking violent confrontations.

Further, while there were (and are) enough black students to be heard and to be disruptive, in the majority of colleges and universities there have not been enough to maintain such coercive tactics over the long haul, particularly in the face of internal division. In addition, it is unclear just how effective coercion actually is. Some evidence suggests that black student protest works only if it is extreme, severe, and prolonged (Astin and Bayer, 1971; Urban Research Corporation, 1970); other evidence suggests that it works only if it is *not* severe or prolonged (Astin, Astin et al., 1975). What is clear is that though black students possess real coercive resources, these are limited in extent and effect.

Thus, the question of resource management—that is, of strategy and tactics—has been central. Katara's ideology stressed black solidarity, brotherhood, and equality. In practice, this meant that Katara (like many other black student unions) operated internally as a participatory democracy, with decisions being made collectively or by committee; the union was structured to minimize bureaucratization and centralization of power. On the other hand, it is precisely these rejected mechanisms of organization and structure that are sometimes necessary for maintaining the internal cohesion and stability important in achieving external success, especially for groups in conflict with a highly organized opponent (Gamson, 1975). This presented Katara with a strategic dilemma of resource management.

There are at least two, rather contradictory, views of black students' general strategy and tactics. Several observers have argued that they were sophisticated, flexible, and effective and achieved notable successes—especially in comparison with their white counterparts (Bell and Kristol, 1969; Horowitz and Friedland, 1970; Lipset, 1971; Trow, 1970). Increased minority admissions and faculty recruitment and the implementation of ethnic studies programs are often cited as demonstrably the results of black student actions.

The late Vivian Henderson (1974:78) presented a rather different, and more critical, view:

> The movement of [black] campus radicalism was short-lived and failed to develop into a genuine youth movement. . . . Its abortive nature resulted, in part, because of wide variations in the character of its operation, demands, and objectives . . . [and] strategies were projected and oriented toward short-term aims. The chief strategy was confrontation politics directed toward rather specific and particular objectives at particular places and at particular times. Campus radicalism was oriented toward winning battles, but not the war.[3]

Examination of events in University College suggests that Henderson's may be the more persuasive view in the long run.

Several of the problems noted earlier—political inexperience, inadequate understanding of the nature of the College, and reliance on ideological conformity and solidary incentives, for example—are relevant to the students' strategic and tactical difficulties. Another problem of the black student movement in University College was its go-it-alone stance.

Throughout its history the black student movement encompassed only black students as members and direct participants. This was a deliberate choice. Only twice was an alliance with other groups sought or achieved: with SDS during the building occupations of the Stone affair, and with El Grito during 1970–71. (Black students did not actively seek to ally themselves with SDS, but were willing to accept its activist support in separate action.) Black students in the College failed to achieve an effective alliance with those at Washington Square. At no point did other, non-black students participate in decision making within the movement. At no point did black students participate in fully integrated joint action with other students, whether on behalf of black issues or in other activist efforts (e.g., the Taylor affair).

Black activists maintained their independence, despite the sympathy for their aims consistently manifested by numbers of white students. They accepted such support but always kept their own efforts separate. They were apparently not interested in firm or long-lasting coalitions with white students. In this, and the consequent failure to utilize fully and effectively such white support, black students in University College were much like those on other white campuses (cf. Anthony, 1971; Donadio, 1968a, 1968b; Edwards, 1970; Horowitz and Friedland, 1970; Napper, 1973).

Why was the black student movement so much a solo effort, particularly since this stance contributed to movement powerlessness? Earl Anthony (1971:4) provides the beginning of the answer. He notes that from 1967 on, an "informal national unanimity" existed among black students around the country that racism, particularly institutional racism, was the primary enemy:

> With this emphasis upon racism as the major problem of black people in America, it became unproductive for the black student movement to remain involved with the white student radical movement. . . . Racism was not an issue that consumed every breathing moment of a young white radical's life, however much he was repelled by it on an abstract level.

Thus, despite the door opened for possible coalition by black acceptance of "Third World" ideologies (see Edwards, 1970), black students felt that they and white students did not have identical perspectives on social reality.

Black students often felt that they could never fully trust white students. Being white, they were inevitably, subtly, perhaps unconsciously involved in racism themselves. Negative experiences with white students, even supposedly liberal or radical ones, served to consolidate these suspicions. (Many of my informants reported such experiences.) The abandonment of the larger civil rights movement by whites after the enunciation of Black Power was often seen by black students as further confirmation of their distrust of white honesty and sincerity. White students could not be trusted to go as far, to take the personal and academic risks, to endure the long-term struggle as black students were prepared to do.[4] Further, the ideology of cooperative, joint action by blacks and whites that characterized the civil rights effort of the early 1960s was no longer accepted and was often explicitly rejected by black students (and other blacks) after 1965.

Non-alliance with white students was also required by "the charter myth of a power-seeking organization," to use Barrington Moore's (1962:10) felicitous phrase. In the light of the movement's history and career in the College, black students' charter myth required non-alliance in another sense.

> A sharp boundary line between those who belong and those who do not aids a movement in preserving its identity in the course of subsequent struggles. The necessity to preserve this boundary line becomes increasingly important the more a movement seeks to control the entire span of an individual member's behavior. (Moore, 1962:15)

Moreover, black students may have avoided alliance with white students out of implicit recognition that authorities tended to react less favorably to black students and their demands when protest issues were diverse and protesters were racially mixed (Astin and Bayer, 1971; Urban Research Corporation, 1970; but cf. the somewhat different findings of Astin, Astin, et al., 1975). Not only were they apparently less likely to accede to the demands of such groups, but they and peace-keeping agents were likely to react more harshly—for example, to call in police who would use MACE and clubs (Urban Research Corporation, 1970).

One reason for this may be the correlated tendency for mixed protest and activism to involve violence more often than unmixed protest

(*Black Scholar*, 1970). Not only does the number of students involved tend to be larger, but perhaps in mixed protest each group has to prove its toughness and commitment to the other, and to itself. That this need may have been greater for white students was suggested by the feeling of many of my black informants in University College that white students were unpredictable and more prone to violent or extreme acts. As one put it, "SDS were maniacs, fanatics; we wanted nothing to do with crazy people like that" (Student Interview no. 6).

In short, black students in University College, and elsewhere, kept their movement a solo effort for practical, ideological, and political reasons. This stance, although probably unavoidable and maybe necessary, ultimately contributed to their long-term powerlessness.

The initial positive responses by the College and the University to the black student movement obscured two crucial facts: first, that administrators will always act to protect the organizational interests of the institution, and, second, that the status of student in the college or university is by its nature relatively powerless. Yet such positive responses confirmed for black students the legitimacy and, more important here, the efficacy of going it alone, dealing with the College as a single group not allied or tied to any other student group.

As Gamson (1968), Lipsky (1968), and Schelling (1956) suggest, coalition and alliance are useful and often necessary for the powerless, including students (see Flacks, 1971*b*).[5] We have, however, seen that for important reasons black students did not seek such alliances with most other student groups then in the College, the great majority of whom were white (there was no appreciable number of Puerto Rican students until 1970–71). Further, earlier black student actions had had the effect of polarizing the campus along racial lines, so that by 1970, when the movement was experiencing real decline and ready to begin seeking an alliance, many white students who had formerly been sympathetic may have been no longer available or willing to participate. At that point, it was too late for coalition. As a result, black students in University College never managed to mobilize effectively the active support of non-radical white students that was crucial for success (Astin, Astin, et al., 1975, for more discussion of this point).

To succeed in their aims, students must also form alliances with off-campus groups, as Richard Flacks (1971*b*) argues, not least because the close connections between the university and the larger society suggest that rapid, fundamental change may not be possible without pressure from outside the institution. As Flacks (1971*b*:100) suggests and the black student movement in University College illustrates, a point is reached in the development of student movements where their isolation and parochialism become self-defeating. At this point alliances on campus and especially off campus become critical. However:

> such alliances are made problematical by the very characteristics of student life that provide collective srength in the first place—their physical isolation, their privileged freedom from the responsibilities and burdens of adult life, and their speech, dress, tastes, and idealistic impatience. (Flacks, 1971b:100)

All of this makes it difficult for off-campus groups to make connections and identify with students, particularly where there are class differences between students and those off campus. Paradoxically, however,

> *the logic of student movements is that they must transcend themselves if the collective consciousness they express is to survive and realize itself.* Youth must find a way to connect its interests with those of other groups that potentially or actually are in motion for radical change. The students' privileged sanctuary in the university must somehow be transcended. (Flacks, 1971b:101; emphasis in original)

This was perhaps even stronger in the period under discussion than before 1965 (cf. Perkins and Higginson, 1971). Efforts by black students to change the relationship of the white university to the large black community represent an attempt, even if largely unwitting, to achieve transcendence. Such efforts have rarely been successful either in directly aiding these black communities or in achieving alliances between black students and community groups. Black students of the early sixties were more successful in these respects, not least because their efforts were aimed at producing benefits for *all* blacks, not just black students. The failure of black students in white colleges after 1965 to transcend the campus suggests the possibility they are *more* disadvantaged and less independent than other black political groups in the larger society. What are the reasons for their failure?

On the one hand, various off-campus developments in ideology, strategy, and tactics (Black Power, nationalism), and the emergence of new groups (the Panthers, the Muslims) did transcend *their* origins. They created a radicalism relevant to a wide variety of blacks, including black students; indeed, these new directions and groups were an important influence in the black student movement after 1965. On the other hand, black students did not—indeed, perhaps could not—create a radicalism clearly and directly relevant to nonstudents. While students' rhetoric, ideology, and, frequently, tactics came from off-campus sources, the reverse influence was largely absent.[6] The university as a setting for political activity is very different from the larger society, and this hampered black students' development of ideologies, strategies, or tactics relevant off campus (see Kauroma, 1971; Perkins and Higginson, 1971). Furthermore, with the possible exception of the Black Panthers and other groups in a few places (see Anthony, 1971; Barlow and Shapiro, 1971; Donadio, 1968a; Lusky and Lusky, 1969), off-campus groups have made few moves to ally with black students directly, despite some initiatives from students.

Moreover, students by definition are more privileged and have higher status, wider options, and greater advantages than the majority of off-campus blacks. Put simply, they are, or are about to be, middle-class. Hence, class differences, distrust, and resentment have been a principal barrier to the creation by the black student movement of a radicalism relevant off campus.[7]

Moreover, only in their efforts to increase the university's community outreach and service activities did black students focus on issues of direct relevance and benefit to the larger black community, and these efforts were limited generally to campuses with a black community nearby. Such efforts faced still another hurdle: they were among the most value-oriented of all black student activities, or at least they were often perceived this way by authorities. As a result, they have been the most resisted and the least likely to implemented by university authorities.

Finally, the one other major "value" black students could offer the larger black community—the promise that they would return to the community, to the ghetto, and place their university-acquired skills at its service for the benefit of all—is also problematic. There is no guarantee that the middle-class professionals and entrepreneurs that these students will become will return to the ghetto (indeed, many black students do not come from the ghetto in the first place), or that they will do so in large enough numbers to have the desired impact, or that they will put racial consciousness above individual or class interests. Many black students do intend to return to the black community to practice their professions. However, the success they desire frequently requires substantial participation in the larger society. Neither should the class differences between the professional and his or her potential clients be minimized. Thus, while it is true that a collective, race-conscious orientation is an important element among blacks, black communities cannot take it for granted in their relations with students. Thus, the tendency to go it alone and the failure to transcend campus origins have been principal elements in the decline of black student activism and the relative powerlessness of black students.

## Movement Continuity

Student life is characterized by constant turnover; every year a new group of students arrives as another leaves. In society people may grow older, move on to other things, or in a variety of other ways leave former allegiances, activities, or relationships. However, they generally do not leave society simultaneously in large, regular cohorts the way students leave college each year.[8] This turnover presents special problems for student movements, black as well as white. Among them is the possibility of a leadership crisis, as described by Weber, each year. There is little time in the four years of undergraduate student life— assuming that students attend college for the traditional four consecutive years, as an increasing number do not—to build up a well-trained, stable, and continuous cadre of leaders. (For example, Paul Hunter's succession to the presidency of Katara was a disaster for the black student movement.)

Each year produces new potential recruits who have different expectations and views; who have no direct experience of the movement's history, goals, and purposes; who have little direct experience or knowledge of the college; and who, at the same time, can have only a temporally limited commitment to the institution or movement. Though these new members may be part of the same chronological generation, they often have different experiences and political socialization and face different historical problems and a different historical "destiny"—they belong, in other words, to separate generational units (cf. Feuer, 1969; Mannheim, 1952; Ryder, 1965). Their presence carries the potential for both change and conflict within the movement. For example, the split within ACCESS that produced Katara was apparently the result of a generational shift following the *first* increase in the number of entering black students, which came in 1966–67. (For further illustration, see Donald, 1970, 1973, for a discussion of the even more critical impact of intergenerational conflict among black students at Cornell in the late 1960s.)

The orientation efforts directed by Katara during the summer and fall of 1968 toward new black students can be seen as an attempt to maintain movement continuity and minimize generational problems. It is significant that after 1968 Katara and the black student movement never again mounted such an extensive and intensive effort to ensure movement continuity and consensus through the socialization of new members. The problem of movement continuity, exacerbated by defection, grew apace after the Stone affair.

Perhaps most critically, constant turnover makes the acquisition of material resources and incentives much more difficult. Hence, not only does the kind of institutionalization posited in the Weber-Michels model of movement development become less likely, but the movement is prevented from using a wider variety of incentives and rewards to facilitate member allegiance and participation. College authorities are generally not willing to grant resources, rewards, and power to a constantly shifting group. Students may make certain demands at one point and, as membership changes and new members seek different rewards, other demands at another point. Even if college authorities grant rewards and resources to a student movement, they have little guarantee that demands and pressures will not be renewed at some future time. Indeed, positive action might simply set precedents for other students demands.

Further, turnover (along with the role demands of the student status) may make the control or subversion of movement goals easier for the authorities. Authorities need only wait or stall—by prolonging discussions for example—and turnover and role demands are likely to ease student pressures. This is how "talking protest to death" operates. It seems to have been a very successful tactic in University College.

## The University as Setting for the Black Student Movement

Despite their lack of coercive power and the limits on their ability to act independently, university administrators may have greater control over internal situations than political authorities in society, because power in the university ultimately rests in the hands of a comparatively small group of individuals, and because in normative organizations the principal mode of exercising power is executive leadership, not participation or even, in many cases, representation. Thus, administrators may hold more power and resources vis-à-vis students than political authorities do vis-à-vis citizens, and in certain circumstances they may have a freer hand in dealing with them. This asymmetry of power and the internal political conditions that resulted were among the sources of white students' push for student power and black students' demands for black control over black studies and other programs.[9] As we have seen, at least in University College, such efforts were generally not successful.

University authorities also find it easier than political ones to subvert or deflect the partisan goals of dissidents.[10] In University College, a clear example of such subversion occurred in the case of the Minority Group Seminar House at the Heights, which opened with a name and official purposes very different from those initially proposed by black students. The same thing seems to have happened in the case of the MLK Student Center and its director at Washington Square. Declining black admissions and resistance to the proposed administrative format of the black studies program are further examples.[11]

Another difference between the university and society lies in the fact that core resources of the former cannot be seized or gotten at in quite the same way as those of the latter. (The history of labor unions and successful revolutionary movements is instructive in this regard.) The university's much greater key resources are well protected from capture by students. In a sense, building occupations, class disruptions, bombings, and so on might be seen as attempts at such seizure. These have an effect on some of the university's resources, but they do not touch its core resources—the faculty or its financial holdings, for example—or have the same impact on the institution's functioning as seizure of production lines or the media of mass communications. Universities have learned to work around building occupations and class disruptions and to isolate them so that they do not seriously impede normal institutional operations.

The building occupations at University College during the Stone affair polarized the campus, strained the social fabric of the campus community, and created significant difficulties for College and University authorities. However, these actions did not gain Stone's reinstatement, nor did they stop many of the College's essential activities. Although student actions such as sit-ins or building occupations have produced some policy changes elsewhere, they generally have not fundamentally altered the relatively powerless condition of students.[12]

## POWER AND RACE: SOME LARGER IMPLICATIONS

Some of the larger implications of this study have to do with the acquisition of power and the production of change by blacks and perhaps other relatively powerless racial groups in the United States.

First, this study suggests that where such groups seek power and change through social movements, it makes a difference whether their efforts take place within an organizational or a societal setting. If the experience of the black student movement in University College is not unique, and in my view it is not, it indicates that the internal forces that tend to produce disunity have a greater negative influence in some settings than in others. Normative organizations such as colleges and universities appear to present special problems—as well as opportunities—for social movements emerging in them. On the one hand, concern for normative consensus may make authorities intitially receptive to some of the movement's demands or aims; on the other hand, the particular character of normative organizations, the status of their members, and their isolation from and special role in society all serve to facilitate the kind of difficulties experienced by the black student movement in University College.

Blacks in the larger society may therefore have greater political advantages and opportunities than black students in white universities. Such advantages include greater numbers, more resources, more possibility for transcendence of locale and parochialism (though the problem of alliance or coalition remains great), more autonomy of action, with political action more likely to enhance the social mobility of activists than to threaten it, and a greater variety of organizations to work through and techniques to employ. These are, of course, only relative advantages, for social change and civil rights efforts in the larger society have not escaped some of the problems faced by black students.

Second, setting makes a difference in the perception of a movement and hence in reactions to it. The normative character of the college has encouraged the tendency to perceive the black student movement as value-oriented—a tendency often shared by outside observers as well as those more directly involved on each campus (see, e.g., Cass, 1969; Record, 1974). Any action or stance that seriously criticizes or opposes the existing normative consensus often seems to strike at basic *values*. Hence, many, both within and without, tend to perceive such actions as value-oriented and threatening. The university's status-allocation function has contributed to this perception. Many have felt that black students should be grateful for the opportunity to attend college, particularly where special efforts have been made to bring them into the institution (see Clift, 1969, and Proctor, 1970, for a clear illustration of such attitudes). Criticism of conditions there appeared to some to be a rejection of the values of those trying to help them.

This perception of the black student movement as value-oriented has an important off-campus analogy. In the larger society black protest and civil rights activity have often been perceived in the same fashion, particularly as these efforts shifted away from legalistic, integrationist goals toward changes in basic institutions and greater equity in the distribution of opportunities and rewards. Some whites view such activities as the result of Communist inspiration or the work of outside agitators or people who want something without working for it. Blacks are seen as somehow "un-American," wanting something for nothing, seeking illegitimate rewards by illegitimate means, wanting too much too soon.

This tendency to perceive black activism as value-oriented reflects a common phenomenon: "publics typically ascribe unannounced broader goals to any movement that attracts attention" (Turner and Killian, 1972:284). More basically, it reflects a clash of what Berger and Luckmann (1966) term "symbolic universes." Such universes are composed of ideologies, values, mythologies, and so on. Black ideologies and demands, whether made by students or others, represent and embody a symbolic universe different from that of whites. The problem is that "the appearance of an alternative symbolic universe poses a threat because its very existence demonstrates empirically that one's own universe is less than inevitable. The confrontation of alternative symbolic universes implies a problem of power" (Berger and Luckman, 1966:100). Because power is involved, the clash between symbolic universes is likely to be perceived as threatening by those whose symbolic universe has heretofore been dominant. This raises the further question of the political process and the arena within which such clashes arise and are worked out.

Without pushing the analogy too far (the university, after all, is not the society), there is an important parallel between the American university and the larger society. As many have noted, the university can be seen as a political institution, particularly in its internal process (Apter, 1974; Baldridge, 1971; Braungart, 1974b). The college is composed of a variety of interest groups and operates through the regulation and adjudication of competition between such groups within a normative consensus.

The political process in society is essentially the same. Under "interest group liberalism," interest groups of all kinds use the political system, directly or through representatives (both elected and lobbyists), to gain their ends. Adjudication and regulation of the resulting competition and conflict is the central process of the system, much as in the university.

This, of course, is true for those groups already in the political arena, as Gamson (1975) demonstrates. Those groups, like blacks, that are either outside the system or only partially included are much less likely to be in the competition or to have their interests met; they are also less likely to play or be bound by the system's rules. This, in itself, is a reason why such groups' actions are perceived by others as especially threatening.

The result is that in both the university and the larger society the political process is often perceived as a zero-sum game. A gain for any one group is seen as a loss for another or a threat to its position. In addition, such gains are perceived by those threatened by them as larger than they actually are: for example, the widespread view that blacks have made massive gains in jobs, income, and so on as the result of affirmative action programs and similar policies, and at the expense of decent, hard-working, average (white) folk. (See Fernandez, 1975, and Levitan, 1975, for illustrations of the distortions involved in such views of black gains.)

Resistance or resentment is likely to be stronger if attempts at change seem to involve methods not legitimized by the existing normative consensus governing political activity. As a consequence, both attempts at change and those who make them are likely to be perceived as illegitimate, "radical," or "militant"—that is, value-oriented. This has been pre-eminently the case for both black students on campus and blacks in the larger society. This situation has been heightened by class differences and racism, with their divisive and corrosive effects on intergroup perceptions and relations. Thus, power-seeking efforts by blacks are likely to provoke special resistance, resentment, or fear on the part of whites, whether in the university or society. This is a problem blacks and other relatively powerless racial groups must face and overcome.

There is a significant irony here, for in the main blacks both on and off campus have been norm-oriented: at times, perhaps, "militant" in their tactics, but not in their basic goals.[13] They have been seeking *inclusion* in American society and its universities, not their destruction. Indeed, both black students and the larger civil rights movement have sometimes been criticized for not being radical or revolutionary enough (see Caplan, 1971; Krueger and Silvert, 1975; Perkins and Higginson, 1971; Rubenstein, 1971; J. Turner, 1971; Wolters, 1975).

The black student movement in University College, as we have seen, is for most of its career best characterized as norm-oriented, even if some of its demands and proposals had a value-oriented element. Its history supports the contention that black students in white colleges have been essentially reformist, not revolutionary. In short, a continuing by-product of black activism has been a crucial misperception of the character of black aims and black gains. The political effects, both on and off campus, of this misperception are still with us.

This study also reinforces the necessity for cohesion and solidarity if power-seeking groups are to maximize their chances for success and continued existence. Certainly the experience of black students in University College confirms the observation that cohesion is critical for the success of relatively powerless groups.

It also provides additional evidence that class and ethnicity can be fragmenting within as well as between racial groups, even within racially homogeneous, supposedly solidary groups. This is a special problem for politically active groups in which class and ethnic differences are insufficiently recognized or deliberately deemphasized. Ideological denial does not eliminate the reality of class and ethnic differences. Instead, by forcing them underground rather than dealing with them head-on, it can intensify their ultimate impact.

We have seen how black students in white colleges and universities may suffer such fragmentation. The work of Fanon (1967, 1968) on non-white independence movements in colonial societies and the experience of the civil rights movement over the past 150 years demonstrate that such fragmentation is a common problem in black political efforts (see also Poussaint and McLean, 1968) and indeed show many parallels with the history of worker insurgency in the United States (see Geschwender, 1977).[14]

In short, in terms of black political action and power, shared blackness is not enough. Even shared ideological beliefs may not be sufficient where these remain vague attitudes rather than behavioral principles in the context of a loosely structured organization attempting to operate on the basis of participatory democracy. While this generalization probably holds true to some extent for many political groups, it seems particularly important for blacks.

## THE FUTURE OF BLACK STUDENT ACTIVISM

A number of forces would appear to militate against an imminent revitalization of the black student movement and large-scale activism nationally. Those factors, both internal and external, instrumental in the demise of the movement in University College after 1971–72 continue to be operative on many campuses. Further, college and university administrators have become adept at handling student concerns, diverting them before the stage of active discontent or open protest is reached or "cooling out" protest once it surfaces.

In addition, the economic crunch of the seventies and early eighties has had a cooling-out effect in itself. Given that blacks, as usual, are suffering disproportionately from these economic difficulties, a college education has taken on added significance for black students. The combination of a tight job market, the government's benign and not so benign neglect of blacks, and their own strong careerism seems to have made many black students more concerned about staying in school and avoiding anything that would jeopardize the completion of their education.

We have also noted the role of off-campus developments in the growth of black campus activism. Black students have been, and remain, very much influenced by the larger civil rights movement. The continuing fragmentation, drift, and weakness of the larger movement in recent years have been a major factor in the apparent absence of black student activism.

I have also suggested that on-campus factors were instrumental in the development of black student protest. Among these was white student activism, which served a precedent-setting and facilitating role, in a sense "legitimizing" black student activities. The decline of white student activism during these years (see Altbach, 1974; Flacks, 1971a, 1971b; Krueger and Silvert, 1975; Miles, 1971, 1974; Statera, 1975) would seem to make the development of black student activism more difficult.

Additionally, black student enrollment continues to be affected by cuts in and increased demands on financial aid programs. Pressures to increase black enrollment appear to have fallen off, so, perhaps, have universities' efforts to recruit and enroll black students. This too is a likely factor in the decline of black student activism.

It is possible that black students now in four-year white colleges and universities are a different kind of black student than those of earlier years: different in socioeconomic background, being more affluent, and different in their political socialization, or at least less willing to engage in direct political action on campus. This certainly seems to be the view of more than a few current black students, and while the evidence for this change is not conclusive, there is some indication that black students now in white colleges and universities do differ on these dimensions (Boyd, 1974*b*; Walters, 1974).

It is also possible that the black student union, the vehicle of political activism and protest in previous years, not only has become a different organization but is viewed differently by current black students. On the one hand, as in University College, the union may be avoided because of a student's desire to avoid conflict, a desire stemming from the union's hard-line reputation or from bad feelings related to its history. On the other hand, the unions on many campuses have been sufficiently institutionalized since 1970–71 that incoming black students perceive them as part of the college, like any other student organization. Hence, the union can be approached, taken or left, like any other student organization. This may be especially likely where the union is no longer highly political. This situation, where it exists, has profound implications for the cohesion, visibility, direction of activity, and revitalization of the union and the movement. Among other things, it means that such unions must compete directly for the allegiance of black students with other organizations on campus. Appeals to racial solidarity, the fundamental mobilization technique of the sixties and early seventies may well be ineffective in this context.

Finally, perhaps Martin Kaplan's assessment (1976: 29–30) of members of the New Left holds true for black students as well; perhaps they have become as conservative as their peers:

> In the seventies, the new conformists, perhaps soon to be our new professional class, have chosen relativism as the best game in town. . . .
> They have chosen the rewards of privatism, self-fulfillment, personal gratification, individualistic autonomy, and the burgherly hearthside virtues of coping, acquiescence, and accommodation. . . . Criticism, for them, will not be a burdensome responsibility.

In short, it would seem that a number of potent forces have been at work to produce the apparent quietism among both white and black students in the last few years. Equally, the black student movement would seem to be permanently over.

And yet things are not quite so simple. The decline of student activism, particularly in the case of black students, is more apparent than real. Students, both black and white, are still concerned about sociopolitical issues, even while they are concerned with jobs, grades, and success (Semas, 1976*a*). As we have noted earlier, it is a mistake to dichotomize careerist and political orientations, particularly for black students (see Gurin and Epps, 1975). In addition, nationwide samples of black students in a variety of institutions indicate that they are still markedly alienated and disaffected from white society and the white college or university (Barol, 1983; Boyd, 1974b; Porter, 1977; Walters, 1974; Willie, 1981; Yankelovich, 1975). Disaffection continues to carry the potential for a revitalization of the black student movement and a renewal of activism.

Third, all of the students interviewed for this study, even those most hostile to the union or the movement itself, believed that black students should exert constant pressure on the white college or university in order to win improvements or maintain those already achieved. As one student put it, "You have to watch them, stay on top of them all the time." This is a view still widely shared among black students (Barol, 1983; Boyd, 1974b; Middleton, 1981; Walters, 1974; Willie, 1981; Yankelovich, 1975).

Further, the continued existence of black student unions on many campuses provides a mechanism for the expression of discontent and the renewal of the movement. It is this organization that the college administration is likely to deal with first on matters of concern to black students. In addition, the union has a political activist heritage, a tradition of success on many campuses and one that can legitimate and support renewed activism. And, of course, the black student union remains a central linkage point between the white campus and the off-campus black community.

Fifth, the image of the quiet campus is as much the result of lessened media coverage of campus events as of any actual decline in student activism. Bayer and Astin (1971) have demonstrated that the campuses in 1970–71, a supposedly quiet year, were not nearly as quiet as popularly supposed. Nor have the years since then been protest-free, especially in the case of black students (Semas, 1976a).

Even if we look only at episodes of black student protest that appeared in the media (primarily the *New York Times*, the *Chronicle of Higher Education*, the *Chicago Tribune*, and various university alumni publications and student newspapers), it is clear that such protest did not disappear after 1970–71. Many of these episodes have involved large-scale protest: sit-ins, building occupations, and other militant tactics.[15]

The misperception that black students have been inactive can also be traced to the view that the salient issues have disappeared because of the alleviation of black grievances and the implementation of substantial

YEAR       SCHOOL

1971–72    Columbia; Harvard; SUNY–Cobleskill
1972–73    Antioch; Boston College; Brandeis; Brown; City College–
           CUNY; Cornell; Harvard, Hunter College–CUNY; MIT;
           Rutgers; U. of California–Santa Barbara; U. of Michigan
1975–76    Columbia; Concordia (Minn.); Cornell; Harvard; Oklahoma U.;
           SUNY–Old Westbury; U. of Alabama–Tuscaloosa; U. of Bridge-
           port (Conn.); U. of California–Berkeley; U. of California–Los
           Angeles; U. of California–San Diego; U. of Massachusetts–
           Amherst; U. of North Carolina–Chapel Hill; U. of Wisconsin–
           Milwaukee
1976–77    Smith; Stanford; U. of California–Berkeley; Vassar
1977–78    Amherst; Harvard; Northwestern; Princeton; U. of California–
           Santa Cruz; U. of Massachusetts–Amherst; Stanford; Wesleyan
           U.; Williams
1978–79    American U.; Amherst; Northwestern; Rutgers; SUNY–Buffalo;
           U. of Michigan; U. of Oregon
1979–80    Augustana College (Ill.); Northwestern; U. of Pennsylvania
1980–81    Harvard; Northwestern; Purdue; Wesleyan U.; Williams
1981–82    Amherst; Cornell; Dartmouth; Harvard; Illinois State U.; North-
           ern Illinois; U. of Illinois–Urbana; U. of Massachusetts–Amherst;
           U. of Wisconsin–Madison
1982–83    Cornell; Harvard; U. of Mississippi; Williams
1983–84    Harvard; Northwestern
1984–85    Columbia; Cornell; Harvard; Northwestern; Rutgers; U. of Cali-
           fornia–Berkeley

changes in campus racial policies (Astin, Astin, et al., 1975). Nevertheless, a number of issues have remained or emerged since 1970: admissions; the recruitment of black faculty members; affirmative action
programs; cut-backs in programs or budgets, especially financial aid
and support programs, and related threats to the presence of black
students on campus; threats to the status of the black student union as a
recognized campus organization; "suddenly" unreasonable or recalci-
trant administrations; Central Intelligence Agency recruiting efforts
aimed at minority students; episodes of open bigotry or racism on
campus; university stockholding in companies operating in South
Africa; and a variety of other issues, local and national. Continuing
black student concern with these issues indicates both the degree to
which movement goals have not been fully achieved and the watch-dog
function of protecting or consolidating movement gains now filled by
many black student unions.

The concern for such issues, continuing black student alienation, and the continued existence of the black student union are conditions making renewed activism likely, even where the movement seems dead or becalmed and organizational vigor and cohesion in the union are low. A good example is provided by University College.

Though their organizational strength had been severely eroded by the fall of 1972, black students in University College became active once more at the start of the semester in opposition to actions of the student government, specifically the publication in the 1972–73 student handbook of a photoengraving depicting black slaves in what black students felt to be a dehumanizing manner. It was meant to symbolize the alleged "slave" status of students and was included in the section of the handbook entitled "University Regulations." Katara demanded its removal. The student government refused. After a week or argument, pressure, and resistance, during which questions of censorship and academic freedom were often raised, the picture was removed and black students received an apology from the student government.

This protest by no means restored Katara's vitality as an organization; nor did it resurrect the movement. However, it illustrates that even where alienated apathy and organizational fragmentation are severe, the movement may re-emerge with the right issue, even if it lapses into a more or less moribund condition thereafter.

From the brief list of protests given above, it is clear that black student activism has not disappeared. Many of these recent episodes have differed from earlier actions in being coalitional. Sometimes they have been "Third World" efforts in which black students have been the central element, but not the sole and separate participants (thus bearing out a prediction made by Edwards, 1970).

This shift has several implications. It may indicate growing political sophistication and realization among black students of the value in certain circumstances (e.g., when issues affecting them also similarly affect others) of allies and coalition politics. Further, it may indicate an ability to mobilize support among potential partisans and sympathizers in the absence of rhetoric or ideologies condemning whites in general. Moreover, it suggests the emergence of issues around which whites and members of other minority groups can rally with black students. Most notable in this regard are demands that colleges and universities divest themselves of stock holdings in companies doing business in South Africa. Also important in creating coalitions have been on-campus episodes of racism (see Middleton, 1981).

An additional difference of some significance is that earlier activism tended to be much more disruptive, and protest incidents were of much longer duration, frequently lasting several days or longer (cf. Astin, Astin, et al., 1975; Barlow and Shapiro, 1971; Cox et al., 1968; Eichel et al., 1970; Urban Research Corporation, 1970). The change partly reflects greater resistance by college authorities and more effective control methods, partly the black gains already made. It may also reflect the current state of the movement—less overtly political and less effectively mobilized. Whatever the reason, there has clearly been a shift in strategy and tactics away from prolonged confrontations and severe disruption (cf. Orum, 1972b).

As Philip Semas (1976b:4) noted in a survey of American campuses, "Even with the demonstrations, much of the new activism can be called—in 1960s terms—'working through the system.' Those who value campus calm should not seek too much comfort in that. The potential for disillusionment still exists." More crucially, as events have demonstrated, the potential for renewed and continued black student activism is likely to persist on white campuses across the country, even if protest is no longer as common as it once was and black students *seem* more privatistic and less political than those of the 1960s.

Despite the changes brought about by previous black student efforts, the potential for continued black student activism remains high. Many conditions have not been materially changed on campus. Interests, programs, and policies of special concern to black students must be protected and maintained. And the lessons of the 1960s are still relevant and available: organize, build solidarity, fight to eradicate inequities or situations adversely affecting black people. These are powerful lessons. White colleges and universities should not assume that they have been forgotten.

# Appendix A
# Innovations in University College
# 1967–68 and 1968–69

I have suggested that campus conditions were an important factor in the development of the black student movement. Among these conditions is the campus atmosphere. In 1967 and 1968, the atmosphere at University College was one of change, produced and indicated by new programs and innovative practices and policies. Among the changes occurring in 1967–68 were the following:

    1. a new department of fine arts established

    2. minors and majors established in Slavic languages and literature, fine arts, and anthropology

    3. experiment with optional pass-fail grading begun

    4. credit point value of honors work increased

    5. joint application made by University College and Fordham (1966–67) for federal support for an Ibero-American program; work going forward (1966–67) on a proposal for a joint program in African studies

    6. interdepartmental minor in African studies established

    7. Metropolitan Leadership Program begun (as the 1966–67 Dean's Report put it: "Proper discontent with the traditional has resulted in approval of the innovating Metropolitan Leadership Program")

    8. the plus-minus grading option approved

    9. a reading week at the end of each semester introduced

    10. right to waive final examinations under certain circumstances granted students and faculty

    11. post of ombudsman created, to be filled by student-elected faculty member

    12. student University College Academic Council established "to provide advice for faculty committees and for the administration in considering student matters and to generate its own ideas which may be fed into the proper College machinery" (Dean's Report, 1967–68)

In 1968–69 such innovations included the following (quotations are from the Dean's Report, 1969):

    1. Curricular Innovation Fund begun

2. cinema and literature course offered for 1969–70

3. literature in translation courses offered for 1969–70

4. Hebrew courses offered for 1969–70

5. Urban Studies Preceptorials (to begin 1969–70): seminar-type courses focused on "topical inter-disciplinary themes related to the urban environment"

6. intensive summer language courses offered in the summer of 1969

7. Probe Courses introduced: course material divided into units and tested by short oral "probes"; students proceed at their own rate; grade determined by the number of probes completed; same probe could be taken several times until mastered

8. University Scholars Seminars augmented with the institution of two-credit seminars, limited enrollment, interdisciplinary and problem-centered courses for 1969–70

9. strengthened departmental majors: history and English increased major requirements from 24 to 30 credits

10. reform of the history curriculum (to begin 1969–70): History of Western Civilization dropped as a required course; students could substitute any of seven courses to fulfill history requirement; curriculum rearranged in a "broad sequential pattern"; a number of one-term seminars introduced of which students majoring in history were required to take two

11. reform of the anthropology curriculum

12. Metropolitan Leadership Program continued

13. Institute for Computer Research in the Humanities continued

14. Curriculum Commission established: large-scale review looking toward reform of the entire College curriculum; report, submitted in fall of 1969, recommended significant reduction in the number and weight of College requirements and restrictions

15. the Four Course Investigation: decision by University College faculty to encourage greater flexibility in designing course weights

16. continuation of reforms introduced in 1967–68: reading period; plus/minus grading system; pass/fail option

17. commissions studying a wide range of issues, including the Stone affair; curriculum; University and College governance; faculty personnel decisions; student affairs

18. departmental reorganization for greater responsiveness to students; student participation on departmental committees

19. sweeping reform of student government; formation of Student Senate

In both years such activity contributed to a general perception that change and innovation were possible. The College presented the image of a flexible, responsive institution. In this sense, these innovations probably encouraged black students in their efforts. The idea that social changes lead to raised expectations and new perceptions of the gap between aspirations and reality, and hence to active protest, is germane here (cf. Brinton, 1965; Gurr, 1970).

# Appendix B
# Comparative Data
# on Black Students

There was a widespread belief in the College that incoming black students were, as a group, both significantly inferior in their academic preparation and much poorer than the typical College student. While they may have been less affluent, they were *not* necessarily from hard-core poverty backgrounds. And if their academic preparation was somewhat inferior, it was not because they went to all-black ghetto high schools. With only two exceptions, the thirty students interviewed reported having attended predominantly white, non-ghetto schools.

Comparative data on black and white students were difficult to obtain, not least because much of the information kept by College offices reportedly was not specific as to race. There were similar difficulties associated with comparing MLK students with other financial aid students or with non–financial aid students. Systematic records and information on MLK students were not kept from 1968 through the spring of 1970. Further, MLK and other financial aid data apparently were affected by changes in personnel, office procedures, filing systems, and so on. (For other difficulties in collecting data, see Appendix C).

It is, however, still possible to make some comparisons between MLK students and other financial aid students on a number of dimensions. These are presented in Table 1. In addition to the limitations noted above, a few other points should be made. The year listed is the academic year starting in September. The mean college grade point average is for second-semester freshmen and upper classmen. Finally, in every year except 1971–72, all, or the majority, of MLK recipients were black.

*Table 1. MLK Recipients*

| | Mean Family Income | | | | Mean Financial Aid Award | | | |
|---|---|---|---|---|---|---|---|---|
| | 1968 | 1969 | 1970 | 1971 | 1968 | 1969 | 1970 | 1971 |
| MLK Recipients | $8,100 | 8,379 | 8,441 | 8,960 | — | 2,025 | 2,248 | 2,200 |
| Other Financial Aid Recipients | $8,937 | 9,810 | 10,736 | 12,251 | 1,417 | 973 | 1,175 | 1,456 |

*and Non-MLK Financial Aid Recipients*

| | Mean SAT Scores: Verbal/math | | | Mean High School Grade Point Average | | | | Mean College Grade Point Average* | | | |
|---|---|---|---|---|---|---|---|---|---|---|---|
| 1968 | 1969 | 1970 | 1971 | 1968 | 1969 | 1970 | 1971 | 1968 | 1969 | 1979 | 1971 |
| — | 360/560 | 528/523 | 535/568 | 3.2 | 3.6 | 3.36 | 2.2 | 3.0 | 2.4 | 2.4 | — |
| 641/661 | 626/630 | 616/630 | 593/617 | 3.5 | 3.6 | 3.6 | 3.5 | 3.0 | 2.9 | 3.1 | 3.0 |

*The predicted average for MLK recipients was 2.18 in each year. The predictions were made by the admissions committee as a means of estimating the likely performance and success of recipients.

# Appendix C
# Research Design and Method

This study has examined the development of the black student movement in University College through two approaches: analysis of archival and documentary materials and direct questioning. The basic aims were (1) a reconstruction of salient events and policies at University College during the period in question (1966–71); (2) the building of a detailed, substantive chronology of events and conditions relating to the black student movement; (3) an account of episodes of activism and protest, as well as the events preceding and immediately following each. On-going activities and relations between black students and others in the College were as important as specific significant events in shaping the social context in which the black student movement developed. Both documentary evidence and direct questioning yielded valuable information in this regard.

As for principal episodes of activism, the actions and views of all parties— black students, white students, faculty, administrators—were again examined through direct questioning and documentary evidence.

Certain difficulties were involved in achieving this reconstruction with accuracy and insight. In the first place, any study that relies heavily on personal views and evaluations, on remembrances and opinions, is faced with the problem of distorted, incomplete, or faulty recollection of the past. This problem can be significant in research on student protest based on retrospective questioning (see Meyer, 1971:259). I endeavored to minimize the problem by using documentary evidence and interview information from a variety of informants as a check on self-reports. I also compared documents with each other (as well as with interview data) to check their reliability, since documents may be as incomplete or selective as individual recall.

A further difficulty was the unavailability or inaccessibility of records and archival sources. Repeated attempts were made to gain access to all necessary documents, but certain kinds were generally unavailable, in particular confidential family and financial aid information. Not surprisingly, neither the financial aid office nor the admissions office would open up its files on individual students. However, some aggregate data were provided by both.

Because of these limitations I had to rely for such information on other documents and interviews. One consequence is the absence of the kind of detailed information on black students' socioeconomic backgrounds and characteristics that would have allowed for more precise and meaningful comparisons within the black student group and between black and white students. Such comparisons might have enabled me to suggest connections between socioeconomic characteristics and the black student movement in University College.

An additional difficulty has to do with the unavailability or inaccessibility of important individuals as informants. There was the problem of reaching persons no longer on campus: former faculty members, administrators, and students. Some of those whom it was particularly important to contact—for example, students who had been influential or notably active—were still in the New York City area and could be reached; others had left the area and could not be contacted; some of those contacted refused to be interviewed. In the latter instances reliance had to be placed on available documentary and interview information.

Finally, there was the crucial difficulty of estimating the number of black students on campus and their characteristics during the period examined. Enrollment statistics may have been misleading, though not in any consistent direction. At the time of the study the state of New York prohibited questions about race or ethnic membership on college admissions forms. Hence, the admissions office and the recorder's office had a limited idea of how many black or other minority students entered with each class or enrolled in classes each term. It is known that the 1968–69 freshmen class had 70 black students, the largest number in a single class in University College before or after. Each subsequent freshman class had fewer black students. Allowing for attrition and basing an estimate on fragmentary aggregate data, there seem to have been no more than 150 black students in the College in 1971–72.

Further, financial aid data before the establishment of the MLK scholarship program were of little help. For example, in the freshmen class entering in 1967 there were reportedly 189 students receiving some form of financial aid. There were 13 black students in that class, but no one had precise information on how many were on financial aid beyond saying "only a few."

Enrollment statistics may not have accurately indicated the number of black students for still other reasons. University College shared the Heights campus with the School of Engineering. Hence, black students enrolled in Engineering were not counted in College statistics, though they were on campus and could join the activities of black students in the College. Moreover, enrollment statistics did not take into consideration that fact that some black students who lived at the Heights were actually enrolled at Washington Square. This was particularly true in the case of athletes. Such resident black students could have participated in on-campus activities, but they did not show up in College statistics. In addition, it is possible that campus residents are more visible and more likely to get counted than students living off campus. In sum, various sources are likely to over- or underestimate the number of black students on campus. The figures used in this study are the best approximations available, drawn from a number of sources.


## THE "SAMPLE"

Given the approach followed in this study, it might seem somewhat misleading to speak of a sample. In some ways its method is as close to that of history as that of sociology. Further, in a case study, one is dealing with informants rather than respondents. At the same time, however, the case study does involve a form of sampling, a decision to choose one case, rather than several others, from the universe of possible cases. I have essentially sampled within a sample: University College is the principal research case, and black students as well as faculty members and administrators are the relevant population in terms of the research case.

NYU's University College was chosen as the research case for several reasons. First, the great increase in black student recruitment and enrollment had occurred recently enough (circa 1966–69) to allow one to trace the beginnings and the development of the movement. Second, NYU's traditional "school of opportunity" philosophy might be expected to predispose it to be receptive and hospitable to blacks. Third, University College seemed fairly typical of white institutions in which black student activism has occurred (see Astin and Bayer, 1971; Bayer, 1971; Bayer and Astin, 1969, 1971; Urban Research Corporation, 1970, for detailed discussions of the characteristics of schools in which student protest, black as well as white, has occurred). Fourth, because of its location, it was accessible to the researcher. Fifth, University College was already somewhat familiar, as were some of the students involved in the study, since I had taught one class part-time in the sociology department in the fall terms of 1970 through 1972. At the same time, I had no strong, pre-existing vested interest in the College. And sixth, the practical question of available research resources made the College a good choice.

The population from which informants were sought within University College comprised all black students on campus (including former students) as well as all faculty members and administrators. I was less concerned with achieving the kind of random sample and representativeness required by survey and other types of research than with finding what Sjoberg and Nett (1968:220) call strategic informants: "Those informants who become the researcher's eyes and ears in indirect observation." Such informants have knowledge, experience, or a valuable perspective on the phenomenon in question. They may be leaders or active participants, as well as active—that is, deliberate—*non*-participants.

Interviews were sought with students who had held or were holding office in Katara or who were deemed leaders or influential by others during the period under study. Almost all of the 1970–72 leadership of Katara was interviewed, as well as leaders from September 1967 to June 1970. Also included in this group of desirable informants were those who had been involved in protests or in the formulation of proposals, demands, negotiations with the University, and so on. I focused especially on students who had been upperclassmen during 1968–69 and 1969–70, the time of greatest black student activity. Comparative information was gathered from some freshmen and sophomores, but the bulk of my informants were juniors and seniors in those years. I also tried, with some limited success, to reach students who had *never* been active in Katara and had taken no part in protest. The same individual sometimes fell into several informant categories simultaneously. Such informants proved to be especially significant.

On the whole, cooperation from students contacted was somewhat better than expected. It is important to note that four students who had been involved in movement activities explicitly refused to be interviewed because the memory was too painful or was part of a past they wanted to forget. This small datum about the personal consequences of movement participation seems significant in connection with the issues of movement decline, failure, disaffection, and internal hostility discussed earlier. A few other students refused to be interviewed on grounds that such information could be used by government agencies, or by the University, against black students. This belief reflects a generalized wariness of white authorities (especially government and law-enforcement agencies) that I have often observed among black students, especially during the period in question, and that is not uncommon in the larger black population.

Concentrating on leaders and influential members, seniors and juniors, active participants, and committed non-participants necessarily limited the number of student interviews, as did occasional unwillingness to be interviewed. I obtained a final total of usable interviews from thirty students (Table 2).

*Table 2. Student Informants*

|  | Freshmen and Sophomores | Juniors | Seniors | Former Students | Total |
|---|---|---|---|---|---|
| Active Participants | 4 | 7 | 8 | 4 | 23 |
| Active Non-Participants | 1 | 3 | 2 | 1 | 7 |
| Total | 5 | 10 | 10 | 5 | 30 |

Clearly, I did not attempt to interview the entire black student population in University College, both because the research design did not require it, and because considerations of time and practicality did not allow it. This, of course, raises the problem of the representativeness of my informants, particularly in the absence of attempts to gather a random sample.

Virtually all of my student informants who had been active in protests appear to be similar to the larger black student population in the College. Hence, though not necessarily representative, they do not seem to have been atypical. All but three were from New York City or its metropolitan area (Long Island, Westchester County, southern Connecticut, and northern New Jersey). This is in line with the statement of a staff member of the admissions office, who observed that in the years since 1967–68, "we've recruited very heavily in the high schools of New York and its environs for black students. This is where most of our students come from" (Administrative/Faculty Interview no. 1).

Six were from West Indian backgrounds, and the rest were American blacks. There are no data on the proportion of College students from West Indian and American backgrounds; hence, the significance of this proportion in terms of the typically of my informants is difficult to assess. It may be worth noting that when freshmen and sophomores are excluded, all but two of the inactive informants were from West Indian backgrounds.

I did not ask about family income and parental occupations in terms of specific dollar amounts or specific jobs, not least because these are touchy subjects for people generally and were especially so for black students during the period examined. However, all but two active informants said that they came from middle- or working-class backgrounds. This seems to be in line with the status of black students in the College; for example, the mean family income of MLK recipients was consistently between $8,000 and $9,000—not affluent, but in those years not poor either.

Half of my informants, both active and inactive, were MLK recipients. This is a somewhat lower proportion than existed in the total black student population: 50 of the 70 black freshmen who entered in 1968 were holders of MLK grants, a proportion that remained much the same in subsequent classes. Almost a quarter of my informants (7), though not MLK recipients, indicated that they either had other financial aid from the College or had taken out loans of various kinds. Again, it is difficult to know how this proportion compares with the total black student body, since the financial aid offices break down financial aid by racial or ethnic categories, as far as I could find, only in the case of the MLK grant program.

Only three student informants had not attended public high schools; these had attended parochial schools. Only two reported having gone to predominantly black high schools, but a few observed that the predominantly white high schools they had attended before 1968 and 1969 had, by 1971–72, either become predominantly black or appeared to be shifting in that direction. Unfortunately, it is impossible to determine whether this high school background is typical; such information was unavailable from the admissions office.

Interviews with faculty members and administrators focused primarily on those who seemed to have been the most involved with black students or most involved in black student actions, especially those who took part in policy decisions and negotiations. These persons were initially determined from a chronology of events based on documentary sources. Members of the offices of the provost and the dean, the counseling office, the student affairs office, faculty committees, and the general faculty were interviewed. Twenty consented to be interviewed out of thirty-five approached.

In many cases informants, both students and faculty members, referred me to or suggested other people with whom I should talk. Such suggestions proved to be an invaluable source of information, especially useful in highlighting important issues and opening up new areas of interest and investigation.

There was a possibility that there would tend to be a uniformity of opinion among those suggesting others to interview and those so suggested. This problem, however, was minimal. Quite frequently the persons suggested proved to hold very different views from the original informants. In many instances they were suggested precisely because they were believed to hold different or opposing views.

## METHODS OF DATA COLLECTION

### Documents, Archives and Published Information

An often invaluable but sometimes neglected source of information for sociologists is found in documents and archival material. The use of such materials has, of course, its limitations. For one thing, bias may be introduced through selectivity and discrimination in what goes into documents, creating problems of "selective deposit and selective survival" (Webb et al., 1966).

The usefulness of journalistic accounts is also limited by the bias that may be introduced by editorial policy and opinion; biased reporting; views of what is "newsworthy"; and, in the case of student newspapers especially, outside control, whether exercised by the administration or a particular student group.

Despite these limitations (which, as noted, were dealt with primarily through the use of a wide variety of documentary sources and interviews as checks), documents were a crucial source of data on a range of issues. Principal documentary and archival sources examined included:

1. admissions, financial aid, and enrollment records and statistics

2. administrative files and accounts where available (President's Reports, Dean's Reports, committee reports and minutes, University and Student Senate reports, minutes of faculty and administrative meetings)

3. university charters, by-laws, faculty handbooks, student handbooks and conduct codes, written regulations

4. college histories, archives, yearbooks, alumni bulletins

5. student newspaper articles, editorials, student activities calendars, files, and archives

6. black student organization documents

*Interviews*

Interviewing was the second important method of data collection employed in this study. As noted, administrators, faculty members, and black students were interviewed. Primary interviewing was carried out between February and June 1972, with some additional interviews gathered during the 1972–73 academic year.

The interviews were focused and semistructured. This procedure assumes that those interviewed have been involved in or have important knowledge of a particular situation; thus, it required looking carefully for key individuals as informants. Some interviews were both focused and objectifying, to use the term coined by Sjoberg and Nett (1968). In such an interview

> the researcher informs the interviewee from the start, as well as at intervals during the questioning process, concerning the kinds of information he is seeking and why. The informant is apprised of his role in the scientific process. . . . Besides examining his own actions, the interviewee is encouraged to observe and interpret the behavior of his associates in his social group. (Sjoberg and Nett, 1968:214)

I used focused, objectifying interviews for informants who were hesitant about being interviewed without knowing specifically what kinds of information were sought and why. This was notably the case with some administrators to whom access is normally limited and with those black students who were suspicious about questioning concerning political actions.

Like any research method, this procedure has certain limitations. There is the possibility that the interviewee will take over the interview and lead it, deliberately or not, in directions other than those emphasized by the researcher. And, as in any interview, there is the possibility that the interviewee may respond with answers that he thinks the researcher wants or expects.

Basically, the questions asked emphasized actions, feelings, evaluations, and beliefs about specified situations and behavior. All questions were asked of all student informants, active and inactive. In each case I tried to avoid too rigid an adherence to the interview schedule, letting the interview flow whenever it seemed appropriate, probing and asking questions not on the schedule to elicit information about issues or statements that seemed especially significant. Though faculty members and administrators were generally asked different questions from students, some parallel questions were asked of both groups about the same events, issues, or situations.

This has been an exploratory case study. My basic aim has been to generate propositions or ideas that can be applied to other cases in order to increase our understanding of the phenomenon of black student activism in the white university. I have tried to promote insight into black student movements by building a sociological history of one case through analytical description and reconstruction.

# Notes

## PREFACE

1. For example: Barlow and Shapiro (1971); Bunzel (1969); Chrisman (1969); Clift (1969); Cobb and McDew (1974); Cohen (1970); W. R. Corson (1970); Donald (1970, 1971, 1973); Foster (1970); Gershman (1969); Ginzberg (1969); Goldman (1970); Harding (1969); Harper (1969, 1971); D. Henderson (1970); Horowitz and Friedland (1970); Karagueuzian (1971); Kilson (1973*a*, 1973*b*); Lipset (1971); Litwak and Wilner (1971); Long (1970*a*); Lusky and Lusky (1969); McEvoy and Miller (1969); Metzger (1970); Obear (1970); Proctor (1970); Strout and Grossvogel (1971); Tarcov (1969); Thelwell (1970); Wisdom and Shaw (1970).

## INTRODUCTION

1. Part of the reason for this decline may be the fact that by the end of 1970–71 almost two-thirds of American colleges and universities offered some kind of program of black or ethnic studies and had instituted increased recruitment of black and other minority students, two central issues in black student activism. Indeed, during the peak period of student activism (January 1968 through June 1970), the most common single cause of protest was the demand for special educational programs of various kinds for blacks and other minorities (Bayer and Astin, 1971; Urban Research Corporation, 1970).

The decline in protest was exaggerated by the change in media coverage. For example, it is often assumed that 1970–71 saw a tremendous falling off in activism and a return of calm to the nation's campuses. However, as Bayer and Astin (1971) demonstrate, this was by no means the case; protest and activism declined in 1970–71 to a level only slightly below that of 1968–69, a peak year for protest. As they point out, the apparent calm on campus was an illusion created by the absence of media coverage. In 1968–69, 40 percent of the campuses experiencing protests got national coverage; in 1970–71, only 10 percent did—hence, the appearance of calm.

2. See Jencks and Riesman (1968); McGrath (1965); and Walters (1974). Ann Jones (1973) suggests that this situation persisted on some black campuses into the 1970s.

3. As I shall argue, perhaps the most significant continuity lies in the goals of black students in each period of the 1960s. That is, both the black activists in the South in the first half of the decade and those on white campuses in the years following were basically reformist rather than revolutionary in their essential aims, despite the tendency of others to misperceive this. As many have noted, black student activists in the southern civil rights struggles were motivated primarily by a desire to remedy their sense of acute and unfair deprivation; they wanted to enjoy the fruits of American society and participate in it as fully as anyone else, and on the same terms (Geschwender and Geschwender, 1973; Matthews and Prothro, 1969; Miles, 1971; Orum, 1972; Rosenthal, 1975; Warren, 1975). They were not out to alter society radically, but only to reform and restructure part of it. Similarly, black student activists on white campuses have not attempted to destroy or radically alter the white university—after all, it is their primary vehicle of social mobility—but only to reform certain aspects of it (Bell and Kristol, 1969; Browne, 1968; Clift, 1969; Horowitz and Friedland, 1970; Lipset, 1971). Black student activist groups have aimed at advancing themselves and other blacks socioeconomically, politically, and perhaps psychologically. Further, black student activists in the late 1960s and early 1970s used tactics, strategies, and often ideas developed by students during the earlier period.

4. The role of spokesmen or campus representatives of the larger black community, especially the more disadvantaged portions of it, is one contemporary black students have often adopted, even if it is not delegated to them by that larger community. In this respect the students' attitude toward fellow blacks in the ghetto is not unlike that of students in underdeveloped countries, first in their identification with those not in college (cf. Lipset, 1967), and second in their view that societal and black problems are intimately interconnected (cf. Bakke, 1967).

## CHAPTER I

1. Here the terms "activism" and "protest" are used interchangeably, even though it might seem that "protest" is a somewhat narrower term, referring to actions taken specifically *against* something. Both terms are used in this study to refer to collective action by students aimed at bringing about change in existing educational, social, and/or political structures, policies, and practices. Included in the definition are a wide variety of behaviors, ranging from calm requests for meetings with officials, through the calling of assemblies and the peaceful presentation of requests, to demands, disruption of classes, occupation of buildings, destruction of property, bodily injury, and clashes with law enforcement agents.

2. Many of the classic writers in sociology have produced important work on various aspects of social movements. Marx, for example, locates the origin of movements and movement values in class conflict. Feuer (1969) and Heberle (1951) provide more extended discussions of this point. Moreover, through his emphasis on dialectical materialism and class conflict as the continuous process of history, Marx indicates that movements and collective actions for change will be recurrent (at least until the final revolution) because they are the expression of rising class consciousness. Tocqueville's study of the *ancien régime* presents one of the first versions of the theory of rising expectations and relative deprivation producing increased discontent and mobilization for remedial action. For important recent work on relative deprivation, see Gurr (1970). Certainly the work of Michels is relevant here; his "Iron Law of Oligarchy" suggests what happens in the process of movement institutionalization. Weber made major contributions to the study of the sources of movement values (in terms of "prophecies"), organization and leadership, transformation via routinization, and the problems of leadership succession, particularly in movements characterized by charismatic leadership. Other important work on the origins and sources of movement beliefs and values may be found in Blumer (1951b, 1953), Cantril (1958), Gusfield (1963), Heberle (1951), Mannheim (1946, 1952), R. Turner (1969), and Wallace (1956). See Oberschall (1973), Turner and Killian (1972), and John Wilson (1973) for comprehensive and useful presentations of ideas and theories about social movements. Charles Tilly (1978) provides an excellent discussion of resource mobilization, one of the newest perspectives on social movements.

3. Most treatments of institutionalization have followed the classic Weber-Michels model. Hiller (1975), Toch (1965), and Zald and Ash (1966) present arguments somewhat different from the classical model and, as we shall see in the final chapters, somewhat more applicable to the black student movement.

4. The question of member commitment, adherence, and participation has concerned many students of social movements (e.g., Blumer, 1953; Cantril, 1958, 1963; Hiller, 1975; Gusfield, 1963; Kanter, 1968; Lanternari, 1963; Toch, 1965; Wallace, 1956).

5. Perhaps the oldest and most common distinction is that between reform and revolutionary movements (e.g., Blumer, 1951b). An elaborated version of this distinction is Cameron's (1966) typology of reactionary, conservative, revisionist, revolutionary, and escapist movements. Wallace (1956) subsumes reform, revolutionary, revivalist, and nationalist movements under the single rubric of revitalization movement. Some discussions have distinguished between violent and non-violent movements (Cameron, 1966; Fanon, 1968; Sorel, 1961), and others between radical and general movements (Mauss, 1971). In general, movement typologies are based on one or some combination of three criteria: (1) purposes, goals, and degree of change sought; (2) degree of organization; and (3) degree of coordination (King, 1961; see also John Wilson, 1973). Regardless of differences in typology, almost all observers agree that societal conditions, perhaps inevitably, produce social movements.

## CHAPTER II

1. See W. O Brown (1931, 1935) and Pitts (1974, 1975) on the importance of race consciousness for political socialization and organized political activity.

2. There is a wealth of work describing and analyzing these developments and their impact on the political socialization of blacks (e.g., Anthony, 1971; Ballard, 1973; Barlow and Shapiro, 1971; Canfield, 1973; K. B. Clark, 1969; Cox et al., 1968; Donadio, 1968a; Donald, 1970, 1971, 1973; Edwards, 1970; Flacks, 1971b; Ginzberg, 1969; Greene and Winter, 1971; Gurin and Epps, 1975; Harding, 1969; Howard, 1971; Krueger and Silvert, 1975; Ladner, 1967; Long, 1970a; McEvoy and Miller, 1969; Miles, 1971; Napper, 1973; National Advisory Commission on Civil Disorders, 1968; Nelson, 1971; Perkins and Higginson, 1971; Pitts, 1975; President's Commission on Campus Unrest, 1971; Pugh, 1972; Rosenthal, 1975; Schuman and Hatchett, 1974; Skolnick, 1969).

3. That is, the first enunciation in its contemporary form: many of its ideas are close to those of such earlier black leaders as Marcus Garvey. See Gerlach and Hine (1970) for a study of the Black Power movement in the United States.

4. Carmichael's views at this point are most cogently presented in the book he coauthored with Charles V. Hamilton (1967), which received wide attention and had great impact.

5. See Krueger and Silvert (1975), Miles (1971), and Pitts (1975) on the impact of various cultural, literary, and intellectual developments in this regard.

6. See Barlow and Shapiro (1971); Bunzel (1969); Goldman (1970). Indeed, by the fall of 1967 San Francisco State was beginning to experience full-fledged, large-scale protest by black and other minority students.

7. Grove, Remy, and Zeigler (1974) provide an indication of the role of organized discontent and dissatisfaction and of the influence of early political socialization on later political beliefs and behavior. See Green (1972) and Pitts (1975) for good discussions of the political socialization of black children and adolescents in terms of these developments.

Protest was widespread in the nation's high schools and even junior high schools in the late 1960s. For example, Liberale and Seligson (1970) note that in the spring of 1969 alone, over 56 percent of the nation's *junior* high schools reported some student protest. The implications of this for college student activism have been inadequately explored. It is possible that at least a significant portion of student activism in colleges and universities results from political socialization and radicalization in the community and in the school (rather than in the family) *before* entry into college (cf. Pitts, 1975). This seems likely for both white and black students; indeed, such pre-college socialization may have been even more important for black students. For example, a significant portion of the protests in junior and senior high schools during the late 1960s involved or were initiated by black students (Lemberg Center, 1968–69). It is also possible that the apparent dramatic decline in student activism after 1970 is partially attributable to the entry into college of students who had participated in protests during high school or earlier. Thus, though not necessarily any less radical or alienated from the college, they had already come to see the limits and ineffectuality of on-campus protest in terms of producing off-campus change. Further, by the time these students arrived on campus, a number of on-campus changes had been produced or attempted by previous college generations. There may have been few remaining issues salient enough to overcome the cynical and alienated apathy of these students.

8. See Berube and Gittell (1969), Harris and Swanson (1970), and Hentoff (1969) for more complete discussion of these controversies and their consequences.

9. One was the NYU–South Bronx Project, begun in 1964 with the aim of providing a comprehensive program of educational help and services for junior high school students in the South Bronx and fighting the poverty and attendant disadvantages so prevalent there. Another was the Neighborhood Tutorial Project. It began as a means of increasing the involvement of students and the College in the surrounding community, promoting understanding between the community and the College, and providing help to a neighborhood rapidly becoming black and Puerto Rican. Though student-initiated and staffed, it was part of an agency operating under Office of Economic Opportunity auspices and thus was not a part of or funded by either the College or the larger University, although it had the College's official sanction and approval.

10. Although these activities expanded throughout the year and were praised by both the dean of the College and the director of student affairs, an assistant dean was moved to complain by mid-spring 1967 of the general apathy on campus. Indeed, this administrator urged students to be active and to agitate, if they felt it necessary, in support of the social issues that concerned and moved them (HDN, 19 March). The endorsement of the assistant dean and the director of student affairs can be seen as providing a kind of official sanction for student activism on social issues.

11. This stance on HDN's part is important in several senses. It is an early instance of a recurring phenomenon: consistent and continual support by HDN (and often student government as well) for the aims and goals, if not the tactics, of black students throughout the period under study. Moreover, the editorial advocated preferential treatment and a large financial expenditure to benefit blacks, even before black students became politically active as a coherent, organized group, and without their specific urging.

12. In the discussions of events in University College in this and subsequent chapters, all names used are pseudonyms, with the exception of James Hester and the late Allan Cartter (president and chancellor of the University, respectively, in the period covered), who may be considered public figures.

13. The suggestion that special achievement tests be required for admission had been narrowly rejected the previous year after much faculty debate (see Dean's Report, 1966–67). It is worth recalling, in this regard, the introduction and use of entrance examinations in University College in an earlier era.

## CHAPTER III

1. Anthony (1971), Barlow and Shapiro (1971), Gurin and Epps (1975), Krueger and Silvert (1975), Lao (1970), Matthews and Prothro (1969), Miles (1971), and Perkins and Higginson (1971) provide interesting discussions of the importance of ideological beliefs. See Gold, Friedman, and Christie (1971) for a more general discussion of the role of attitudes and beliefs in political, and especially protest, behavior; and Grove, Remy, and Ziegler (1974) for a discussion of political attitudes and ideologies as a source of on-campus educational discontent.

2. Astin (1970b); Bayer (1972, 1973); Bayer and Boruch (1969a, 1969b); Bell and Kristol (1969); Boyd (1947b); Bradley (1967); Centra (1970a); Davis, Loeb, and Robinson (1970); Gaier and Watts (1969); Gist and Bennett (1963); Hedegard (1972); Morgan (1970); K. Wilson (1969); Yankelovich (1975).

In addition to studies directly comparing black and white students, there are many that focus on black students: e.g., Astin and Cross (1981); Attman and Snyder (1971); Banks (1970); Bayer and Boruch (1969a); Blumenfeld (1968); Bowles and DeCosta (1971); Boyd (1981); Caliver (1971); Clark and Plotkin (1963); Egerton (1969); Gurin and Epps (1975); Gurin, Gurin, Lao, and Beattie (1969); Miller (1969); Stanfiel (1976); Willie and McCord (1972).

Some of these studies on educational aspiration and performance were done before there were large numbers of black students in the schools studied and before the implementation of open-enrollment policies in some public colleges and universities. The question clearly calls for more research.

3. Centra (1970a); Donaldson and Pride (1969); Forbes and Gipson (1969); Stanfiel (1976); Yankelovich (1972, 1975). There is evidence (Orum and Cohen, 1973) that such political orientations develop in black children as early as eleven years of age. This suggests that the political socialization of black and white children may be very different (cf. also Green, 1972). It also points up the impact of race in a racially stratified society and the role of off-campus developments in the black student movement as noted earlier. See also Pitts (1975) in this latter regard.

Several observers have noted that this political awareness and militance are often expressed in a go-it-alone, autonomous style (Anthony, 1971; Donadio, 1968a; Edwards, 1970; Horowitz and Friedland, 1970). This style is often combined with high vocationalism; "in this way, two main ambitions of the black students are served: upward mobility in the economic world and ideological purity in the political world" (Horowitz and Friedland, 1970:199).

4. These discussions of black student characteristics prior to 1967 are based on aggregate College statistical data; student and alumni interviews; information in published College and University documents; and interviews with members of the College admissions committee and the counseling and student affairs offices.

5. This is likely true even for those who attended integrated schools or lived

in integrated neighborhoods. Even for those students, the white college, especially the residential college, is the first situation in which they live intimately and continuously with whites. Although he does not specify how it happens, Orbell (1967:466) suggests that "proximity to the white culture increases the likelihood of protest involvement." Two reasons for this might be suggested: an increased sense of alienation, and an increased sense of relative deprivation. Also see Willie (1981) for a discussion of the stressful consequences of increased black and white interaction.

6. For example: Boyd (1974b, 1981); Burbach and Thompson (1971); Clift (1969); Gurin, Gurin, Lao, and Beattie (1969); Harper (1971); Hedegard (1972); Hedegard and Brown (1969); Kleinbaum and Kleinbaum (1976); Miller (1969); Naughton (1972); Pugh (1972); Walters (1974); Willie (1981); Willie and McCord (1972); Yankelovich (1972, 1975).

In addition to experienced discontinuity and disjuncture, black student alienation may also be determined in part by the widespread alienation from white society and its institutions among blacks in general (Gottlieb, 1969; Middleton, 1963; Paige, 1971; Schuman and Hatchett, 1974; D. I. Warren, 1975), and the fact that student alienation seems to be an integral part of university or college life (Apter, 1974; Etzioni, 1961a; Miles, 1974).

7. See J. P. Clark (1959); Dean (1961); Gould (1969); Josephson and Josephson (1962); Nettler (1957); Seeman (1959, 1971). A useful discussion is found in Middleton (1963), who delimits six meanings and forms of alienation: powerlessness, meaninglessness, normlessness, cultural estrangement, social estrangement, and estrangement from work. Interestingly, he found that on every dimension except cultural estrangement blacks are more alienated than whites. Gamson (1968) has suggested that alienation may be a matter of a sense of one's perceived efficacy (individually or collectively) and/or a trust orientation and, along with Etzioni (1961a), that it may also be a matter of commitment to and involvement in formal organizations. Both the Gamson and the Etzioni conceptions may be seen as aspects of "system" alienation rather than as simply psychological states. Finally, the idea of alienation as self-estrangement should be added to the list of meanings.

8. For a discussion of authenticity focusing on both its structural and its sociopsychological dimensions see Trilling (1972).

9. Gurin, Newcomb, and Cope (1968) indicate the degree of strain such conditions place on personal resources, and Neal and Seeman (1974) suggest the frequency with which organization is a response to these conditions.

10. At the same time, it must be emphasized that the organization can also play a *coercive* role in the realm of beliefs and behavior, rewarding the expression of certain views and actions while punishing others. This tendency toward coercion seems to be not uncommon in movement organizations (Bittner, 1963; D. E. Morrison, 1973), particularly in power-oriented as opposed to participation-oriented ones (D. E. Morrison, 1973; Turner and Killian, 1972). Unfortunately, as we shall see, such insistence on ideological and behavioral conformity and social solidarity has been a major force for disunity among black students (see Napper, 1973). More generally, Gamson (1975) indicates that reliance on

solidary incentives alone, even if coercively applied, may not be sufficient to prevent disunity.

11. This sense of their own efficacy was also increased by political and ideological developments off campus (see Flacks, 1969, on the legacy of the civil rights movement in this regard); and by positive college actions vis-à-vis black students (see McEvoy and Miller, 1969).

12. See Caplan (1971), Forward and Williams (1970), and Paige (1971) for empirical support of this idea in terms of off-campus black populations. Jackson (1971a) presents a rather different view of the relation of a sense of political efficacy to protest efforts among black students. Jackson found that a high sense of political efficacy produces *traditional* kinds of political activity and that political cynicism was associated with *protest* activity. If cynicism is associated with lost trust, the point argued in this study and suggested by Gamson (1968) is supported.

13. The organization by this point had already begun the practice of not announcing its meetings to the general campus public via the student activities calendar in HDN. This announcement was the last time that committees of the organization would publicly announce their plans or activities, except when the organization sponsored an event for which general campus attendance or participation was desired.

14. The two-month delay between the opening of the school year and indication of the demise of ACCESS illustrates the degree to which black students kept to themselves information about their meetings or activities. This was standard procedure for Katara at this point in its career.

15. These developments—the split within ACCESS, the appearance of Katara, the "loin-girding" and consciousness-raising silence of black students through most of 1967–68, coupled with occasional militant (but non-programmatic) public statements—are all to be expected in the early stage of a movement (cf. Killian, 1964). As Miles (1971:226) points out, this tendency to "endorse the radical doctrines in advance of any direct engagement with university authorities" was typical of black students in a number of colleges and universities, perhaps because "racial solidarity is one appeal, if effectively developed, which can mobilize support for the black left in an otherwise unsympathetic environment."

## CHAPTER IV

1. The Hall of Fame of Great Americans was located on the University Heights campus of NYU (now the campus of Bronx Community College of the City University of New York), administered by NYU though under federal jurisdiction. Nomination and election to membership in the Hall of Fame is made by a college of electors. This body, composed of 156 members representing all fifty states, is selected by the NYU University Senate. Candidates for the Hall of Fame may also be nominated by the general public. Normally, to be

eligible, candidates must have been dead for twenty-five years or more. Election is by majority vote of the electors.

2. This demand was eventually fulfilled a few years later. By this point there were probably few, if any, black students interested in joining a white fraternity of any sort. The demand is significant as an indication of students' determination to remove all vestiges of overt discrimination and racism from the College.

3. As of spring 1968 the University had approximately 1,850 black students enrolled in its various divisions (out of a total student enrollment in excess of 40,000), 1,100 as regular students and 750 as special students. University College had one of the lowest black enrollments, especially in comparison with other undergraduate divisions of the University.

4. Among the many assumptions apparently operating here was a belief that these new students would come predominantly from poor academic and socioeconomic backgrounds. See Appendix B for data comparing black students receiving MLK aid with other financial aid students in University College.

5. This last was in response to a late Katara proposal brought up between 10 and 17 April. The idea involved was not unlike the one behind the demands for community control and decentralized local school boards then agitating the city. Essentially, the students were endorsing a Harlem CORE project. The significance of the formulation of these six committees, and the apparent enthusiasm for them on campus, lies in the fact that once again, this time at the "local" level (i.e., the College), response to black students was swift and positive.

6. Evidence for the norm-oriented, essentially reformist orientation of the movement at this stage may be seen in the fact that Katara's demands were, for the most part, local, College-oriented, and not fundamentally challenging of the basic philosophy or functioning of the institution—with the possible exception of the demand that it set up a community center over which it would have no control.

7. This initial effort at fostering the growth of common beliefs, by raising collectively shared expectations as well as producing similar evaluations of themselves and the College, helped produce the seeming near-unanimity with which black students later responded to confrontations with College authorities.

8. See Davies (1962, 1971) and Gamson (1968, 1975) for theoretical discussion of the importance of such "revolutionary cramp" in producing active protest and revolt.

9. At least eleven new students were not recipients of MLK aid, either paying their own way or having other financial support. MLK grants ranged from very modest aid to full support, so it seems likely that several of these new students were *not* from hard-core poverty backgrounds. Given the tendency (noted by college and university financial aid offices) for students and their families (white and black) to underreport family income and available financial support, it seems likely that most black students entering University College in 1968 and subsequent years came from working-class or middle-class backgrounds. The

MLK program may have functioned to help NYU compete with other institutions for such students. MLK money does not seem to have reached the real ghetto population, the "underclass."

10. This statement, in addition to the explicit aims it indicates, is further evidence of the raised expectations of black students and of Katara's self-confidence. It also indicates that Katara itself may have raised students' expectations about its *own* competence and responsiveness.

11. Todd Little outlined Katara's plans in some detail in the 30 September HDN. Activities would focus on several areas: (1) recruiting of black students; (2) the institution of black courses in the curriculum; (3) a Black Culture week; (4) social and educational work in the community; (5) tutoring for freshman; (6) hiring more black faculty members and administrators; (7) exploring the possibilities of cooperation with other student societies on campus; (8) political action in the communities surrounding the campus. This announcement served to bolster the request for an enlarged budget by publicizing the extensive activities planned. In this way, it was a kind of appeal for public support. Further, this is the first and almost the only time Katara explicitly and publicly indicated a willingness to work or cooperate with other student groups on campus. In all this the movement remained essentially moderate and reformist.

12. It is interesting to speculate briefly on why some administrators were sympathetic. They may have believed in the seriousness and worth of the request and the proposed uses of the money. They may also have wished to preserve the College's record of responsiveness in dealing with black students, as well as the harmony reached at the end of the 1967–68 school year. Or they may have wished to prevent dissatisfaction and potential trouble—this was, after all, the period in which black student protests were reaching a peak on white campuses nationally, and tensions were then on the rise in NYU as a result of a controversial administrative appointment (to which we will turn shortly).

13. This was the first public indication that such a center was being contemplated for the Heights. Just where the impetus for such a center came from is unclear; it was not part of the demands made in the aftermath of the King assassination. The idea may have come from the College in response to the formation of such a center downtown, or black students in the College may have feared that the downtown center would not serve their needs very well, if only because of its location.

14. Because of the complexity of the Stone affair, the following account draws upon several sources: interviews, documents, and the official College account, the *Report of the Commission on Campus Disorders*, hereinafter to be termed the Haines Commission Report after its faculty chairman.

15. How Stone became the leading candidate of black students for the position at NYU is not clear. The Ocean Hill–Brownsville controversy over community control and decentralization of the schools was reaching its climax at this period. Hence, persons engaged in educational ventures in New York City's black communities, especially those involving issues of community control, may have been more locally visible.

16. This was an organization composed of the presidents of student organizations from all the undergraduate divisions of the University.

17. A full account of the decision and its consequences can be found in the report of the special faculty commission appointed to investigate these developments. Unless otherwise noted, all direct quotations are from the Haines Commission Report.

18. The purpose of the center that this statement presents is different from the one that black students had in mind when proposing it and also from the one that the University ostensibly accepted. Further, reconciliation among groups does not seem to have been a central aim of the center once it began operations. This is the first of several instances in which programs and policies proposed by black students with one aim in mind are accepted, justified, and implemented—not to say used—by school authorities with other aims and for other purposes.

19. This and similar incidents raise the question of who controlled HDN. No clear ties between the editors of HDN and the more radical student groups could be found. None, for example, appear to have belonged to SDS. Clearly it was controlled neither by black students nor by the administration.

20. This was the first clear formulation of specific demands by black students in University College during the controversy over Stone. There is some divergence from those presented by black students at Washington Square earlier the same day. This was neither the first nor the last divergence between black students at the two campuses.

21. Sometime during the same night, Little and others drove to Columbia to consult with black student leaders there about the tactics and problems of building occupations and responding to police actions. Columbia had had massive protests in the previous spring, and both black and white students from University College had been there as observers. In that instance, too, black and white protesters occupied seperate buildings.

22. Among those who did not participate were: (1) those who lived off-campus and either were not contacted or did not get to the campus in time; (2) those who stayed out to plan and participate in the protest scheduled for later that Friday morning outside the Student Center; (3) those who disagreed with the decision to occupy the building or resented the tactics used to mobilize participation; (4) those who were afraid of the consequences of participation or unsure of the wisdon of such action, or were forced by their parents to come home or stay in the dorm. Students whose homes were in the city and who were female and/or freshmen seem to have been most subject to these counterpressures. A few, when faced with the decision whether or not to take part, either stood outside and became quietly hysterical, as one woman student did, or left the campus for three days, as one male student did. Others locked themselves in their rooms and did not answer their doors.

23. Freshmen, black or white, are incompletely socialized into college and campus political cultures, especially in their first semester, and are often unsure of themselves, their beliefs, the world around them, and their place in it. Moreover, these black freshmen had been in the college less than a month when

they were asked to engage in these serious actions. Thus, protest came *before* many had developed generalized beliefs strong enough to enable them to handle the anxiety naturally attendant to such situations, despite Katara's efforts over the summer and during orientation week. This reversal of Smelser's (1963) prediction that protest participation comes *after* the development of generalized beliefs was to have important consequences in the form of intramural dissension.

24. The rule of thumb in the New York City Police Department for such operations was that there should be four policemen for each demonstrator; thus, if there were fifty people in the building, two hundred policemen would be required to end the occupation.

25. As in similar situations in other colleges and universities, a large proportion of those wanting to throw black students out seem to have been fraternity men and athletes (cf. Cox et al., 1968).

26. It is unclear what caused BASA's reversal. It is possible that Katara's more extreme action in support of Stone caused black students downtown to rethink their own position.

27. The split within ACCESS during the spring of 1967 was the first crisis of the movement. It was an internal conflict successfully resolved, though at the price of the disaffection of some black students. However, nearly three-fourths of the black students on campus in 1968–69 had not been there in 1966–67 and so had not been affected by this earlier crisis.

28. The "lessons of isolation" learned by Katara occasioned not a little resentment and distrust among black students in the College toward black students downtown. As we shall see, this was to have important effects on later actions by Katara. In the weeks to follow, Katara would pursue a seemingly contradictory policy. While trying to maintain the maximum coordination and consensus with BASA, it would at the same time adhere to an increasingly independent course.

29. Except where black interests were directly and specifically concerned, at no time did Katara engage in activism over such student power issues as university governance, participation in policy making, faculty committees, hiring, and tenure. This non-participation is typical and seems to have occurred on most white campuses experiencing black protest (cf. Astin, 1971; Astin and Bayer, 1971; Bayer and Astin, 1969; Foster, 1970; Harper, 1971; Horowitz and Friedland, 1970; Lipset, 1971; Long, 1970a; Matthews and Prothro, 1969; Trow, 1970).

In addition to providing an occasion for white students to support the grievances of black students, the Stone crisis spawned a number of new white activist groups at the Heights. By 15 October there were, in addition to SDS, the Committee for Constructive Change (CCC), the Committee of Activist Students (CAS), Students for a Restructured University (SRU), and the Committee of the People (COP). All of these groups, like SDS, were supportive of black students, but most were equally concerned, if not more concerned, with changes in the College or University.

30. The Noteboard in the 16 October HDN announced that Katara was presenting the first in its series of lectures by black speakers, a series planned before the Stone crisis arose. The notice is an interesting indication that in addition to its protest activities, Katara intended to carry out the programs and plans it had already scheduled—that in spite of the protest, other activities serving the black student population would continue on schedule.

31. On that day the Undergraduate Engineering Council of the School of Engineering, in the first public statement of its views, released a statement criticizing Katara for not promoting racial understanding, and the CCC, along with other groups, issued a call for a broad "restructuring of the University." This is one more indication of the role played by the Stone affair in the growth of organization and radicalism among white students and their push for student power and participation.

# CHAPTER V

1. Just why HDN felt it necessary at this point to suggest further steps to meet black student grievances is a matter for speculation. Perhaps it recognized that the settlement downtown left important concerns of black students uptown untouched. Perhaps it was responding to the great dissatisfaction among black students in the College. Perhaps the editors felt that such steps would help relieve interracial tensions on campus. In any case, the editorial is evidence of continuing support for black students.

2. A private meeting would serve several Katara purposes. First, it would symbolize black students' seriousness of purpose and reasonableness of approach and their willingness to negotiate rather than demonstrate. Second, such a meeting might make positive administrative response easier. The College would not seem to have bowed to overt student pressure but to have proposed or enacted changes because of its sincere concern. Third, if this approach worked, Katara would be able to announce several accomplishments of its own and would have come out of the Stone affair with tangible gains. And fourth, if the issues embodied in the fifteen demands could be settled without protest, then Katara would be spared the difficult task of mobilizing black students once more in the face of internal problems still not fully resolved. At the same time, Katara was wary of relying solely on the generosity or receptivity of College authorities. After all, authorities might regard all issues involving black students as settled with the settlement of the Stone crisis.

3. The demand for biweekly reports can be interpreted as an attempt to increase pressure on the administration to respond favorably and publicly. Public response would commit the administration more firmly than private agreements. Reports would also inform black students of developments affecting their interests. This demand is another legacy of the isolation faced by Katara during the Stone controversy.

4. The fact that HDN took this position even though the demands had been

presented peacefully (though a demand itself is not necessarily a peaceful form), and only after there had been no response to them when presented privately, suggests continuing support for Katara's general aims but some waning of support for protest as a means to achieve them.

5. Katara's willingness to begin negotiations immediately rather than pushing for acceptance of all its demands points to the norm-oriented character of the movement. It may well indicate in addition the internal state of the organization, which made actual protest difficult to mobilize.

6. Note that by this point the center was no longer to be named in honor of Martin Luther King, Jr. Whether the change was the result of student or administrative initiative is unknown.

7. Complicating these problems were class tensions among black students, to be presented in more detail shortly, and suspicion that some of their number were in reality undercover agents of the police or FBI. Though there seems to be little evidence that this was true, such paranoia clearly did not help internal organizational difficulties or enhance cohesion.

8. Students protesting included SDS, the various activist student groups formed during the Stone crisis, and a number of previously unaffiliated and non-activist students. All were banded together into a single umbrella group, the Committee for Improved Educational Values (CIEV), or operated under its aegis. In many respects this controversy was even more extensive and divisive than the Stone affair of the previous semester. As resistence continued to the students' initial aim—which was simply to discuss with the English Department its decision—the situation changed drastically. Requests gave way to demands. The single issue of tenure for Taylor expanded into a whole range of issues: student power and participation, faculty hiring and firing procedures, curricula, restructuring the College, and the University's involvement in the Vietnam War, among others. There was a similar escalation of tactics: from requests for meetings to demonstrations, rallies, sit-ins, and the occupation of buildings on at least two different occasions, the second occupation ending only after the College obtained a court injunction against the occupiers. Both the College Chapel and the Engineering Library were firebombed.

9. Chapter VIII discusses some of the factors responsible for this situation on white campuses where black protest has occurred (cf. Anthony, 1971; Astin and Bayer, 1971; Donadio, 1968a; Lipset, 1971).

10. As originally proposed, the program required the combination of a traditional departmental major with a concentration in African and Afro-American Studies—in effect a double major. Minors in African Studies and Afro-American Studies would be introduced. The program also proposed the formation of a black studies center at the Heights to begin operation in September 1969. This would have its own core faculty as well as faculty drawn from existing departments. The center would serve as a liaison with the MLK Institute downtown and with existing departments, and would promote the College's relations with the surrounding community (New York University, 1969b).

11. Administrative resistance to this part of the proposal is not difficult to understand. Many college administrators have resisted arrangements establishing the principle of student control of an academic program of any size and importance. In University College, moreover, the Taylor affair was reaching its apogee at this time in both intensity and scope. Student power and participation in policy making were central issues in these protests. The proposed Coordinating Committee would provide students with real power in an academic program. Hence, in addition to its opposition on principle, the administration may have felt that it could not possibly accede to this proposal without "legitimizing" and conceding the same principle to white students. Miles (1971) provides a good discussion of the general failure of black students nationally to achieve autonomous ethnic studies programs in which students had a real role in decision-making. Eichel et al. (1970) discuss what happened in a parallel case in the spring of 1969 at Harvard.

12. The administration's opposition may well have been especially radicalizing in the context of the Taylor affair, which centered on the student power principle that black students were trying to establish. This was the one time, ironically, when black students pushed this issue intensively. Basically, the movement failed to become value-oriented at this point for two reasons: the efforts of Little and other leaders who felt that they could still gain their goals through negotiation, and the internal state of Katara. In the political judgment of Katara's leaders, it would be wiser not to protest but to continue presenting Katara as reasonable and serious and keep the threat of protest in reserve as a final coercive resource. They also feared that the black studies issue would get lost in the larger Taylor affair (see Astin and Bayer, 1971, on joint protests by black and white students with different aims and the tendency for black issues to be submerged and diverted). Moreover, the original lack of unanimity on black studies made potential mobilization more difficult.

This crisis for the administration may well have been the optimal time to push, and push vigorously, for black studies (see Gamson, 1975:112 on such crisis situations as opportune times for protest). Certainly several black students believed this.

13. It is, of course, impossible to judge the accuracy or fairness of this assessment of administrators' attitudes, but it is a view, I found, that black students also often held. That it was believed by faculty members as well as students gives some indication of the emotions involved and the atmosphere on campus at the time.

14. Of the thirty-nine freshman recipients of MLK aid, not all were black (as they had been the year before); approximately a quarter belonged to other racial or ethnic groups, with Puerto Rican students the largest group after blacks. It is possible that the proportion of black students from middle-class backgrounds may have *risen* in the second year of the MLK program in the College. The decline in the total number of black students admitted may be related to the institution of open admissions at the City University of New York; the cutback of MLK funds that resulted from the Stone affair; or simply

less effective or reduced recruiting efforts by the College. It may also reflect a decline in the total size of the freshman class that occurred at the same time: in 1968–69, 610 freshmen entered University College; in 1969–70, 577.

15. Black students at the Heights the year before had rejected the practice (as well as the principle) of relying on non-local authorities to reach solutions to local problems that affected them alone. This is a partial explanation for the hostility and distrust many black students at the Heights felt toward Allen as the year progressed and a black studies program failed to materialize. Many attributed this failure to unconcern about the Heights, and this feeling further estranged blacks at the Heights from those at Washington Square.

16. Both the Student Senate and the Committee on Student Affairs were new entities, formed in the overall revamping of student government that followed the protests of 1968–69. The Student Senate replaced previous forms of student government and was responsible for the recognition and funding of student groups, among its other functions. The Committee on Student Affairs, composed of faculty members, students, and the director of student affairs, became the superior authority over the Student Senate.

17. This frequent use of the "Noteboard" illustrates the state of Katara in 1969–70. A review of the "Noteboards" for September through February shows that Katara regularly used this means to announce its meetings and activities. This is in marked contrast to the previous two years: Katara used the Noteboard to announce its meetings only twice in 1967–68. In 1969–70 such announcements became more frequent as the year progressed. This seems to be an indication of the Katara's increasing difficulties in maintaining itself as a viable, solidary organization and retaining the interest of black students. The continuing failure over black studies simply made matters worse.

18. Their efforts on behalf of EDCEP at a time when black studies was foundering increased resentment toward Little and Chambers, who was regarded by some as in the administration's pocket.

19. According to Todd Little, strenuous efforts were made to get Katara, or at least a number of black students, actively involved in sponsoring the proposal. He says that he talked with every black student on campus before the proposal was written up, trying to get ideas and, more important, help. Only fifteen people worked on it wholeheartedly and continuously, an indication, perhaps, of the divisions plaguing black students.

20. Notably, Fordham University, Manhattan College, and Lehman College of the City University of New York; only the last is a public institution.

21. The tactics used on behalf of EDCEP not only provide evidence of the norm-oriented character of the movement, but indicate a certain political sophistication on the part of its student proponents. Enlisting the administration in the process of formulating details, although it tends to produce less radical programs, also helps to produce some prior institutional commitment. The role of supplicant may be quite effective in institutions that have traditionally been both liberal and paternalistic, as many American colleges and

universities are. The forums, along with extended discussions and maintenance of the position of calm reason, were good public relations vis-à-vis students and faculty. Attempts to enlist off-campus support put further pressure on the College.

22. This is another example of the subversion and deflection of black student goals in the process of administrative implementation; we have seen it before, most notably in the differing interpretations by students and University authorities of Stone's essential role and responsibilities.

23. The number of freshmen, as in the year before, was 577. The number of incoming Puerto Rican students increased, another possible factor in the decline in black admissions since the two groups were sharing a finite amount of financial aid. Unfortunately, exact figures on Puerto Rican enrollment are not available.

24. Connected with the School of Continuing Education, the program in 1970–71 was entering its third year of operation with 150 students. They were enrolled in one or another of the four-year undergraduate divisions downtown (the School of the Arts, the School of Commerce, the School of Education, and Washington Square College). The program included Chinese, Puerto Rican, Cuban, Panamanian, Dominican, Jewish, and West Indian as well as American black students.

25. See, e.g., Cameron (1966), King (1961), Smelser (1963), and Zald and Ash (1966).

26. In this latter regard the essentially careerist orientation of many black students seems especially relevant (many of the members of the Sickle Cell Anemia Association were pre-med students). The formation of SCAA is also an indication of the tendency among black students to combine a careerist orientation—ordinarily individualistic—with concern for the welfare of the larger black community (see Edwards, 1970; Glazer, 1970a; D. M. Henderson, 1970).

27. The formation of these groups is additional indication of the career orientation of black students and the tendency for career concerns to predominate in the absence of a strong activist organization.

28. Though some Katara members and other black students took part in the protest, no black students from the Heights seem to have been consulted or to have played a role in subsequent negotiations, continuing the familiar pattern of isolation from the Square. Katara itself made no coherent effort to play any significant role either in the protest or in the negotiations that followed.

29. The amnesty issue was especially important because under New York State Law, any student convicted on criminal trespass charges could legally be prohibited from receiving federal or state financial aid for up to two years. Thus, if any of the forty-six were convicted and found to be on financial aid, they could find their careers at University College disrupted and be unable to transfer to other schools.

## CHAPTER VI

1. One of the community outreach programs, aimed at providing local residents with training in bookkeeping and accounting, failed at least in part because of lack of community interest. This may, however, reflect a lack of serious planning on the part of the College to ascertain the needs and interests of the community.

2. The EDCEP/ESP (Educational Development and Community Enrollment Program/Educational Support Program) can be called a successful policy change promoted by black and Puerto Rican students, but because it was implemented only in 1971–72, as the plans for merging University and Washington Square Colleges were being announced, its long-term success cannot be judged.

3. See Institute for the Study of Educational Policy (1975) for a good discussion of problems related to statistics on black enrollment. This increase in black enrollment in white colleges and universities was made at the expense of the black colleges in two senses. First, "in large measure the white campuses were drawing from the black ones, rather than enlarging the pool of black collegians" (Egerton, 1975). By the 1974–75 school year, only about a quarter of the total black student enrollment was to be found in black colleges. Moreover, in a kind of "brain-drain" process, the more talented, better prepared, and more affluent are likely to be found in white colleges, not black ones (Harnett, 1970; Peterson and Peterson, 1974).

4. See Smelser (1963) for a more theoretical discussion of control methods used to encourage a movement to remain norm-oriented.

5. Willie and McCord (1972) provide a good discussion of many aspects of the on-campus world of black students in white colleges and universities.

## CHAPTER VII

1. Relative deprivation here refers to black students' experience of alienation and racism in the context of a changing College that they perceive as insufficiently responsive to their needs and interests as blacks and as black students.

2. Mobilization on the basis of dashed expectations and a thwarted vision of a changed social reality is a distinguishing feature of value-oriented movements.

3. Lyons and Lyons (1973) provide a good discussion of the basic incompatibility between university interests and those of any student group.

4. The concepts of institutional racism and white resistance may have helped prepare black students for the University's failure to meet their expectations. More important, they provided an explanation for Stone's dismissal that was highly useful in movement mobilization.

5. The dismissal also indicates that blacks and black students are not as powerful or politically important as other groups within or outside the white university. While this may or may not be an indication of direct racism, it does reflect the relatively powerless status of blacks in the United States and illustrates one dimension of institutional racism. In any case, this basic conflict of interest is a lesson current and future black students would do well to remember.

6. Coser (1967), Gamson (1975), and Tilly (1969) provide good discussions of the degree to which extreme protest action may be rational and instrumental, even when seeming most irrational.

7. I am not here denying the validity of such beliefs or the reality of racism, both institutional and personal, in the University. Rather, I am suggesting an additional, organizational dimension to the issue.

8. Mobilization may have been easier to the extent that freshmen are often more tentative in their opinions, less informed about issues and events, more eager to be accepted and to prove themselves, and therefore more open to manipulation and pressures for solidarity. Yet the uncertainties and insecurities of being a freshman may lead many to avoid unfamiliar and stressful action.

9. Use of forceful curtailment may present an additional problem in the case of black students. Because of the "white liberal" tendency and self-image of many colleges and universities, authorities may hesitate before taking actions against blacks that they would readily take against white students (cf. Donadio, 1968a; Lusky and Lusky, 1969). Though black students have not always capitalized on it, this tendency may provide them with a kind of moral resource in their dealings with authorities who possess greater resources of other kinds.

10. "Non-negotiable" demands, building take-overs, disruption of classes, and so on are not part of the usual operating modes of the university; they are both non-formal and extralegal methods in this context. This is an important reason for their potency (and perhaps their ultimate limitation as well) as a set of tactics, and the control problems they present to the university as a normative setting.

11. Baldridge (1971), Glazer (1969), Horowitz and Friedland (1970), Kornstein and Weissenberg (1970), Metzger (1970), and Platt and Parsons (1969) make important observations on the significance of bargaining and exchange in resolving conflicts within the university, including those involving student discontent.

12. Police entrance on campus has served to radicalize student protest movements, both black and white, throughout the country. Astin and Bayer (1971), Bayer and Astin (1969), and Urban Research Corporation (1970) provide national evidence; Bunzel (1969) discusses this effect at San Francisco State, Cox et al. (1968) at Columbia, Eichel et al. (1970) and Meyer (1971) at Harvard, and Lipset and Wolin (1965) and Napper (1973) at Berkeley. As both Lipset (1971) and Meyer (1971) point out, student protesters in many cases deliberately provoked police entrance because of its radicalizing effect on the rest of the campus (students and faculty), as well as on their own supporters.

13. Toch's conception should be modified to include movements that are *not*

successful externally and/or internally. It is reasonable to suppose that the attempt to survive through the kind of expediency and pragmatism Toch implies may be *most* probable in the case of movements whose success is limited. Such a view is more adequate to explain the movement in University College, without, I believe, doing violence to Toch's theoretical framework.

14. Zurcher and Curtis (1973) also argue that the Weber-Michels model of movement transformation, despite its dominant position in American sociology, nonetheless describes only *one* possible transformation. (See Ash, 1972, and Hiller, 1975, for further discussion of alternatives to the Weber-Michels model.)

15. See Nelson (1974) for an excellent discussion of the effects of pre-movement factors particularly at important junctures (often crises or turning points) in the movement's history, in the transformation of the movement, and the fate of the movement organization, especially in terms of schism and factionalization. Pre-movement factors include the composition of membership, methods of recruitment and retention in the organization, and leadership structures.

16. See Cameron (1966); Smelser (1963); Toch (1965); Turner and Killian (1972); Zald and Ash (1966).

17. See also Schein (1969) for additional discussion of such permeation. Black student unions are not only exclusive organizations, but share many traits with what Lewis Coser (1974) has called "greedy institutions." As he puts it, "greedy institutions are always exclusive" (Coser, 1974:8).

18. For further theoretical support for the fragmenting role of heterogeneity, especially when suddenly increased, see Hagstrom and Selvin (1965), Tsouderos (1955), and Turner and Killian (1972). See Marx and Useem (1971) and Nelson (1974) for the role of membership heterogeneity in a movement's career.

19. In order to avoid the difficulties and intraracial discord stemming from small populations, Willie and McCord (1972:15) suggest that the minimum number of black students in white colleges should be around two hundred, "since the quality of campus social life for black students is directly related to the number of black students enrolled and not to the ratio of black and white students." At University College, there were apparently never this many black students on campus in any one year.

20. For a somewhat different interpretation of surface conformity to ghetto styles, see Donald (1973), who argues that this role-playing often tended to have a politicizing, radicalizing, and mobilizing impact on black students. That is, what may have begun as playacting often ended as authentic behavior reflecting true belief. Of course, "true belief" originating this way *may* make movement failure or crisis even more disillusioning for some, since their commitment did not come before movement activity. And role-playing obviously provides an excuse for those not wishing to join or who wish to leave the movement to do so with less guilt.

21. Ethnic strain and tension have also occurred on some campuses between American blacks and Africans (see T. Becker, 1973).

22. North American black students appear to be just as career-oriented (Boyd, 1974b; Gaier and Watts, 1969; Gurin and Epps, 1975; Walters, 1974). However, they seemed to show greater acceptance of ideologies of black solidarity and the necessity for skilled, trained blacks to return to the community to work for the good of all blacks, rather than their own individual benefit. This provided them with a rationale for engaging in activism and giving time to the movement, at least initially.

23. See Boyd (1974b); Donald (1970, 1971); Edwards (1970); Gaier and Watts (1969); Gurin and Epps (1975); V. Henderson (1974); Obatala (1972); Walters (1974).

24. This conflict between individual and collective orientations indicates the possible role in the black student movement of what Burton Clark (1961) has termed precarious values—that is, values that are undefined and provide unclear or contradictory behavioral cues.

25. See Scott (1965) on the role of shared moral values in maintaining commitment and sustaining a course of action, even in the face of adversity. Kanter (1968) gives an excellent general discussion, highly relevant to this study, of the dimensions, types, and mechanisms of commitment. D. E. Morrison (1973), Olson (1965), and Useem (1973) indicate that member commitment is always a major problem in movements seeking change in the world rather than in members.

26. Here I am following the distinction made by Blumer (1953). In the case of esprit de corps, members' adherence is based on the gratification they get from simply participating with other members. In the case of morale, commitment is based on belief in and acceptance of the ideology and program of the movement.

27. All of these are more or less in line with Blumer's (1953:206) more theoretical description of techniques for developing and maintaining esprit de corps.

28. Many black students seem to have expected to find what Hagstrom and Selvin (1965) call sociometric cohesion. That is, they expected that most, if not all, of their friends would be found among black students and particularly within the black student organization.


CHAPTER VIII


1. See Astin, Astin, et al. (1975), Gamson (1975), and Lipsky (1968) on the general effectiveness of protest as a means of gaining political and other goals.

2. See Donald (1970, 1971), Napper (1973), and Willie and McCord (1972). Attacks on "bourgeois niggers" and the blacker-than-thou syndrome illustrate the kind of exaggeration of the causes of frustration that Smelser

(1963) attributes to norm-oriented movements faced with failure and dissensus. Such division has not been uncommon among nonstudent black groups.

3. See, for example, Browne (1968), Caplan (1971), and Perkins and Higginson (1971) for applications of this view.

4. This may have been an especially important consideration given that black student protest has tended to result in the arrest of protesters more frequently than white student protest (Urban Research Corporation, 1970).

5. While several observers have made a persuasive case for the importance of coalition or alliance for change-seeking groups, including students, the empirical evidence in the case of *black* students is rather inconsistent, as noted above.

6. These off-campus sources often served as reference points for black students. Black student activism can in some respects be looked at as an attempt by black students to prove themselves to an off-campus audience suspicious of their "bourgeois" proclivities. It is possible that this off-campus audience also included black students on other campuses.

7. See Edwards (1970, 1971), Krueger and Silvert (1975), and Perkins and Higginson (1971) for further discussion of this issue.

8. In the United States constant quadrennial changeover is another component of the heterogeneity of the student population (white as well as black) adding generational differences to those of class, ethnicity, and so on. See Ryder (1965) on the cohort as a concept in the study of social change. See Bengtson, Furlong, and Lauer (1974), Braungart (1974a, 1974b), Eisenstadt (1956), Feuer (1969), Gusfield (1957), Lipset and Ladd (1971a, 1971b), Mannheim (1952), Turner and Killian (1972), and Westby and Braungart (1968) for empirical and theoretical discussions of the importance of generational unit analysis, historical consciousness, and generational problems and issues in social movements, especially youth movements. See Donald (1970, 1971, 1973) for a discussion of both intergenerational and intragenerational conflict within the black student movement after 1965, particularly at Cornell.

9. This structure of power in the university and student dissatisfaction with it were also a major reason for the development during the late 1960s of elaborate legalistic conduct and disciplinary codes, in University College and elsewhere. These are means of creating and maintaining student rights in settings where they have traditionally had few, without fundamentally altering the asymmetrical power balance between authorities and students.

10. Subversion or deflection of movement goals by authorities is not limited to movements in universities or other complex organizations. Smelser (1963), for example, argues that it is a technique frequently used to control a norm-oriented movement in society.

11. Subversion of student goals may be most likely to be attempted when the changes sought are opposed by significant others in the university or go against its organizational interests.

12. See Astin, Astin, et al. (1975) for a discussion of the general failure of sit-ins to produce change in the racial policies of white colleges and universities.

13. This, of course, is not to deny that the successful accomplishment of black goals might well increase competition for good jobs, opportunities, and rewards of all kinds, and that some who now benefit from the status quo might not do so well. Furthermore, to the extent that racist beliefs and practices are pervasive and integral in the society, perceptions of black activism as value-oriented are not always entirely inaccurate.

14. Earlier I noted that such fragmentation also occurs in student movements not involving blacks. Non-student movements and political efforts not involving blacks have also been plagued with fragmentation on the basis of ethnic or class cleavage. Almond (1954), for example, shows how this has happened in Communist parties in a number of countries. Numerous examples might be cited in the United States: for example, the Know-Nothing Party and movement of 1854–57; various farmers' movements in the last quarter of the nineteenth century; experiments in utopian communal living in the last century and this one; and the reform movement in the New York City Democratic Party during the last twenty or so years. Most of the nationalistic or independence movements around the world have had to face such fragmentation. A good example was the nationalist movement in India, especially during the 1920s, which faced not only ethnic and religious factionalism, but caste fragmentation as well (Smelser, 1963).

15. This listing includes primarily the more elite and well-known colleges and universities, which are most likely to receive media attention outside the local area. As a result, I believe it is safe to assume that this is *not* in any sense a comprehensive listing, lending further support to the argument that black student activism has persisted well past the time when it was supposed to have disappeared.

# References

Abeles, Elvin
    1969    *The Student and the University*. New York: Parent's Magazine Press.

Aberle, David
    1966    *The Peyote Religion Among the Navaho*. Chicago: Aldine.

Abram, Morris B.
    1970    "Reflections on the University in the New Revolution." *Daedalus* 99:122–40.

Afro-American Studies and Research Program
    1982    "1982–83 Academic Year Promises New Gains in Black Studies." *Afro-Scholar Newsletter* no. 8. Urbana-Champaign: University of Illinois.

Allen, Robert L.
    1974    "Politics of the Attack on Black Studies." *Black Scholar* 6 (September):2–7.

Almond, Gabriel
    1954    *The Appeals of Communism*. Princeton: Princeton University Press.

Altbach, Philip G.
    1967    "Students and Politics." Pp. 74–96 in S. M. Lipset (ed.), *Student Politics*. New York: Basic Books.
    1970    *A Selected Bibliography on Students, Politics and Higher Education*, rev. ed. Cambridge, Mass.: Center for International Affairs, Harvard University.
    1974    *Student Politics in America*. New York: McGraw-Hill.

Altbach, Philip G., and David Kelley
    1973    *American Students: A Selected Bibliography on Student Activisim and Related Topics*. Lexington, Mass.: D. C. Heath.

Altbach, Philip G., and Patti Peterson
    1971    "Before Berkeley: Historical Perspectives on American Student Activism. *Annals* 395 (May):1–14.

American Council on Education
    1973     *Fact Book on Higher Education.* Loose-Leaf Reporting Series. Washington, D.C.
    1976     *National Norms for Entering College Freshmen.* Cooperative Institutional Research Program, Graduate School of Education, University of California at Los Angeles.
American Sociological Association
    1982     "Minorities and Women." *Footnotes* 10 (November):4.
*Annals*
    1971     Special issue on student protest. Vol. 395 (May). *Annals of the American Academy of Political and Social Science.*
Anthony, Earl
    1971     *The Time of the Furnaces: A Case Study of Black Student Revolt.* New York: Dial.
Apter, David E.
    1974     "An Epitaph for Two Revolutions That Failed." *Daedalus* 103:85–103.
Aptheker, Herbert
    1969     "The Negro College Student in the 1920s." *Science and Society* 33 (Spring):150–67.
Aron, William S.
    1971     "Ideology and Behavior as Components of Radicalism." Paper presented at the annual meeting of the American Sociological Association, September, Denver.
Ash, Roberta
    1972     *Social Movements in America.* Chicago: Markham.
Astin, Alexander W.
    1965     *Who Goes Where to College?* Chicago: Science Research Associates.
    1968     *The College Environment.* Washington, D.C.: American Council on Education.
    1970*a*    "Determinants of Student Activism." Pp. 89–101 in Julian Foster and Durward Long (eds.), *Protest!* New York: William Morrow.
    1970*b*    "Racial Considerations in Admissions." Pp. 15–42 in Edgar A. Epps (ed.), *Black Students in White Schools.* Worthington, Ohio: Charles A. Jones.
    1971     "New Evidence on Campus Unrest, 1969–70." *Educational Record* 51 (Winter):41–46.
    1982     *Minorities in American Higher Education.* San Francisco: Jossey-Bass.
Astin, Alexander W.; Helen S. Astin; Alan E. Bayer; and Ann S. Bisconti
    1975     *The Power of Protest.* San Francisco: Jossey-Bass.

Astin, Alexander W., and Alan E. Bayer
  1971      "Antecedents and Consequents of Disruptive Campus Protests."
            *Measurement and Evaluation in Guidance*, pp. 18–30.
Astin, Alexander W.; Margo R. King; and Gerald T. Richardson
  1975      *The American Freshman: National Norms for Fall 1975.* Los
            Angeles: Cooperative Institutional Research Program, American
            Council on Education, University of California at Los Angeles.
Astin, Helen S., and Patricia H. Cross
  1981      "Black Students in Black and White Institutions." Pp. 30–45 in
            Gail E. Thomas (ed.), *Black Students in Higher Education.*
            Westport, Conn.: Greenwood Press.
Attman, R. A., and P. O. Snyder (eds.)
  1971      *The Minority Student on Campus.* Boulder, Colo.: Western
            Interstate Commission for Higher Education.
Bailey, Ronald E.
  1984      "Consolidating Academic Excellence and Social Responsibility
            in Black Studies." Oxford, Miss.: Afro-American Studies Pro-
            gram, University of Mississippi.
Baker, S. R.
  1966      "The Relationship Between Student Residence and Perception of
            Environmental Press." *Journal of Educational Psychology*
            52:308–16.
Bakke, E. Wight
  1967      "Roots and Soil of Student Activism." Pp. 54–73 in S. M. Lipset
            (ed.), *Student Politics.* New York: Basic Books.
Baldridge, J. Victor
  1971      *Power and Conflict in the University.* New York: Wiley.
Ballard, Allen B.
  1973      *The Education of Black Folk.* New York: Harper and Row.
Baltzell, E. Digby
  1964      *The Protestant Establishment.* New York: Random House.
Banks, Henry A.
  1970      "Black Consciousness: A Study Survey." *Black Scholar* 2
            (September):44–51.
Barlow, William, and Peter Shapiro
  1971      *The End to Silence: The San Francisco State College Student
            Movement in the '60s.* New York: Pegasus.
Barol, William
  1983      "Why They Choose Separate Tables." *Newsweek on Campus.*
            March.
Barton, Alan H.
  1963      "The College as a Social Organization." *College Admissions*
            10:31–45.

1968       "The Columbia Crisis: Campus, Vietnam and the Ghetto." *Public Opinion Quarterly* 32:333–62.

Barzun, Jacques

1968       *The American University*. New York: Harper.

Bay, Christian

1967       "Political and Apolitical Students: Facts in Search of a Theory." *Journal of Social Issues* 23:76–91.

Bayer, Alan E.

1971       "Institutional Correlates of Faculty Support of Campus Unrest." *Research Report* 6 (no. 1). Washington, D.C.: Office of Research, American Council on Education.

1972       "The Black College Freshman." *Research Report* 7 (no. 3). Washington, D.C.: Office of Research, American Council on Education.

1973       "The New Student in Black Colleges." *School Review* 81:415–26.

Bayer, Alan E., and Alexander W. Astin

1969       "Violence and Disruption on the U.S. Campus, 1968–1969." *Educational Record* 50:337–50.

1971       "Campus Unrest, 1970–71: Was It Really All That Quiet?" *Educational Record* 52:301–13.

Bayer, Alan E., and Robert F. Boruch

1969*a*       *The Black Student in American Colleges*. Washington, D.C.: Office of Research, American Council on Education.

1969*b*       "Black and White Freshman Entering Four-Year Colleges." *Educational Record* 50:371–86.

Becker, Howard S., and Irving L. Horowitz

1972       "Radical Politics and Sociological Research." *American Journal of Sociology* 78:48–66.

Becker, Tamar

1973       "Black Africans and Black Americans on an American Campus." *Sociology and Social Research* 57:168–81.

Bell, Daniel, and Irving Kristol (eds.)

1969       *Confrontation*. New York: Basic Books.

Bengston, Vern L.

1970       "The Generation Gap: A Review and Typology of Social-Psychological Perspectives." *Youth and Society* 2:7–32.

Bengston, Vern L.; Michael J. Furlong; and Robert S. Laufer

1974       "Time, Aging, and the Continuity of Social Structure." *Journal of Social Issues* 30 (Spring):1–30.

Bereday, George Z. F.

1967       "Student Unrest on Four Continents." Pp. 97–123 in S. M. Lipset (ed.), *Student Politics*. New York: Basic Books.

Berger, Peter L., and Thomas Luckmann
1966     *The Social Construction of Reality.* Garden City, N.Y.:
         Doubleday.
Berube, Maurice R., and Marilyn Gittell
1969     *Confrontation at Ocean Hill–Brownsville.* New York: Praeger.
Bisconti, Ann S.
1970     "Events in Protest." Washington, D.C.: American Council on
         Education.
Bittner, Egon
1963     "Radicalism and the Organization of Radical Movements."
         *American Sociological Review* 28:928–40.
*Black News*
1968–71  Newsletter published irregularly by Katara, New York Uni-
         versity.
*Black Scholar*
1970     "Student Strikes, 1968–69." *Black Scholar* 1 (January/
         February):65–75.
Blackwell, James E.
1982     "Demographics of Desegregation." Pp. 28–70 in Reginald Wil-
         son (ed.), *Race and Equity in Higher Education.* Washington,
         D.C.: American Council on Education.
Blau, Peter M.
1955     *The Dynamics of Bureaucracy.* Chicago: University of Chicago
         Press.
1956     *Bureaucracy in Modern Society.* New York: Random House.
1964     *Exchange and Power in Social Life.* New York: Wiley.
1973     *The Organization of Academic Work.* New York: Wiley.
1974     "Parameters of Social Structure." *American Sociological Review*
         39:615–35.
Blau, Peter M., and W. Richard Scott
1962     *Formal Organizations.* San Francisco: Chandler.
Blau, Peter M., and Ellen L. Slaughter
1971     "Institutional Conditions and Student Demonstrations." *Social
         Problems* 18:475–87.
Block, Jeanne H.; Norma Haan; and M. Brewster Smith
1968     "Activism and Apathy in Contemporary Adolescents." Pp. 198–
         231 in J. F. Adams (ed.), *Contributions to the Understanding of
         Adolescence.* Boston: Allyn and Bacon.
1969     "Socialization Correlates of Student Activism." *Journal of Social
         Issues* 25:162–67.
Blumenfeld, W. S.
1968     "College Preferences of Able Negro Students: A Comparison of
         Those Naming Predominantly Negro Institutions and Those

Naming Predominantly White Institutions." *College and University* 43:330–41.

Blumer, Herbert

1951*a* "Collective Behavior." Pp. 167–222 in A. M. Lee (ed.), *Principles of Sociology*. New York: Barnes and Noble.

1951*b* "Social Movements." Pp. 199–220 in A. M. Lee (ed.), *New Outline of the Principles of Sociology*. New York: Barnes and Noble.

1953 "Collective Behavior." Pp. 204–20 in A. M. Lee (ed.), *New Outline of the Principles of Sociology*. New York: Barnes and Noble.

1954 "What Is Wrong with Social Theory?" *American Journal of Sociology* 19:3–10.

1956 "Sociological Analysis and the 'Variable.'" *American Sociological Review* 21:683–90.

Bowes, Harry P.

1964 "University and College Student Rebellion in Retrospect and Some Sociological Implications." Ph.D. Thesis, School of Education, University of Colorado.

Bowles, Frank, and Frank DeCosta

1971 *Between Two Worlds: A Profile of Negro Higher Education*. New York: McGraw-Hill.

Boyd, William M.

1974*a* "Black Student, White College." *Williams Alumni Review* 66 (Spring):207.

1974*b* *Desegregating America's Colleges*. New York: Praeger.

1981 "The Forgotten Side of the Black Undergraduate." Pp. 142–51 in Gail E. Thomas (ed.), *Black Students in Higher Education*. Westport, Conn.: Greenwood Press.

Bradley, Nolan

1967 "The Negro Undergraduate Student." *Journal of Negro Education* 36:15–23.

Brager, George

1969 "Commitment and Conflict in a Normative Organization." *American Sociological Review* 34:482–91.

Braungart, Richard G.

1971 "Family Status, Socialization, and Student Politics." *American Journal of Sociology* 77:108–30.

1974*a* "The Sociology of Generations and Student Politics." *Journal of Social Issues* 30:31–54.

1974*b* "Youth and Social Movements." Paper presented at the annual meeting of the American Sociological Association, August, Montreal.

Brinton, Crane

1965 *The Anatomy of Revolution*. Englewood Cliffs, N.J.: Prentice-Hall.

Brouillete, John, and E. L. Quanrantelli
1971    "Types of Patterned Variation in Bureaucratic Adaptations to Organized Stress." *Sociological Inquiry* 4:39–46.

Brown, Donald R.
1967    "Student Stress and the Institutional Environment." *Journal of Social Issues* 23:92–107.

Brown, W. O.
1931    "The Nature of Race Consciousness." *Social Forces* 10:90–97.
1935    "Race Consciousness Among South African Natives." *American Journal of Sociology* 40:569–81.

Browne, Robert L.
1968    "The Challenge of Black Student Organizations." *Freedomways* (Fall), pp. 12–23.

Bundy, McGeorge
1970    "Were Those the Days?" *Daedalus* 99:531–67.

Bunzel, John
1969    "Black Studies at San Francisco State." Pp. 22–44 in Daniel Bell and Irving Kristol (eds.), *Confrontation*. New York: Basic Books.

Burbach, H. J., and M. A. Thompson
1971    "Alienation Among College Freshmen: A Comparison of Puerto Rican, Black and White Students." *Journal of College Student Personnel* 12:248–52.

Caliver, Ambrose
1971    *A Background Study of Negro College Students*. Westport, Conn.: Greenwood.

Cameron, William Bruce
1966    *Modern Social Movements*. New York: Random House.

Canfield, Roger B.
1973    *Black Ghetto Riots and Campus Disorders*. San Francisco: R and E Research Associates.

Cantril, Hadley
1958    *The Politics of Despair*. New York: Basic Books.
1963    *The Psychology of Social Movements*. New York: Wiley.

Capen, S. P.
1953    *The Management of Universities*. Buffalo: Foster and Stewart.

Caplan, Nathan
1971    "Identity in Transition: A Theory of Black Militancy." Pp. 143–65 in Robert Aya and Norman Miller (eds.), *The New American Revolution*. New York: Free Press.

Carmichael, Stokeley, and Charles V. Hamilton
1967    *Black Power*. New York: Vintage.

Cass, James
1969    "Can the University Survive the Black Challenge?" *Saturday Review* 52 (no. 25, 21 June):68–71, 83–84.

Centra, John A.

1970a   "Black Students at Predominantly White Colleges." *Sociology of Education* 43:325–37.

1970b   *The College Environment Revisited*. Princeton: Educational Testing Service.

Chrisman, Robert

1969   "Observations on Race and Class at San Francisco State." Pp. 222–32 in James McEvoy and Abraham Miller (eds.), *Black Power and Student Rebellion*. Belmont, Calif.: Wadsworth.

Clark, Burton R.

1961   "Organizational Adaptation and Precarious Values." Pp. 158–67 in Amitai Etzioni (ed.), *Complex Organizations*. New York: Holt, Rinehart and Winston.

Clark, Burton R., and Martin Trow

1966   "The Organizational Context." Pp. 17–70 in T. M. Newcomb and E. K. Wilson (eds.), *College Peer Groups*. Chicago: Aldine.

Clark, J. P.

1959   "Measuring Alienation Within a Social System." *American Sociological Review* 24:849–52.

Clark, Kenneth B.

1969   "Black Youth Search for Identity." Pp. 268–73 in Alexander Klein (ed.), *Natural Enemies: Youth and the Clash of Generations*. Philadelphia: Lippincott.

Clark, Kenneth B., and Lawrence Plotkin

1963   *The Negro Student and Integrated Colleges*. New York: National Scholarship Service and Fund for Negro Students.

Cleaver, Eldridge

1968   *Soul on Ice*. New York: Dell.

Clift, Virgil A.

1969   "Higher Education of Minority Groups in the United States." *Journal of Negro Education* 38:291–302.

Clignet, Remi

1974   *Liberty and Equality in the Educational Process*. New York: Wiley.

Cobb, Jewel Plummer, and Carolyn McDew (eds.)

1974   *The Morning After: A Retrospective View of a Select Number of Colleges and Universities with Increased Black Student Enrollment in the Past Five Years*. Storrs, Conn.: Racine Printing.

Cohen, Michael

1970   *Guns on Campus: Student Protest at Cornell*. Chicago: Urban Research Corporation.

Coles, Robert

1964   "Social Struggle and Weariness." *Psychiatry* 27:305–15.

Conway, Jill

1970   "Styles of Academic Culture." *Daedalus* 99:43–55.

Corson, J. J.
    1960        *Governance of Colleges and Universities*. New York: McGraw-
                Hill.
Corson, William R.
    1970        *Promise or Peril: The Black College Student in America*. New
                York: Norton.
Corwin, Ronald G.
    1974        *Education in Crisis*. New York: Wiley.
Coser, Lewis
    1967        *Continuities in the Study of Social Conflict*. New York: Free
                Press.
    1974        *Greedy Institutions: Patterns of Undivided Commitment*. New
                York: Free Press.
Couch, Carl
    1968        "Collective Behavior." *Social Problems* 15:310–22.
Coughlin, Ellen K.
    1976        "Minority Enrollment Up 11.7 Pct. in 2 Years." *Chronicle of
                Higher Education* 13 (8 November):7.
Cox, Archibald; Hylan Lewis; Simon H. Rifkind; Dana L. Farnsworth; Jeffer-
son B. Fordham; and Anthony G. Amsterdam.
    1968        *Crisis at Columbia*. New York: Vintage.
Crawford, Thomas J., and Murray Naditch
    1970        "Relative Deprivation, Powerlessness, and Militancy: The
                Psychology of Social Protest." *Psychiatry* 3:208–23.
Cruse, Harold
    1967        *The Crisis of the Negro Intellectual*. New York: Apollo.
*Daedalus*
    1968        Students and Politics. Vol. 97.
    1969        Dialogues. Vol. 98.
    1970a       The Embattled University. Vol. 99.
    1970b       Rights and Responsibilities: The University's Dilemma. Vol. 99.
    1974        American Higher Education: Toward an Uncertain Future. Vol.
                103.
    1975        American Higher Education: Toward an Uncertain Future, II.
                Vol. 104.
Daniel, Jack
    1973        "Black Academic Activism." *Black Scholar* 4:44–52.
Daniel, Philip. T. K., and Admasu Zike
    1983        *The National Council for Black Studies—Northern Illinois Uni-
                versity Black Studies Four-Year College and University Survey*.
                DeKalb: Northern Illinois University.
Davies, James C.
    1962        "Toward a Theory of Revolution." *American Sociological Re-
                view* 6:5–19.
    1971        *When Men Revolt and Why*. New York: Free Press.

Davis, Samuel C.; Jane W. Loeb; and Lehmann F. Robinson
1970    "A Comparison of Characteristics of Negro and White College Freshman Classmates." *Journal of Negro Education* 39:359–66.

Dean, Dwight
1961    "Alienation." *American Sociological Review* 26:753–58.

Dean's Report
1967–70    *The Annual Report of the Dean*. University College of Arts and Sciences. University Heights Center, New York University.

deGraaf, Lawrence B.
1970    "Howard: The Evolution of a Black Student Revolt." Pp. 319–44 in Julian Foster and Durward Long (eds.), *Protest!* New York: William Morrow.

DeMott, Benjamin
1972    "On Counter-Culture and Over-the-Counter Culture." *New York Times*, 10 January, Educational Supplement:11.

Donadio, Stephen
1968a    "Black Power at Columbia." *Commentary* 46:67–76.
1968b    "Columbia: Seven Interviews." *Partisan Review*:354–92.

Donald, Cleveland, Jr.
1970    "Cornell in Crisis." *Essence* 1:22–27.
1971    "Cornell: Confrontation in Black and White." Pp. 135–84 in Cushing Strout and David I. Grossvogel (eds.), *Divided We Stand*. Garden City, N.Y.: Doubleday.
1973    "Black Students." Pp. 377–92 in P. I. Rose, S. Rothman, and W. J. Wilson (eds.), *Through Different Eyes: Black and White Perspectives on American Race Relations*. New York: Oxford University Press.

Donaldson, Robert H., and Richard A. Pride
1969    "Black Students at a White University: Their Attitudes and Behavior in an Era of Confrontation." *Journal of Social and Behavioral Sciences* 15:22–38.

Douglas, J. D.
1970    *Youth in Turmoil*. Washington, D.C.: U.S. Government Printing Office.

Dunlap, Riley
1970    "Radical and Conservative Student Activism." *Pacific Sociological Review* 13:171–81.

Edwards, Harry
1970    *Black Students*. New York: Free Press.
1971    "The Reluctant Revolutionaries: Types of Black Student Activists." In Gary Marx (ed.), *Racial Conflict*. Boston: Little, Brown.

Egerton, John
1969    *State Universities and Black Americans*. Atlanta: Southern Education Foundation.

1971      "The White Sea of Higher Education." Pp. 35–41 in R. A.
          Attman and P. O. Snyder (eds.), *The Minority Student on Cam-
          pus*. Boulder, Colo.: Western Interstate Commission for Higher
          Education.
1975      "Adams vs. Richardson: Can Separate Be Equal?" *Change* 6
          (Winter):29–36.
Eichel, Lawrence; Kenneth W. Jost; Robert D. Luskin; and Richard M.
Neustadt
1970      *The Harvard Strike*. Boston: Houghton Mifflin.
Eisenstadt, S. N.
1956      *From Generation to Generation*. Glencoe, Ill.: Free Press.
1972      "Intellectuals and Traditions." *Daedalus* 101:1–19.
Eliot, Thomas H.
1970      "Administrative Response to Campus Turmoil." Pp. 181–94 in
          David C. Nichols and Olive Mills (eds.), *The Campus and the
          Radical Crisis*. Washington, D.C.: American Council on Educa-
          tion.
Epstein, Cynthia Fuchs
1973      "Positive Effects of the Multiple Negative: Explaining the Suc-
          cess of Black Professional Women." *American Journal of Sociol-
          ogy* 78:912–35.
Erikson, Erik H.
1970      "Reflections on the Dissent of Contemporary Youth." *Daedalus*
          99:154–96.
Etzioni, Amitai
1961a     *A Comparative Analysis of Complex Organizations*. New York:
          Free Press.
1961b     *Complex Organizations*. New York: Holt, Rinehart and Win-
          ston.
1964      *Modern Organizations*. Englewood Cliffs, N.J.: Prentice-Hall.
1968a     *The Active Society*. New York: Free Press.
1968b     "Mobilization as a Macro-Sociological Conception." *British
          Journal of Sociology* 19:240–50.
Eustace, Rowland
1969      "The Government of Scholars." Pp. 51–61 in David Martin
          (ed.), *Anarchy and Culture: The Problem of the Contemporary
          University*. New York: Columbia University Press.
Evans, Robert R. (ed.)
1973      *Social Movements*. Chicago: Rand McNally.
Exum, William H.
1975      "The University-Church Analogy." Paper presented at the
          annual meeting of the American Sociological Association, Au-
          gust, San Francisco.
1983a     "Climbing the Crystal Stair." *Social Problems* 30:383–99.
1983b     "The Partly Open Door: Conflict of Values and Limited Access

in Higher Education." Paper presented at the jointly sponsored annual meetings of the Association of Black Sociologists and the Society for the Study of Social Problems, August, Detroit.

1984 "Academia as an Internal Labor Market." Paper presented at the annual meeting of the Educational Research Association, New Orleans.

Exum, William H.; Robert J. Menges; Bari Watkins; and Patricia Berglund

1984 "Making It to the Top." *American Behavioral Scientist* 27:301–24.

Fanon, Franz

1967 *Black Skins, White Masks*. New York: Grove Press.

1968 *The Wretched of the Earth*. New York: Grove Press.

Feldman, Kenneth A.

1971 "Some Methods for Assessing College Impacts." *Sociology of Education* 44:135–50.

Feldman, Kenneth A., and Theodore M. Newcomb

1969 *The Impact of College on Students*. San Francisco: Jossey-Bass.

Fernandez, John

1975 *Black Managers in White Corporations*. New York: Wiley.

Festinger, Leon; Stanley Schacter; and Kurt Back

1950 *Social Pressures in Informal Groups*. New York: Harper.

Feuer, Lewis S.

1969 *Conflict of Generations*. New York: Basic Books.

Fisher, Bernice M.

1972 "Education in the Big Picture." *Sociology of Education* 45:233–57.

Fiske, Edward B.

1981 "After Steady Rise, the Number of Black Doctoral Students Falls." *New York Times*, 21 July.

1983 "For Black Studies, the Fight Goes On." *New York Times*, 13 January.

Flacks, Richard

1967 "The Liberated Generation." *Journal of Social Issues* 23:52–75.

1968 "Social and Cultural Meanings of Student Revolt." Paper presented at the annual meeting of the American Association for the Advancement of Science, Dallas.

1969 "Protest or Conform: Some Psychological Perspectives on Legitimacy," *Journal of Applied Behavioral Sciences* 5:127–50.

1970 "Who Protests: The Social Bases of the Student Movement." Pp. 134–58 in Julian Foster and Durward Long (eds.), *Protest!* New York: William Morrow.

1971a "Revolt of the Young Intelligentsia." Pp. 223–59 in Robert Aya and Norman Miller (eds.), *The New American Revolution*. New York: Free Press.

1971b    *Youth and Social Change.* Chicago: Markham.
Forbes, Gordon B., and Marilyn Gipson
1969     "Political Attitudes and Opinions, Need for Social Approval, Dogmatism and Anxiety in Negro and White College Students." *Journal of Negro Education* 37:61–63.
Forward, John R., and Jay Williams
1970     "Internal-External Control and Black Militancy." *Journal of Social Issues* 26:75–92.
Foster, Julian
1970     "Student Protest: What Is Known, What Is Said." Pp. 27–58 in Julian Foster and Durward Long (eds.), *Protest!* New York: William Morrow.
Foster, Julian and Durward Long
1970a    "The Dynamics of Institutional Response." Pp. 419–46 in Julian Foster and Durward Long (eds.), *Protest!* New York: William Morrow.
Foster, Julian, and Durward Long (eds.)
1970b    *Protest!: Student Activism in America.* New York: William Morrow.
Freeman, Richard, and J. Herbert Holloman
1975     "The Declining Value of College Going." *Change* 7 (September):24–31, 62.
Friedenberg, Edgar Z.
1970     "The University Community in an Open Society." *Daedalus* 99:56–74.
Friedman, Myles I., and M. Elizabeth Jacka
1969     "The Negative Effect of Group Cohesiveness on Intergroup Negotiation." *Journal of Social Issues* 25:181–94.
Gaier, E. L., and W. A. Watts
1969     "Current Attitudes and Socialization Patterns of White and Negro Students Entering College." *Journal of Negro Education* 38:342–50.
Gamson, William A.
1968     *Power and Discontent.* Homewood, Ill.: Dorsey Press.
1975     *The Strategy of Social Protest.* Homewood, Ill.: Dorsey Press.
Gerald, Debra, and Audrey Weinberg
1984     "Higher Education." Pp. 61–102 in National Center for Education Statistics, *The Condition of Education.* Washington, D.C.: U.S. Department of Education.
Gerlach, Luther P., and Virginia H. Hine
1970     *People, Power, Change: Movements in Social Transformation.* Indianapolis: Bobbs-Merrill.
Gershman, Carl
1969     "Black Separatism: Shock of Integration." *Dissent*:294–97.

Gerth, Hans
    1940     "The Nazi Party: Its Leadership and Composition." *American Journal of Sociology* 45:517–41.
Geschwender, Barbara N., and James A. Geschwender
    1973     "Relative Deprivation and Participation in the Civil Rights Movement." *Social Science Quarterly* 54:403–11.
Geschwender, James A.
    1977     *Class, Race and Worker Insurgency.* New York: Cambridge University Press.
Ginzberg, Eli
    1969     "Black Power and Student Unrest: Reflections on Columbia University and Harlem." *George Washington Law Review* 37:835–47.
Gist, Noel, and William S. Bennett, Jr.
    1963     "Aspirations of Negro and White Students." *Social Forces* 42:40–80.
Glazer, Nathan
    1969     "'Student Power' in Berkeley." Pp. 3–21 in Daniel Bell and Irving Kristol (eds.), *Confrontation.* New York: Basic Books.
    1970a    *Remembering the Answers: Essays on the American Student Revolt.* New York: Basic Books.
    1970b    "The Six Roots of Campus Trouble." *Harvard Alumni Bulletin* 73 (September):23–30.
Gold, Alice R.; Lucy N. Friedman; and Richard Christie
    1971     "The Anatomy of Revolutionaries." *Journal of Applied Social Psychology* 1:26–43.
Goldman, Ralph M.
    1970     "San Francisco State: The Technology of Confrontationism." Pp. 271–92 in Julian Foster and Durward Long (eds.), *Protest!* New York: William Morrow.
Gottlieb, David
    1969     "Poor Youth: A Study in Forced Alienation." *Journal of Social Issues* 25:91–119.
Gould, Lawrence T.
    1969     "Conformity and Alienation: Two Faces of Alienation." *Journal of Social Issues* 25:39–63.
Gouldner, Alvin W.
    1954     *Patterns of Industrial Democracy.* Glencoe, Ill.: Free Press.
Graham, Edward K.
    1969     "The Hampton Institute Strike of 1927." *American Scholar,* pp. 668–83.
Grant, W. Vance, and Thomas D. Snyder
    1984     *Digest of Education Statistics, 1983–84.* Washington, D.C.: National Center for Education Statistics.
Green, Eugene
    1972     "The Political Socialization of Black Inner-City Children."

Pp. 180–94 in A. M. Orum (ed.), *The Seeds of Politics*. Englewood Cliffs, N.J.: Prentice-Hall.

Greene, D. L., and David G. Winter
1971    "Motives, Involvement and Leadership Among Black College Students." *Journal of Personality* 39:319–32.

Grier, William H., and Price Cobbs
1968    *Black Rage*. New York: Basic Books.
1969    "Foreword." Pp. ix–xiv in Jerome Skolnick, *The Politics of Protest*. New York: Simon and Schuster.

Gross, Edward
1968    "Universities as Organizations." *American Sociological Review* 33:518–44.

Grove, D. John; Richard C. Remy; and L. Harmon Zeigler
1974    "Political Socialization and Political Ideolgy as Sources of Educational Discontent." *Social Science Quarterly* 55:411–24.

Gurin, Gerald; Theodore M. Newcomb; and R. G. Cope
1968    "Characteristics of Entering Freshmen Related to Attrition in the Literary College of a Large State University." Office of Education, U.S. Department of Health, Education and Welfare Project No. 1938. Ann Arbor: Survey Research Center, Institute for Social Research, University of Michigan.

Gurin, Patricia, and Edgar Epps
1975    *Black Consciousness, Identity and Achievement*. New York: Wiley.

Gurin, Patricia; Gerald Gurin; Rosina C. Lao; and Muriel Beattie
1969    "Internal-External Conflict in the Motivational Dynamics of Negro Youth." *Journal of Social Issues* 25:29–54.

Gurr, Ted Robert
1970    *Why Men Rebel*. Princeton: Princeton University Press.

Gusfield, Joseph R.
1957    "The Problem of Generations in an Organizational Structure." *Social Forces* 35:323–30.
1963    *Symbolic Crusade: Status Politics and the American Temperance Movement*. Urbana: University of Illinois Press.
1966    "Functional Areas of Leadership in Social Movements." *Sociological Quarterly* 7:137–56.
1971    "Student Protest and University Response." *Annals of the American Academy of Political and Social Science* 395 (May):26–38.

Gusfield, Joseph R. (ed.)
1970    *Protest, Reform and Revolt*. New York: Wiley.

Haan, Norma; M. Brewster Smith; and Jeanne H. Block
1968    "The Moral Reasoning of Young Adults." *Journal of Personality and Social Psychology* 10:183–201.

Hagstrom, W. O., and Hannan C. Selvin
1965    "The Dimensions of Cohesiveness in Small Groups." *Sociometry* 27:30–43.

Haines Commission Report
1968    *Report of the Commission on Campus Disorders*. University College of Arts and Sciences, University Heights Center, New York University.

Hajda, Jan
1961    "Alienation and Integration of Student Intellectuals." *American Sociological Review* 26:758–66.

Hamilton, Charles V.
1969    "Minority Groups." Pp. 20–23 in Robert H. Connery (ed.), *The Corporation and the Campus*. Proceedings of the Academy of Political Sciences, no. 30.

Harding, Vincent
1969    "Black Students and the 'Impossible' Revolution." *Ebony* 24 (August):141–48.

Harper, Frederick D.
1969    "Black Student Revolt on the White Campus." *Journal of College Student Personnel* 10:291–95.
1971    "Media for Change: Black Students in the White University." *Journal of Negro Education* 40:255–65.

Harris, Louis, and Bert E. Swanson
1970    *Black-Jewish Relations in New York City*. New York: Praeger.

Hartnett, Rodney
1970    "Differences in Selected Attitudes and College Orientations Between Black Students and Attending Traditionally Negro and Traditionally White Institutions." *Sociology of Education* 43:419–36.

*Harvard Magazine*
1975    "Fewer Blacks in College." Vol. 77 (March):10.

Heberle, Rudolf
1951    *Social Movements*. New York: Appleton-Century-Crofts.

Hechinger, Fred M.
1971    "Black Colleges: Dispute Over a Rescue Attempt." *New York Times*, 17 October.
1980    "Black Studies Come of Age." *New York Times Sunday Magazine*, 13 April.

Hedegard, James M.
1972    "Experiences of Black College Students at Predominantly White Institutions." Pp. 43–59 in E. A. Epps (ed.), *Black Students in White Schools*. Worthington, Ohio: Charles A. Jones.

Hedegard, James M., and Donald R. Brown
1969    "Encounters of Some Negro and White Freshmen with a Public Multiversity." *Journal of Social Issues* 25:131–44.

*Heights Daily News*
1966–71  Vols. 36–40.

Henderson, Algo D., and Jean G. Henderson
1974    *Higher Education in America.* San Francisco: Jossey-Bass.
Henderson, Donald M.
1970    "Black Student Protest in White Universities." Pp. 157-70 in John F. Szwed (ed.), *Black America.* New York: Basic Books.
Henderson, Vivian W.
1974    "Blacks and Change in Higher Education." *Daedalus* 103:72–79.
Henshel, Ann Marie, and Richard L. Henshel
1969    "Black Studies Programs." *Journal of Negro Education* 38:423–29.
Hentoff, Nat
1969    *Black Anti-Semitism and Jewish Racism.* New York: Richard W. Baron.
Heyns, Roger W.
1968    "Stress and Administrative Authority." Pp. 163–72 in G. K. Smith (ed.), *Stress and Campus Responses.* San Francisco: Jossey-Bass.
Hiller, Henry H.
1975    "A Reconceptualization of the Dynamics of Social Movement Development." *Pacific Sociological Review* 18:342–60.
Hodgkinson, Harold
1970    "Student Protest—An Institutional and National Profile." *Teachers College Record* 71:537–55.
Hofstadter, Richard, and C. DeW. Hardy
1952    *The Development and Scope of Higher Education in the United States.* New York: Columbia University Press.
Homans, George
1961    *Social Behavior.* New York: Harcourt, Brace and World.
Horowitz, Irving Louis, and William H. Friedland
1970    *The Knowledge Factory.* Chicago: Aldine.
Howard, Lawrence C.
1971    "Black Consciousness and Identity Crisis." Pp. 177–206 in H. L. Hodgkinson and M. B. Bloy, Jr. (eds.), *Identity Crisis in Higher Education.* San Francisco: Jossey-Bass.
Institute for the Study of Educational Policy
1975    *Equal Opportunity for Blacks in U.S. Higher Education: An Assessment.* Washington, D.C.: Howard University.
Jackson, John S., III
1971a   "The Political Behavior, Attitudes and Socialization of Selected Groups of Black Youths." Ph.D. dissertation, Vanderbilt University.
1971b   "The Political Behavior and Socio-Economic Background of Black Students: The Antecedents of Protest." *Mid-West Journal of Political Science* 15:661–86.

Janssen, P. A.

1972 "Higher Education and the Black American." *Chronicle of Higher Education* (30 May):1–2.

Jencks, Christopher

1979 "The Social Basis of Unselfishness." Pp. 63–86 in Herbert Gans et al. (eds.), *On the Making of Americans.* Philadelphia: University of Pennsylvania Press.

Jencks, Christopher, and David Riesman

1968 *The Academic Revolution.* Garden City, N.Y.: Doubleday.

Jenkins, J. Craig

1979 "What Is to Be Done: Movement or Organization?" *Contemporary Sociology* 8:222–28.

Jennings, M. Kent, and Richard Miemi

1974 *The Political Character of Adolescence.* Princeton: Princeton University Press.

Jessor, Richard

1968 *Society, Personality, and Deviant Behavior.* New York: Holt, Rinehart and Winston.

Johnson, Harry M.

1960 *Sociology.* New York: Holt, Rinehart and Winston.

Jones, Ann

1973 *Uncle Tom's Campus.* New York: Praeger.

Jones, Thomas Francis

1933 *New York University: 1832–1932.* New York: New York University Press.

Josephson, Eric, and Mary Josephson

1962 *Man Alone: Alienation in Modern Society.* New York: Dell.

Kahn, Roger

1971 *The Boys of Summer.* New York: Signet.

Kanter, Rosabeth Moss

1968 "Commitment and Social Organization." *American Sociological Review* 33:499–517.

1972 *Commitment and Community: Communes and Utopias in Sociological Perspective.* Cambridge: Harvard University Press.

Kaplan, Martin

1976 "The Ideologies of Tough Times." *Change* 8 (August):22–31.

Karagueuzian, Dikran

1971 *Blow It Up!: The Black Student Revolt at San Francisco State and the Emergence of Dr. Hayakawa.* Boston: Gambit.

Kauroma, Yusuf

1971 "Right On! . . . Where?: Historical Contradictions of the Black Student Movement." Pp. 63–73 in R. A. Attman and P. O. Snyder (eds.), *The Minority Student on Campus.* Boulder, Colo.: Western Interstate Commission for Higher Education.

Keniston, Kenneth
  1968a    *Young Radicals*. New York: Harcourt, Brace and World.
  1968b    "Youth, Change and Violence." *American Scholar* 37:227–45.
  1973     *Radicals and Militants: An Annotated Bibliography of Empiri-
            cal Research on Campus Unrest*. Lexington, Mass.: D. C. Heath.
Keniston, Kenneth, and Michael Lerner
  1971     "Campus Characteristics and Campus Unrest." *Annals of the
            American Academy of Political and Social Science* 395
            (May):47–54.
Kerlinger, Fred
  1967     *Foundations of Behavioral Research*. New York: Holt, Rinehart
            and Winston.
Kerpelman, Larry C.
  1970     "Student Activism and Ideology in Higher Education Institu-
            tions." Office of Education, Project No. 8-A-208. Amherst:
            University of Massachusetts.
  1972     *Activists and Nonactivists*. New York: Behavioral Publications.
Kerr, Clark
  1963     *The Uses of the University*. Cambridge: Harvard University
            Press.
  1970a    "Governance and Functions." *Daedalus* 99:108–121.
  1970b    "Student Dissent and Confrontation Politics." Pp. 3–10 in Julian
            Foster and Durward Long (eds.), *Protest!* New York: William
            Morrow.
Killian, Lewis
  1964     "Social Movements." Pp. 426–55 in R. E. L. Faris (ed.), *Hand-
            book of Modern Sociology*. Chicago: Rand McNally.
Kilson, Martin
  1973a    "Blacks at Harvard: Crisis and Change." *Harvard Bulletin* 75
            (April):24–27.
  1973b    "Blacks at Harvard: Solutions and Prospects." *Harvard Bulletin*
            75 (June):31–32, 41–42.
King, C. Wendell
  1961     *Social Movements in the United States*. New York: Random
            House.
Kleinbaum, David G., and Anna Kleinbaum
  1976     "The Minority Experience at a Predominantly White Univer-
            sity." *Journal of Negro Education* 45:312–328.
Kornberg, Alan, and Mary L. Brehm
  1971     "Ideology, Institutional Identification, and Campus Activism."
            *Social Forces* 49:445–59.
Kornstein, Daniel, and Peter Weissenberg
  1970     "Social Exchange Theory and the University." Pp. 447–56 in
            Julian Foster and Durward Long (eds.), *Protest!* New York:
            William Morrow.

Kriesberg, Louis
   1973    *The Sociology of Social Conflicts*. Englewood Cliffs, N.J.: Prentice-Hall.

Krueger, Marlis, and Frieda Silvert
   1975    *Dissent Denied: The Technocratic Response to Protest*. New York: Elsevier.

Kruytbosch, Carlos E., and Sheldon L. Messinger (eds.)
   1969    *The State of the University*. Beverly Hills: Sage.

Ladner, Joyce
   1967    "What Black Power Means to Negroes in Mississippi." *Transaction* 5 (Spring):7–15.

Lang, Kurt, and Gladys Engel Lang
   1970    "Collective Behavior Theory and the Escalated Riots of the Sixties." Pp. 94–110 in Tamotsu Shibutani (ed.), *Human Nature and Collective Behavior*. Englewood Cliffs, N.J.: Prentice-Hall.

Lanternari, Vittorio
   1963    *The Religions of the Oppressed*. New York: Mentor.

Lao, Rosina C.
   1970    "Internal-External Control and Competent and Innovative Behavior Among Negro College Students." *Journal of Personality and Social Psychology* 14:263–76.

Lavin, David E.; Richard D. Alba; and Richard A. Silberstein
   1981    *Right versus Privilege: The Open Admissions Experiment at the City University of New York*. New York: Free Press.

Law, Kim S., and Edward J. Walsh
   1983    "The Interaction of Grievances and Structures in Social Movement Analysis." *Sociological Quarterly* 24:123–36.

Lazarsfeld, Paul, and Wagner Theilens, Jr.
   1958    *The Academic Mind*. Glencoe, Ill.: Free Press.

Lefton, Mark
   1968    "Race, Expectations and Anomia." *Social Forces* 46:347–52.

Lemberg Center for the Study of Violence
   1968–69    *Riot Data Review*, no. 105. Waltham, Mass.: Brandeis University.

Levinson, Daniel J.
   1958    "Role, Personality and Social Structure in the Organizational Setting." Expanded version of paper presented at the meetings of the American Sociological Association, August. Mimeographed, Harvard University.

Levitan, Sar A.
   1975    *Still a Dream: The Changing Status of Blacks Since 1960*. Cambridge: Harvard University Press.

Liberale, Marc, and Tom Seligson (eds.)
   1970    *The High School Revolutionaries*. New York: Random House.

Lipset, Seymour Martin (ed.)
    1967    *Student Politics*. New York: Basic Books.
    1971    *Rebellion in the University*. Boston: Little, Brown.
Lipset, Seymour Martin, and Philip G. Altbach
    1967    "Student Politics and Higher Education." Pp. 199–252 in S. M.
           Lipset (ed.), *Student Politics*. New York: Basic Books.
Lipset, Seymour Martin, and Everett C. Ladd, Jr.
    1971*a*  "College Generations and Their Politics." *New Society*
           (7 October):654–57.
    1971*b*  "College Generations—From the 1930's to the 1960's." *The
           Public Interest* 25:99–113.
Lipset, Seymour Martin, and Earl Raab.
    1970    *The Politics of Unreason: Right Wing Extremism in America,
           1790–1970*. New York: Harper and Row.
Lipset, Seymour Martin, and Gerald Schaflander
    1971    *Passion and Politics: Student Activism in America*. Boston: Lit-
           tle, Brown.
Lipset, Seymour Martin, and Sheldon S. Wolin
    1965    *The Berkeley Student Revolt*. Garden City, N.Y.: Doubleday.
Lipsky, Michael
    1968    "Protest as a Political Resource." *American Political Science
           Review* 62:1144–58.
Litwak, Lee, and Herbert Wilner
    1971    *College Days in Earthquake Country—Ordeal at San Francisco
           State*. New York: Random House.
Lodhi, Abdul Qaiyum, and Charles Tilly
    1973    "Urbanization, Crime, and Collective Violence in Nineteenth-
           Century France." *American Journal of Sociology* 79:296–318.
Lomax, Louis
    1963    *The Negro Revolt*. New York: Signet.
Long, Durward
    1970*a*  "Black Protest." Pp. 459–82 in Julian Foster and Durward Long
           (eds.), *Protest!* New York: William Morrow.
    1970*b*  "Wisconsin: Changing Styles of Administrative Response."
           Pp. 246–70 in Julian Foster and Durward Long (eds.), *Protest!*
           New York: William Morrow.
Lowe, Gilbert A., Jr., and Sophia F. McDowell
    1971    "Participant-Nonparticipant Differences in the Howard Uni-
           versity Student Protest." *Journal of Negro Education* 40:81–90.
Lowi, Theodore
    1969    *The End of Liberalism*. New York: Norton.
Lukas, J. A.
    1968    "The Negro at an Integrated College." *New York Times*, 3 June.
Luria, S. E., and Zella Luria
    1970    "The Role of the University." *Daedalus* 99:75–83.

Lusky, Louis, and Mary H. Lusky
1969    "Columbia, 1968." *Political Science Quarterly* 84:169–288.
Lyons, James E.
1973    "The Adjustment of Black Students to Predominantly White Campuses." *Journal of Negro Education* 42:462–66.
Lyons, Morgan, and Judith Lyons
1973    "Power and the University." *Sociology of Education* 46:37–58.
Lystad, Mary
1973    *As They See It: Changing Values of College Youth.* Morristown, N.J.: General Learning Press.
McAdam, Doug
1983    "Tactical Innovation and the Pace of Insurgency." *American Sociological Review* 48:735–54.
McCarthy, John d., and Mayer N. Zald
1973    *The Trend of Social Movements in America.* Morristown, N.J.: General Learning Press.
McEvoy, James, and Abraham Miller (eds.)
1969    *Black Power and Student Rebellion.* Belmont, Mass.: Wadsworth.
McFee, Ann
1961    "The Relation of Students' Needs to Their Perceptions of a College Environment." *Journal of Educational Psychology* 52:25–29.
McGill, William J.
1972    "Small-Scale Protest Is Big on Columbia Campus." *New York Times,* 10 January, Education Supplement:16.
1974    "Facing the Fires of September." *Change* 6 (March):42–46.
McGrath, Earl J.
1965    *The Predominantly Negro Colleges and Universities in Transition.* New York: Teachers College, Columbia University.
Mackay-Smith, Anne
1984    "Large Shortage of Black Professors in Higher Education Grows Worse." *Wall Street Journal,* 12 June.
Madge, John
1965    *The Tools of Social Science.* Garden City, N.Y.: Doubleday.
Mankoff, Milton, and Richard Flacks
1976    "The Changing Social Base of the American Student Movement." *Annals of the American Academy of Political and Social Science* 395 (May):54–67.
Mannheim, Karl
1946    *Ideology and Utopia.* New York: Harcourt, Brace and World.
1952    "The Problem of Generations." Pp. 276–322 in Karl Mannheim, *Essays on the Sociology of Knowledge.* New York: Oxford University Press.

Marcus, Philip M.
1960    "Expressive and Instrumental Groups." *American Journal of Sociology* 66:54–59.

Martin, David (ed.)
1969    *Anarchy and Culture: The Problem of the Contemporary University.* New York: Columbia University Press.

Marx, Gary, and Michael Useem
1971    "Majority Involvement in Minority Movements." *Journal of Social Issues* 27:81–104.

Matthews, Donald, and James Prothro
1969    "Negro Students and the Protest Movement." Pp. 379–418 in James McEvoy and Abraham Miller (eds.), *Black Power and the Student Rebellion.* Belmont, Mass.: Wadsworth.

Mauss, Armand C.
1971    "On Being Strangled by the Stars and Stripes: The New Left, the Old Left, and the Natural History of American Radical Movements." *Journal of Social Issues* 27:183–202.

Meier, August, and Elliott Rudwick
1973    *CORE.* New York: Oxford University Press.

Menges, Robert J., and William H. Exum
1983    "Barriers to the Progress of Women and Minority Faculty." *Journal of Higher Education* 54:123–44.

Merton, Robert K.
1965    "Problem Finding in Sociology." Introduction to Robert K. Morton, Leonard Broom, and Leonard S. Cottress, Jr. (eds.), *Sociology Today,* vol. 1. New York: Harper and Row.

Metzger, Walter P.
1970    "The Crisis of Academic Authority." *Daedalus* 99:568–608.

Meyer, Marshall W.
1971    "Harvard Students in the Midst of Crisis." *Sociology of Education* 44:245–69.

Middleton, Lorenzo
1981    "New Outbreaks of Cross-Burnings and Racial Slurs Worries Colleges." *Chronicle of Higher Education* 21 (12 January):12.

Middleton, Robert
1963    "Alienation, Race, and Education." *American Sociological Review* 28:973–76.

Miles, Michael
1971    *The Radical Probe.* New York: Atheneum.
1974    "Student Alienation in the U.S. Higher Education Industry." *Politics and Society* 4:311–41.

Miller, Albert A.
1969    "Problems of the Minority Student on Campus." *Liberal Education* 55:18–23.

Moore, Barrington, Jr.
    1962      *Political Power and Social Theory.* New York: Harper.
    1978      *Injustice: The Social Bases of Obedience and Revolt.* White
              Plains, N.Y.: M. E. Sharpe.
Morgan, Gordon Daniel
    1970      *The Ghetto College Student.* Iowa City: American College Test-
              ing Service.
Morgan, William R.
    1972      "Campus Conflict as Formative Influence." Pp. 278–91 in J. F.
              Short, Jr., and M. E. Wolfgang (eds.), *Collective Violence.* Chi-
              cago: Aldine.
Morrison, Denton E.
    1973      "Some Notes Toward Theory on Relative Deprivation, Social
              Movements, and Social Change." Pp. 103–15 in R. R. Evans
              (ed.), *Social Movements.* Chicago: Rand McNally.
Morrison, Robert S.
    1970      "Some Aspects of Policy-Making in the American University."
              *Daedalus* 99:609–44.
Napper, George
    1973      *Blacker Than Thou: The Struggle for Campus Unity.* Grand
              Rapids: Eerdmans.
Nasatir, David
    1968      "A Note on Contextual Effects and the Political Orientation of
              University   Students."   *American   Sociological   Review*
              33:210–19.
National Advisory Commission on Civil Disorders
    1968      *The Report of the National Advisory Commission on Civil
              Disorders* (The Kerner Report). New York: Bantam.
National Advisory Committee on Black Higher Education
    1981      *A Losing Battle.* Washington, D.C.: Department of Education.
National Center for Education Statistics
    1983      *Participation of Black Students in Higher Education.* Washing-
              ton, D.C.: U.S. Department of Education.
    1984      *Digest of Education Statistics, 1983–84.* Washington, D.C.: U.S.
              Department of Education.
National Council for Black Studies
    1984      "NCBS Statement on the Structural Integrity of Black Studies
              Units." *Voices in Black Studies* 8 (Spring):2.
Naughton, Ezra
    1972      "What You See Is What You Get: Black Student–White Cam-
              pus." Pp. 49–66 in David Vermilye (ed.), *The Expanded Cam-
              pus.* San Francisco: Jossey-Bass.
Neal, Arthur G., and Melvin Seeman
    1974      "Organizations and Powerlessness." *American Sociological Re-
              view* 29:216–26.

Nelson, Harold A.

1971    "Leadership Change in an Evolutionary Movement: An Analysis of Change in the Leadership Structure of the Civil Rights Movement." *Social Forces* 49:353–71.

1974    "Social Movement Transformation and Pre-Movement Factor-Effect." *Sociological Quarterly* 15:127–42.

Nettler, Gwynn

1957    "A Measure of Alienation." *American Sociological Review* 22:670–77.

New York University

n.d.*a*    "Broadsides, circulars, documents, letters and reports on student activism at University Heights Center, 1968–70." Collected by the New York University Library.

n.d.*b*    "University College: A Small College of Liberal Arts." Office of Admissions.

1956    *The Self-Study.* New York: New York University Press.

1963    "A Presentation to the Ford Foundation." Mimeographed.

1971    *The Martin Luther King, Jr., Grant Program After Two Years.* Office of Institutional Research.

New York University, University Heights Center

1969*a*    "Memorandum." Educational Policy and Planning Committee, University College of Arts and Sciences.

1969*b*    "Proposal for the Establishment of a Major and Minor in African and Afro-American Studies, University Heights Campus, New York University, 1969." Mimeographed. University College of Arts and Sciences.

1969*c*    *Heights and Student Handbook, 1969–70.*

1969*d*    Minutes of the Meetings of the Faculty, University College of Arts and Sciences.

1970*a*    "Educational Support Program Committee Proposal." Mimeographed.

1970*b*    "Interim Report on the Educational Support Program." Mimeographed. Educational Policy and Planning Committee, University College of Arts and Sciences.

1970*c*    Minutes of the Meetings of the Faculty, University College of Arts and Sciences.

1970*d*    "Report of the Educational Policy and Planning Committee." Mimeographed. University College of Arts and Sciences.

1970*e*    "Rules Regulating Student Disciplinary Procedures at University Heights." Memo from the provost.

1971    "Report of the Educational Policy and Planning Committee." Mimeographed. Submitted jointly by the Educational Policy and Planning Committee and the Educational Support Program Committee, University College of Arts and Sciences.

Newcomb, Theodore, and Everett K. Wilson (eds.)
    1966    *College Peer Groups*. Chicago: Aldine.

Nickson, Sheila J.
    1983    "Status of Minority Professionals on Majority Campuses." Pp. 50–54 in Julia Elam (ed.), *Blacks on White Campuses*. Lanham, Md.: National Association for Equal Opportunity in Higher Education, University Press of America.

Obatala, J. K.
    1972    "Black Students: Where Did Their Revolution Go?" *Nation* (2 October):272–74.
    1974    "Black Students Stop the Shouting and Go to Work." *Smithsonian* 5 (December):46–53.

Obear, Frederick W.
    1970    "Student Activism in the Sixties." Pp. 11–26 in Julian Foster and Durward Long (eds.), *Protest!* New York: William Morrow.

Oberschall, Anthony
    1973    *Social Conflict and Social Movements*. Englewood Cliffs, N.J.: Prentice-Hall.

Olive, Betsy Ann
    1967    "The Administration of Higher Education." *Administrative Science Quarterly* 2:617–77.

Olson, Mancur
    1965    *The Logic of Collective Action*. Cambridge: Harvard University Press.

Orbell, John
    1967    "Protest Participation Among Southern Negro College Students." *American Political Science Review* 61:446–56.

Orum, Anthony M.
    1972*a*    *Black Students in Protest*. Washington, D.C.: Arnold and Caroline Rose Monograph Series, American Sociological Association, 1722 N Street, N.W.
    1972*b*    "Patterns of Protest: The Politics of Black Youth in the 1960s." Pp. 271–81 in A. M. Orum (ed.), *The Seeds of Politics*. Englewood Cliffs, N.J.: Prentice-Hall.

Orum, Anthony M. (ed.)
    1972*c*    *The Seeds of Politics*. Englewood Cliffs, N.J.: Prentice-Hall.

Orum, Anthony M., and Roberta S. Cohen
    1973    "The Development of Political Orientation Among Black and White Children." *American Sociological Review* 38:62–74.

Otten, C. Michael
    1970    *University Authority and the Student*. Berkeley: University of California Press.

Paige, Jeffrey
    1971    "Political Orientation and Riot Participation." *American Sociological Review* 36:810–20.

*Palisades*
1970    *Heights Student Handbook, 1970–71.* University Heights Center, New York University.
1971    *Heights Student Handbook, 1971–72.* University Heights Center, New York University.

Parsons, Talcott
1969    "The Academic System" Pp. 159–83 in Daniel Bell and Irving Kristol (eds.), *Confrontation.* New York: Basic Books.

Perkins, W. E., and G. E. Higginson
1971    "Black Students: Reformists or Revolutionaries?" Pp. 195–222 in Robert Aya and Norman Miller (eds.), *The New American Revolution.* New York: Free Press.

Peterson, Marvin W.; Robert T. Blackburn; Zelda F. Gamson; Carlos H. Arce; Roselle W. Davenport; and James R. Mingle
1978    *Black Students on White Campuses.* Ann Arbor: Survey Research Center, Institute for Social Research, University of Michigan.

Peterson, Richard E.
1968a    *The Scope of Organized Student Protest in 1967–68.* Princeton: Educational Testing Service.
1968b    "The Student Left in American Higher Education." *Daedalus* 97:293–317.
1970    "The Scope of Organized Protest." Pp. 59–80 in Julian Foster and Durward Long (eds.), *Protest!* New York: William Morrow.

Peterson, Roy P., and Juanita Betz Peterson
1974    "Southern White Institutions and Black Students." *Educational Record* 55:13–22.

Pifer, Alan
1974    "How Well Has Higher Education Served Black Americans?" *Change* 6 (April):8–9.

Pinkney, Alphonso
1975    *Black Americans,* 2d ed. Englewood Cliffs, N.J.: Prentice-Hall.

Pinner, Frank A.
1971    "Students—A Marginal Elite in Politics." *Annals of the American Academy of Political and Social Science* 395:127–38.

Pitts, James
1974    "The Study of Race Consciousness." *American Journal of Sociology* 80:665–87.
1975    "Self-Direction and the Political Socialization of Black Youth." *Social Science Quarterly* 56:93–104.

Platt, Gerald, and Talcott Parsons
1969    "Decision-Making in an Academic System." In C. E. Kruytbosch and S. L. Messinger (eds.), *The State of the University.* Beverly Hills: Sage.

Porter, Horace
    1977      "Reflections of a Black Son." *Change* 8 (February):34–39.
Potter, P.
    1965      "Student Discontent and Campus Reform" Pp. 71–78 in O. W. Knorr and W. J. Minter (eds.), *Order and Freedom on the Campus.* Boulder, Colo.: Western Interstate Commission for Higher Education.
Poussaint, Alvin F., and Linda R. McLean
    1968      "Black Roadblocks to Black Unity." *Negro Digest* 17 (November):10–75.
President's Commission on Campus Unrest
    1971      *The Report of the President's Commission on Campus Unrest.* New York: Avon.
Proctor, Samuel D.
    1970      "Racial Pressures on Urban Institutions." Pp. 43–58 in David C. Nichols and Olive Mills (eds.), *The Campus and the Racial Crisis.* Washington, D.C.: American Council on Education.
Pugh, Roderick W.
    1972      *Psychology and the Black Experience.* Monterey, Calif.: Book/Cole.
Record, Wilson
    1974      "White Sociologists and Black Students in Predominantly White Universities." *Sociological Quarterly* 15:164–82.
Riley, Matilda White
    1963      *Sociological Research.* New York: Harcourt, Brace and World.
Ritterband, Paul
    1974      "Ethnic Power and the Public Schools." *Sociology of Education* 47:251–67.
Roche, J. P. and S. J. Sachs
    1955      "The Bureaucrat and the Enthusiast: An Exploration of the Leadership of Social Movements." *Western Political Quarterly* 8:248–61.
Rosenberg, Morris
    1968      *The Logic of Survey Analysis.* New York: Basic Books.
Rosenthal, Joel
    1975      "Southern Black Student Activism." *Journal of Negro Education* 44:113–29.
Rothbart, George S.
    1970      "The Legitimation of Inequality: Object Scholarship vs. Black Militancy." *Sociology of Education* 43:159–74.
Rubenstein, Richard E.
    1971      "Rebels in Eden." Pp. 97–172 in Robert Aya and Norman Miller (eds.), *The New American Revolution.* New York: Free Press.

Rubington, Earl
  1973      *Alcohol Problems and Social Control.* Columbus: Charles E.
            Merrill.
Rudolph, Frederick
  1965      *The American College and University.* New York: Vintage.
  1966      "Neglect of Students as a Historical Tradition." Pp. 40–60 in
            L. E. Dennis and J. F. Kaufman (eds.), *The College and the
            Student.* Washington, D.C.: American Council on Education.
Runciman, W. G.
  1966      *Relative Deprivation and Social Justice.* Berkeley: University of
            California Press.
Ryder, Norman B.
  1965      "The Cohort as a Concept in the Study of Social Change."
            *American Sociological Review* 30:843–61.
Schein, Edgar H.
  1961      *Coercive Persuasion.* New York: Norton.
  1969      "The Passion for Unanimity." Pp. 279–89 in Barry McLaughlin
            (ed.), *Studies in Social Movements.* New York: Free Press.
Schelling, Thomas C.
  1956      "An Essay on Bargaining." *American Economic Review*
            46:281–306.
Schuman, Howard, and Shirley Hatchett
  1974      *Black Racial Attitudes.* Ann Arbor: Institute for Social Research,
            University of Michigan.
Schwab, Joseph H.
  1969      *College Curriculum and Student Protest.* Chicago: University of
            Chicago Press.
Scott, William A.
  1965      *Values and Organization: A Study of Fraternities and Sororities.*
            Chicago: Rand McNally.
Seeman, Melvin
  1959      "On the Meaning of Alienation." *American Sociological Review*
            24:783–91.
  1971      "Alienation and Estrangement." Pp. 467–527 in Angus Camp-
            bell and Philip Converse (eds.), *The Human Meaning of Social
            Change.* New York: Russell Sage.
Selznick, Philip
  1961      "Foundations of the Theory of Organization." Pp. 18–31 in
            Amitai Etzioni (ed.), *Complex Organizations.* New York: Holt,
            Rinehart and Winston.
Semas, Philip W.
  1976a     "The Student Mood, 1976." *Chronicle of Higher Education* 12
            (26 April):7–8.
  1976b     "Student Activism Shows New Sophistication." *Chronicle of
            Higher Education* 12 (3 May):3–4.

Silvern, Louis, and Charles Y. Nakamura
    1971      "Powerlessness, Social-Political Action, Social-Political Views: Their Interrelation Among College Students." *Journal of Social Issues* 27:137–57.

Simmel, Georg
    1950      *The Sociology of Georg Simmel*. Glencoe, Ill.: Free Press.

Simon, R. J.
    1969      "Selective Evaluation of Their University by Negro and White Undergraduates." *Phylon* 30 (Spring):11–16.

Sjoberg, Gideon, and Roger Nett
    1968      *A Methodology for Social Research*. New York: Harper and Row.

Skolnick, Jerome
    1969      *The Politics of Protest*. New York: Simon and Schuster.

Smelser, Neil J.
    1963      *Theory of Collective Behavior*. New York: Free Press.

Smith, Robert B.
    1972      "Campus Protests and the Vietnam War." Pp. 250–77 in J. F. Short, Jr., and M. E. Wolfgang (eds.), *Collective Violence*. Chicago: Aldine.

Snyder, Benson R.
    1963      "College as a New Environment." Pp. 76–86 in Leonard J. Duhl (ed.), *The Urban Condition*. New York: Simon and Schuster.

*Sojourner*
    1971      Monthly paper put out by the Martin Luther King, Jr., Institute of Afro-American Affairs of New York University. 2 issues (May and June).

Sorel, Georges
    1961      *Reflections on Violence*. New York: Collier.

Sowell, Thomas
    1972      *Black Education*. New York: McKay.

Spiegel, John P.
    1972      "Cultural Value Orientations and Student Protest." Pp. 236–49 in J. F. Short, Jr., and M. E. Wolfgang (eds.), *Collective Violence*. Chicago: Aldine.

Stanfiel, James D.
    1976      "A Profile of the 1972 Freshman Class at Howard University." *Journal of Negro Education* 45:61–69.

Staples, Robert
    1984      "Racial Ideology and Intellectual Racism: Blacks in Academia." *The Black Scholar* 15 (March-April):2–17.

Statera, Gianni
    1975      *Death of a Utopia: The Development and Decline of Student Movements in Europe*. New York: Oxford University Press.

Steinberg, Stephen
1971 "How Jewish Quotas Began." *Commentary* 52 (September):67–76.
1973 *The Academic Melting Pot: Catholics and Jews in American Higher Education.* New York: McGraw-Hill.
Stinchcombe, Arthur
1964 *Rebellion in a High School.* Chicago: Quadrangle.
1965 "Social Structure and Organizations." Pp. 142–93 in J. G. March (ed.), *Handbook of Organizations.* Chicago: Rand McNally.
Stroup, Herbert H.
1966 *Bureaucracy in Higher Education.* New York: Free Press.
Strout, Cushing, and David I. Grossvogel (eds.)
1971 *Divided We Stand: Reflections on the Crisis at Cornell.* Garden City, N.Y.: Doubleday.
Synnott, Marcia Graham
1979 *The Half-Opened Door.* Westport, Conn.: Greenwood Press.
Tarcov, Nathan
1969 "Four Crucial Years at Cornell." Pp. 128–44 in Daniel Bell and Irving Kristol (eds.), *Confrontation.* New York: Basic Books.
Thelwell, Michael
1970 "Black Studies and White Universities." Pp. 538–48 in William M. Chace and Peter Collier (eds.), *Justice Denied.* New York: Harcourt, Brace and World.
Thiessen, Victor, and Mark Intocovich
1970 "Some Comments on Edward Gross's 'Universities as Organizations: A Research Approach.'" *American Sociologist* 5:252–54.
Thompson, Daniel C.
1973 *Private Black Colleges at the Crossroads.* Westport, Conn.: Greenwood Press.
Tilly, Charles
1969 "Collective Violence in European Perspective." Pp. 4–44 in Hugh D. Graham and Ted R. Gurr (eds.), *Violence in America.* New York: Bantam Books.
1978 *From Mobilization to Revolution.* Reading, Mass.: Addison-Wesley.
Toch, Hans
1965 *The Social Psychology of Social Movements.* New York: Bobbs-Merrill.
Tocqueville, Alexis de
1955 *The Old Regime and the French Revolution.* Garden City, N.Y.: Doubleday.
Trilling, Lionel
1972 *Sincerity and Authenticity.* Cambridge: Harvard University Press.

Trow, Martin
    1969      "Conceptions of the University." Pp. 27–44 in C. E. Kruytbosch and S. L. Messinger (eds.), *The State of the University*. Beverly Hills: Sage.
    1970      "Reflections on the Transition from Mass to Universal Higher Education." *Daedalus* 99:1–42.

Tsouderos, John E.
    1955      "Organizational Change in Terms of a Series of Selected Variables." *American Sociological Review* 20:206–10.

Turner, James
    1971      "Social Origins of Black Consciousness." Pp. 166–94 in Robert Aya and Norman Miller (eds.), *The New American Revolution*. New York: Free Press.

Turner, Ralph H.
    1969      "The Theme of Contemporary Social Movements." *British Journal of Sociology* 20:390–405.
    1970      "Determinants of Social Movement Strategies." Pp. 145–64 in Tamotsu Shibutani (ed.), *Human Nature and Collective Behavior*. Englewood Cliffs, N.J.: Prentice-Hall.
    1972      "Campus Peace: Harmony or Uneasy Truce?" *Sociology and Social Research* 57:5–21.

Turner, Ralph H., and Lewis Killian
    1972      *Collective Behavior*. 2d ed. Englewood Cliffs, N.J.: Prentice-Hall.

Tygart, Clarence and Norman Holt
    1971      "A Research Note on Student Leftist Political Activism and Family Socioeconomic Status." *Pacific Sociological Review* 14:121–28.

Udy, Stanley H., Jr.
    1959      "'Bureaucracy' and 'Rationality' in Weber's Organization Theory." *American Sociological Review* 24:781–95.

United States Department of Health, Education and Welfare
    1979      *Access of Black Americans to Higher Education*. Washington, D.C.: Government Printing Office.

United States Office for Civil Rights
    1978      *Racial and Ethnic Enrollment Data from Institutions of Higher Education*. Washington, D.C.: Government Printing Office.

University College of Arts and Sciences
    1971      "Proposal for an Undergraduate Major in African and Afro-American Studies." Ad Hoc Committee on African and Afro-American Studies. Mimeographed.

Urban Research Corporation
    1970      *Student Protests 1969*. Chicago: Urban Research Corporation.

Useem, Michael
    1973      *Conscription, Protest and Social Conflict*. New York: Wiley.

Vesey, Laurence R.
1965    *The Emergence of the American University.* Chicago: University of Chicago Press.
Wade, Harold, Jr.
1976    *Black Men at Amherst.* Amherst, Mass.: Amherst College Press.
Wallace, Anthony F. C.
1956    "Revitalization Movements." *American Anthropologist* 58:264–81.
Walters, Ronald W.
1974    "The Mood of Black Youths." *Encore* 3 (September):15–19.
Warren, Donald I.
1975    *Black Neighborhoods.* Ann Arbor: University of Michigan Press.
Warren, Robert Penn
1965    *Who Speaks for the Negro?* New York: Random House.
Webb, Eugene; Donald T. Campbell; Richard D. Schwartz; and Lee Sechrest
1966    *Unobtrusive Measures.* Chicago: Rand McNally.
Weber, Max
1965    *The Theory of Social and Economic Organization.* New York: Free Press.
Wegner, Eldon L.
1975    "The Concept of Alienation." *Pacific Sociological Review* 18:171–93.
Weinberg, Michael
1977    *Minority Students: A Research Appraisal.* Washington, D.C.: Government Printing Office.
Westby, D. L., and R. G. Braungart
1968    "The Alienation of Generations and Status Politics: Alternative Explanations of Student Political Activism." In Roberta S. Segal (ed.), *Political Socialization.* New York: Random House.
Wheeler, Stanton
1966    "The Structure of Formally Organized Socialization Settings." Pp. 51–116 in O. G. Brim and Stanton Wheeler (eds.), *Socialization After Childhood.* New York: Wiley.
Wiggens, Jefferson
1970    *White Cross—Black Crucifixion.* New York: Exposition Press.
Wilkins, Roger
1975    "Black Studies: What's Left Is No Small Achievement." *New York Times*, 16 March.
Willie, Charles V.
1981    *The Ivory and Ebony Towers.* Lexington, Mass.: D. C. Heath.
Willie, Charles V., and Joan D. Levy
1972    "Black Is Lonely." *Psychology Today* 5 (March):50–52, 76–80.
Willie, Charles V., and Arline S. McCord
1972    *Black Students at White Colleges.* New York: Praeger.

Wilson, James Q.
    1961    "The Strategy of Protest: Problems of Negro Civic Action."
            *Journal of Conflict Resolution* 3:291–303.
    1965    "The Negro in Politics." *Daedalus* 94 (Fall):949–73.
Wilson, John
    1973    *Introduction to Social Movements.* New York: Basic Books.
Wilson, Kenneth M.
    1969    *Black Students Entering* CRC *Colleges.* College Research Center
            Research Memorandum 69-1. Poughkeepsie, N.Y.: Vassar College.
Winter, J. Alan
    1970    "On the Mixing of Morality and Politics." *Social Forces*
            49:36–41.
Wisdom, Paul E., and Kenneth A. Shaw
    1970    "Black Challenge to Higher Education." Pp. 96–109 in David C.
            Nichols and Olive Mills (eds.), *The Campus and the Racial
            Crisis.* Washington, D.C.: American Council on Education.
Wolff, Robert Paul
    1969    *The Ideal of the University.* Boston: Beacon Press.
Wolters, Raymond
    1975    *The New Negro on Campus: Black College Rebellions of the
            1920s.* Princeton: Princeton University Press.
Wood, James L.
    1974    *The Sources of American Student Activism.* Lexington, Mass.:
            D. C. Heath.
Wuthnow, Robert
    1979    "On Suffering, Rebellion, and the Moral Order." *Contemporary Sociology* 8:212–15.
Yankelovich, Daniel
    1972    *The Changing Values on Campus.* New York: Washington
            Square Press.
    1975    "The New Morality." *Equal Opportunity* 8 (Spring):12–21, 24.
Zald, Mayer N., and Roberta Ash
    1966    "Social Movement Organizations: Growth, Decay and
            Change." *Social Forces* 44:327–40.
Zald, Mayer N., and Michael A. Berger
    1978    "Social Movements in Organizations." *American Journal of
            Sociology* 83:823–61.
Zald, Mayer N., and John D. McCarthy (eds.)
    1979    *The Dynamics of Social Movements.* Cambridge, Mass.:
            Winthrop.
Zinn, Howard
    1965    SNCC: *The New Abolitionists.* Boston: Beacon Press.
Zurcher, Louis A., and Russell Curtis
    1973    "A Comparative Analysis of Propositions Describing Social
            Movement Organizations." *Sociological Quarterly* 14:175–88.

# Index